BERKLEE PRESS

THE

3RD EDITION

SELF-PROMOTING
MUSICIAN

STRATEGIES FOR
INDEPENDENT MUSIC
SUCCESS

Peter Spellman

Berklee Press

Editor in Chief: Jonathan Feist
Vice President of Online Learning and Continuing Education: Debbie Cavalier
Assistant Vice President of Operations for Berklee Media: Robert F. Green
Assistant Vice President of Marketing and Recruitment for Berklee Media: Mike King
Dean of Continuing Education: Carin Nuernberg
Editorial Assistants: Matthew Dunkle, Amy Kaminski, Zoë Lustri, Sarah Walk
Cover Design: Small Mammoth Designs

ISBN 978-0-87639-139-6

DISTRIBUTED BY

HAL•LEONARD®
CORPORATION
7777 W. BLUEMOUND RD. P.O. BOX 13819
MILWAUKEE, WISCONSIN 53213

1140 Boylston Street
Boston, MA 02215-3693 USA
(617) 747-2146

Study with
■ **BERKLEE ONLINE**

Visit Berklee Press Online at
www.berkleepress.com

online.berklee.edu

Visit Hal Leonard Online at
www.halleonard.com

Berklee Press, a publishing activity of Berklee College of Music, is a not-for-profit educational publisher.
Available proceeds from the sales of our products are contributed to the scholarship funds of the college.

CONTENTS

ACKNOWLEDGMENTS iv

PART I. Prepare 1

Chapter 1. Beyond the New Music Business 3

Chapter 2. Getting Ready to Do Business 17

Chapter 3. Plan Your Work, Work Your Plan..................... 35

Chapter 4. Smart Management for the
Professional Musician 61

PART II. Go Forward.. 99

Chapter 5. Networking in the New Music Economy 100

Chapter 6. Essentials of Music
Promotion and Marketing 114

Chapter 7. Finding Gigs in All the Right Places:
Tapping the Sources of
Lesser-Known Music Work 126

Chapter 8. Playing the Clubs:
Getting Your Foot in the
Door without Getting It Slammed.................. 138

Chapter 9. Fifteen Ways to Get the
Most Out of Every Gig 148

PART III. Rise Up 157

Chapter 10. Mapping Your Media Plan 158

Chapter 11. Working Your Media Plan 180

Chapter 12. The Self-Promoting Songwriter
and Composer... 203

Chapter 13. Expanding and Deepening
Your Music Career 225

APPENDIX. RESOURCE DIRECTORY 254

INDEX..274

ABOUT THE AUTHOR... 284

ACKNOWLEDGMENTS

So many people have had a hand in helping this book come to life, whether directly or through their support.

For their contributions to independent music the author wishes to thank Greg Arney, Moses Avalon, Bob Baker, John Braheny (RIP), Dave Cool, Wendy Day, Rik Emmett, Eric de Fontenay, Jeri Goldstein, Dave Herlihy, Keith Holzman, Bruce Houghton, Ariel Hyatt, Dan Kimpel, Steve Lurie, Jodi Krangle, Gerd Leonard, Darcie Nicole, Mark Northam, Panos Panay, Ravi, Derek Sivers, and Jenny Toomey.

For inspiration: Thanks to Angela Myles-Beeching, Larry Bethune, Julia Bingham, Dwight Heckelman, Gilli Moon, Scooter Scudieri, Amanda Hunt-Taylor, Steve Kirby, Rich Meitin, Matt Jenson, Grey Larsen, Joe Miglio, Bob Mulvey, Lauren Passarelli, Erik Privert, Jay Rinaldi, Shea Rose, Tom Stein, Stan Swiniarski, Tess Taylor, Carl Whitaker, the Underwater Airport crew, and all other indie musicians who are working the trade.

Thanks to Berklee College of Music for continuing to provide a lab in which contemporary musicians can prepare, thrive, and launch. It is the inspiring example of musicians themselves (not always valued in a society that measures success by mutual fund performance) that has informed the writing of this book. Many thanks to musicians everywhere who have lived and taught the "independent" way.

I would also like to acknowledge the enthusiasm and support of Berklee Press as they shepherded this project along from rough manuscript to finished product. Special thanks to Editor in Chief Jonathan "Eagle Eye" Feist for his patience and consummate copyediting skills. Finally, I wish to thank my wife and family for their support and enthusiasm through the writing of this book and beyond. It is with great love and appreciation that this book is dedicated to them.

—Peter Spellman, 2000/2008/2013

PART I

Prepare

CHAPTER 1

Beyond the New Music Business

The music business stands at a historical crossroads. Almost every aspect of the way people create, consume, and listen to popular music is changing, dwarfing even the seismic shift in the 1890s when music lovers turned from sheet music and player pianos to wax cylinders and later, in 1915, newfangled 78 rpm phonograph records.

Radio used to be the primary channel for music promotion. Today, in lieu of constrictive radio playlists, we have touring, blogs, ringtones, podcasts, downloads, Internet and satellite radio, videogame tie-ins, alliances with brand marketers, film and television exposure, sponsorships, and placements in commercials, all growing in value.

The career of singer-songwriter Ingrid Michaelson serves as illustration of this shifting musical landscape.

Ingrid Michaelson is a poster child for the Age of the Indie Artist. Her rise to success as a singer-songwriter began on the Internet and was propelled through a television show. And she's done it all without the help of a record label.

Michaelson began her music career in 2002 while she was waiting tables at the Muddy Cap, a coffee bar and performance space near her home in Staten Island, New York. She would perform weekly at the club, and by 2003, she had self-produced her first album. By 2007, she was performing in larger local clubs but was still living with her parents. That was when she decided to load her songs onto her MySpace page. A talent scout in Los Angeles listened to one of her songs there, and was so impressed with the quirky, heartfelt nature of Michaelson's music that she arranged to have three of her songs used on the hit television show, *Grey's Anatomy*.

At that point, things started to happen quickly. Old Navy chose one of her songs for a sweater commercial. VH1 selected her for its artist discovery program, making her the first unsigned artist to appear on the channel. Radio stations added her songs to their playlists, and her second album reached number 2 on the iTunes pop chart. She was soon on a cross-country music tour in which many of her concerts sold out without advertising.

The producers of *Grey's Anatomy* even asked her to write a song specifically for the show, which became "Keep Breathing." The song played through the closing minutes of the 2008 season finale with the last line, "all we can do is keep breathing," repeating over each dramatic scene that closed each character's story for the season.

Michaelson knows her rise to fame was sudden and outside the music industry's usual path to stardom. "I worry this is all going to disappear in a few months, and I'll have to wait tables again," she said. "I get anxiety-ridden, and I can't relax." She added, "I should sing my own songs to myself."

Ingrid Michaelson's rise to stardom exemplifies the positive changes that are happening in the music industry today, as well as the uncertainties within it. The business model, techniques of promotion, and means of distribution are all changing rapidly.

THE MUSIC BUSINESS AT A CROSSROADS

Here are some revolutionary developments for artists, from the past few years:

- Letting fans choose how much to pay for your album.

- Leaving the label you've called home for your entire career to hook up with a concert-promotions giant for a $100 million-plus deal.

- Recording iTunes-only one-off singles not slated for inclusion on an album.

- Offering "artist subscriptions" to fans, who pay a flat annual fee for more intimate access to their favorite acts.

- Serving up the millions of songs in your label's catalog to MP3 players and cell phones for one all-you-can-listen-to price per month.

All of the above are straws blowing in the wind, indicators of development, barometers registering the sea change in music industry dynamics.

Let's delve a little deeper into these changes and look for ways you can set your sail on these tumultuous waters.

When I talk about "trends," I don't mean the common definition of "trendy, faddish, or fashionable." Those are usually short-lived, "flavor-of-the-week" happenings that grip the market's attention for a time and then quickly fade into oblivion. Beanie Babies, the Macarena, and 8-track tapes fall into this category.

What I'm referring to when I say "trends" are emerging meta-currents in our social and cultural lives that herald new ways of living and thinking. These developments have been gradual and sometimes difficult to arrest and analyze. Nevertheless, they are very real and are changing the world, especially the world of the independent music provider. It wouldn't be extreme to say that for the past fifty years, the world has been experiencing a comprehensive global restructuring of economic and social life.

Let's consider some of the most ground-shaking and enduring "megatrends" currently reshaping the music business.

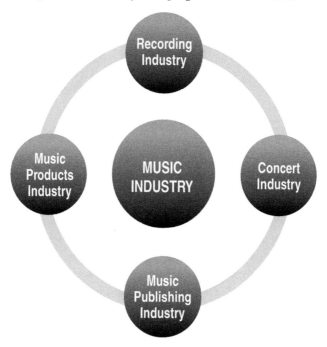

Fig. 1.1. The Music Industry's Four Main Sectors

MEGATREND 1. EMPOWERED MUSIC CONSUMERS

● Music Publishing: $3.8 Billion

● Music Products (Physical Items, ex. CDs): $5.7 Billion

● Music Recordings (Virtual Products, ex. MP3): $12.4 Billion

○ Concert Industry: $10.3 Billion

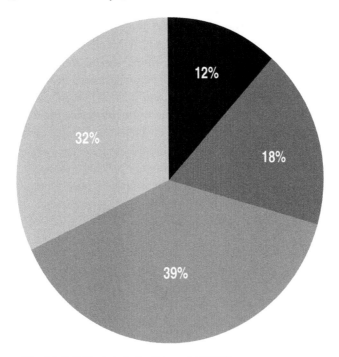

Fig. 1.2. U.S. Music Industry Revenues (2011)

Today may be the very best time to be a music fan, especially one looking for a connection to a favorite artist, or guidance and access to the exotic or rare.

Be it the iPad, alluring satellite radio services such as XM, the fan-beloved minutiae posted on websites, the availability of live music performances on NPR, the esoteric music videos streaming off Launch.com, or the self-tailored satisfaction of burning a home-made mix on CD at home, there is a singular zest to the modern fan experience today.

It's becoming increasingly more difficult for companies to treat us like "mass market" ciphers. The trend is towards "mass customization" where consumers' preferences are primary. Some marketing gurus call this trend "the 1-to-1 Future," and the companies that can respond creatively to it will prosper.

The public is now driving the market. And the challenge to the industry is to respond positively in such a way as to secure the future of music while satisfying customer demand and providing choice.

What You Can Do About It

- Get to know your fans. They are your chief assets, going forward. The better you know them, the better you can communicate with them, build loyalty, and enlist them in lending their support to you and your music projects.

- Involve them, empower them, mobilize them, let them co-create with you. None of us knows what all of us know. Build a community, a fan club, a subscription service, and learn how to pool the wisdom of your following.

- Provide potential customers with as much choice as possible.

- Learn the technologies that will help you customize your communications with customers and fans.

MEGATREND 2: EVERY BUSINESS IS BECOMING AN ENTERTAINMENT BUSINESS

Mountain Dew started a record label. So did Artois Brewery, Toyota, and Levi's Jeans. Apple Computer, Red Bull, and Nike—three companies outside the orbit of the traditional music business—have spearheaded successful initiatives in the music space that record companies themselves seem constitutionally incapable of carrying out.

Pharmaceutical giant Lilly has chosen music as the primary platform to convey marketing and educational messages to middle-aged men concerning its sexual dysfunction treatment Cialis. The Holiday Inn hotel chain launched its own music label, with its first "signing" being Nashville singer/songwriter Kyle Andrews. Holiday Inn used his song as part of its campaigns in markets around the globe.

If you look closely enough, you will notice that "the Hollywood organizational model" is quickly being adopted by a number of the cutting-edge industries of the twenty-first century. In his book *Jamming: The Art and Discipline of Business Creativity,* John Kao of Harvard Business School urges CEOs to integrate the Hollywood network model into their long-term strategic plans. "You need to act like today's version of a Hollywood studio," says Kao, "and practice business like an 'improvisational jazz band.'"

It's no mere coincidence that other industries try to model the way the entertainment industry is organized. The cultural industries—including the recording industry, the arts, television, and radio—commodify, package, and market *experiences* as opposed to physical products or services. Their stock and trade is selling short-term access to simulated worlds and altered states of consciousness. The fact is, they are an ideal organizational model for a global economy that is metamorphosing from commodifying goods and services to commodifying cultural experience itself.

Companies way outside the orbit of the traditional music business are awakening to this all around the planet. In early 2008, Bacardi announced that it would help the English electronic duo Groove Armada pay for and promote its next release. Caress, the body-care line owned by Unilever, commissioned the Pussycat Dolls singer Nicole Scherzinger to record a version of Duran Duran's "Rio" that it gave away on its website to promote its "Brazilian body wash" product. What we are seeing here is every business is becoming an entertainment business. One result of this is musical artists are no longer beholden to traditional "music industry companies" to achieve success.

Most would agree the major record companies served their purpose well; they made recorded music available to us on a vast scale for seventy-plus years, instilling an insatiable appetite for music in the process.

As a result, music *sells.* It has accompanied just about every product that's come to market since the 1930s. In fact, today some of the most interesting music is heard more readily on television commercials than on the radio. Wherever we go we hear music. Why? Because we love it and we want it. We want it when we drive, eat breakfast, shower, work, make love, shop for stuff—it's the aural landscape of our lives.

We hear music on recordings, on our computers, at concerts, on commercials, and at the airport; we listen to music over the phone and in our video games, Walkmen, iPods, Zunes, and cell phones. The global demand for music is chronic and ever-expanding.

We're purchasing music just about everywhere too. Twenty-five years ago you bought records at record stores; today you can get them at record stores, grocery stores, drug stores, book stores, consumer electronic stores, department stores, plant stores, tattoo parlors, bars, gyms, museum shops, through the mail, over the Internet, at kiosks, at the airport, at McDonald's, at Starbucks, at Victoria's Secret, thru 800 numbers, and hundreds of other places—MUSIC IS EVERYWHERE!

Why?

Because music is a universally loved value and activity, and companies across the board are looking to associate themselves with music and its fans.

What You Can Do About It

- These trends require a new way of thinking about the "music business" and "music industry careers." It's time to stretch our minds and get outside the box of traditional music business models. The "digital common" brings all kinds of non-music businesses into a space where creative partnerships can develop. Nonmusic partners are fresh and unjaded, and excited about associating with musical and entertainment arts as a way of adding value to what they're offering.

- Try reflecting on where musical products and services are *used* rather than on where they have traditionally been *sold*. For example, think of companies you personally resonate with and then focus on those that may have an affinity with the kind of music product you offer. Make an alliance and use that alliance to market your music. Consider Craig Dory and Brian Levine of Dorian Recordings who got their recordings played on all the new hardware at consumer electronics shows. Smart alliances.

- Remember, the economic structures of the last century are being torn apart. The rules are being rewritten. Anything goes in the business world today. Therein lie many opportunities *for you.*

MEGATREND 3:
NEW BUSINESS MODELS REPLACING THE OLD

The writing is on the wall for traditional music companies. The record industry grew rapidly, matured, and is now in the throes of transformation. How successful this transformation will be depends on how creatively the musical industrial complex can dance with all the changes spiraling around it.

Unfortunately, so much of the music industry is beholden to corporate owners, itchy for quick profits, and driven by rigid corporate imperatives. This wreaks havoc with *artist* development; heck, it wreaks havoc with *business* development, and necessitates high turnover of both artists and employees. Major labels are also saddled with legacy problems regarding production and retail. Thus, the geologic tempo of industry change.

But the same forces undoing the larger music companies are empowering individual musicians and microbusinesses.

As with most modern industries, a silent computer on a desk is the wildcard that makes so much tradition redundant. Perhaps the term "record company" itself is becoming outdated—"music company" might be more relevant. Many music biz execs echo the words of Steve Becket of Warp Records when he says, "I think we'll mutate into a new type of company—mixture of artist management, publisher, marketing consultant, agent, and promoter." "We're a communications company," agrees Marc Jones of Wall of Sound, "and that's what we're becoming more everyday. I don't think the model for a traditional record label will exist in this environment anymore."

But we don't have to solve the dilemma for the mainstream music business about which future to embrace. We're living the side-stream music movement that may inspire the majors, but God willing, will never be completely controlled by them.

Unlike mainstream commercial music, the farther you get out onto the fringes, the more helpful people become. The more participants, the greater the chances that something truly interesting will emerge from the collective rabble.

A new generation of music entrepreneurs is rising with a power in its corner it has never had before. The times are ripe for change and these creators are the spearhead.

What You Can Do About It

- The appetite for music only grows around the globe and you can satisfy it. You'll need to employ your maverick instincts over conventional "business rules", take fuller responsibility for your own success, and beware of "standard industry practices" that can handcuff your career.

- Your fans are the "coin of the realm" and your potential patrons of support. Explore how you can engage them with special projects underwritten by a crowd-funding service like Artistshare, Kickstarter, or Pledgemusic (see chart below).

- It's time to think outside the normal channels of business and imagine new kinds of companies. We should think outside the box of the musical industrial complex and explore fresh possibilities. What new shapes can *your* company take?

Creative alliances and partnerships are the key. Combining high-quality music, cheap, global distribution, creative event-making, and business savvy almost guarantees success in today's music-hungry world.

CROWDFUNDING
FROM "TOP DOWN" TO "BOTTOM UP"

TRADITIONAL RECORD LABEL MODEL	CROWDFUNDING MODEL
Lawyers & managers negotiate a support deal with...	Fans & audience decide their own deal to provide...
✦	✦
Record company that supplies...	Artist support
✦	
Artist support revenue so artist can build...	
✦	
Fans/ Audience	

MEGATREND 4: SEGMENTING MUSIC MARKETS AND NICHE MUSIC CULTURES

I often hear musicians moaning about how consolidation and the monopolization of the media by companies like Clear Channel and Viacom threaten musical diversity. Yet, I can hear and obtain more interesting music today than I could ever hope to in the 1950s.

The menu of music choices and styles expands daily.

Consider this: When the GRAMMYs started in 1958, there were 28 categories of awards. In 2011, there were 109! Even the pop charts, which have made room in recent years for Gym Class Heroes, Modest Mouse, Arcade Fire, Diana Krall, and Franz Ferdinand, suggest there's an audience starving for something other than musical junk food. Check out the "Music Styles" page at Allmusic. com, and you'll find over forty styles of music, *each* with a drop-down menu of several "substyles."

The music market continues to segment, and each segment is a "world"—a portal through which small companies can create value and success.

While good news for niche companies, this is bad news for the musical industrial complex. The major labels cannot justify going after these smaller markets, because they are optimized instead for the larger, pop mainstream. These niche music cultures can't generate the sales needed to float the major label boat. While 20,000 unit sales are a cause to celebrate at a microlabel, they hardly register a blip on big company radar screens.

The times call for focus. Mass customization and a segmenting market encourage the development of products and services of a "niche" nature. Since few of us have the time, money, or energy to mount national marketing campaigns, it is in our best interest to discover and concentrate on a niche—a segment that we can explore towards successful enterprise. Whether your specialty is house, trance, bluegrass, or neosoul, learn to work that niche and scope out relationships and opportunities within it.

What You Can Do About It

- What is *your* niche? Maybe it's arranging music, or the history of rock, or the intricacies of music software. Whatever it is, it will lie at the crossroads where your most compelling desires intersect with your background resources and current opportunities in the real world.

- What is *your music's* niche? If your music can be slotted into an established category, then master that area both musically and businesswise. Know the inlets and outlets for your music, become familiar with the influencers and tastemakers in that realm, and start communicating with them. If your music defies categorization, then lead with that.

MEGATREND 5: THE NEXT "BIG THING" IS SMALL

The analogy is television. Thirty years ago, the three broadcast networks (ABC, CBS, and NBC) had a 90 percent share of the viewing audience. Today, it's less than 40 percent. Where's the other 50 percent? Watching cable channels. Though cable channels have miniscule ratings, they're profitable. Why? Because they've discovered and developed their specialized audiences.

And this is what smaller, indie labels do. The Americana sounds of New West Records, Red House Records' focus on singer/songwriters, the creative acid jazz of Instinct Records, and the deep reggae catalog of Trojan all ensure listeners that they can expect quality discs from each company within their respective niches. The indie music market is not only healthy—it's thriving. In fact, independent labels are dominating the music scene, garnering the lion's share of 2011's GRAMMY Awards.

Lacking vision beyond their own profit lines, major record companies fail to see that the revolution in music delivery occurred in reaction to the industry's mismanagement, not to mention its complicity in force-feeding the public a flavorless diet of sonic pabulum. With the increasingly conservative (read, "risk-averse") stance of the majors today, indie market niches become all the more important to the creative development of music.

The implosion of the musical industrial complex has also resulted in the availability of many formerly signed artists and talented executives. The past ten years have seen veteran artists like the Pretenders, Rod Stewart, Foreigner, Aimee Mann, Sinead O'Connor, Carole King, Sammy Hagar, Dolly Parton, Hall & Oates, Hanson, Steve Vai, Sophie B. Hawkins, and dozens of others either starting their own labels or signing on with smart indies.

We are now looking at a historical crossroad. The state of affairs we now find ourselves in isn't so much an end of the recording industry as it is a new beginning. Today's indies, like Fueled By Ramen, Nuclear Blast, Dangerbird, Thirty Tigers, Definitive Jux, Stones Throw, Domino, Beach Street, and MapleCore, are all making themselves felt in this shaky marketplace for recorded music.

What You Can Do About It

- The paternalisms of yesterday have given way to personal responsibility for your own success. The Holy Grail is *not* a record deal; it's waking up to your own power.

- Signing with a major label today in most cases is a career *risk*. These divisions-within-corporations are generally unstable and anti-art environments, and best avoided by aspiring recording artists.

- If you're up for it, start your own company and release your music through it. If you want to delegate the heavy lifting, seek out a successful indie label to partner with. But only do so when you've achieved a level of success appealing to a business partner (that is, you're showing net profit for an extended period of time).

Record company bosses think society's top priority today must be restoring record-company revenue and profits. But music lovers and musicians have a different perspective. They want to know how musicians can exploit the extraordinary technology of the Internet to expand the audience and enable more musicians to make a living doing what they love, and improve the quality of life of consumers.

In a sense, musicians may be in a better place today than they've ever been before. Taking a cue from the cyber-bard John Perry Barlow, I believe we could be seeing a paradigm shift from the domination of the "music business" to that of the "musician business."

The more things go digital, the more we crave authentic, roots-based music. The more music that's available to us, the more we seek niches that provide meaning and navigation through all the choices. And the more worldwide radio shows through satellite radio, the more we desire shared cultural experience via local DJs.

If we had to, all of these trends can be placed under one banner that reads, "the larger the world economy, the more powerful its smallest players."

NEW BEGINNINGS IN THE NEW MUSIC ECONOMY

If you were to judge the health of the recording industry by the mainstream press, you'd have to conclude that things do look pretty bleak. Industry trade groups like the RIAA and the IFPI continue parading their woeful data on global CD sales, and there are no signs of improvement. In real dollars, the industry has been flatlining for ten straight years.

And it's not just the recording industry that's ailing. Other sectors of the biz—music publishing, music products, and the concert industries—are also registering declines.

But the key word here is "industry." It's important for those in the biz to make the distinction between the music "industry" and the music "trade." The former is primarily the domain of transnational corporations and organizations, like the RIAA and the major music companies; the latter is the domain of most musicians and a tremendous diversity of small music enterprises, most "under the radar" and perceived by the former as basically insignificant in the larger picture.

It's anybody's guess if the "industry" will re-emerge to its former financial glory. (I doubt it). There are forces at work taking the rug of necessity out from under large sectors of the corporate side of the biz—and not just the music industry, either. The same is happening in film, design, hedge funds, travel, insurance, publishing, real estate, and almost every other industry sector you can name.

Interestingly, the very same forces undoing longstanding industries are encouraging small-scale players. There is power in the corner of individuals today that there has never been before. In music, it's particularly acute.

To flip Paul Simon's lyrics from the song "Can't Run," "the music *business* suffers while the *music* thrives." It's nothing new that the coolest stuff has always come from outside the industry. But now, the music trade has a chance to control its own processes too, apart from the pressures of corporate imperatives.

And that's exactly what it's doing.

What are these powers music workers now have? How about:

- the means to both produce and distribute music on a global scale

- new business models to partner with in the world of music and beyond

- the Internet pipeline that has clearly become an open mic to the world

- lightweight plug-and-play software infrastructures providing musicians with ways to have the look, reach, and efficiencies of larger companies.

We have the power to galvanize global audiences and build a network of support for the rest of our careers. Sounds pretty good, huh?

It should.

But remember the timeless words of Uncle Ben to Peter Parker: "With great power comes...great responsibility."

And that's the rub.

The current difficult climate serves as a form of reckoning. The tougher the times, the more clarity you gain about the difference between what really matters and what you only pretend to care about.

No one knows where all the cards will fall in this industry-wide shakeup, but the good thing about radical change is that, during those times, the little person has a chance to make a big difference. It is the time when big ideas are brought to life, big names are made, and, yes, even big money is made.

Read on.

STAYING AHEAD OF THE CURVE

Wired Magazine:	www.wired.com
Digital Music News:	www.digitalmusicnews.com
Hypebot:	www.hypebot.com
Media Futurist:	www.mediafuturist.com

CHAPTER 2

Getting Ready to Do Business

The new music economy has little room for those who cannot read, write, compute, frame and solve problems, use technology, manage resources, work in teams, and continue to learn on the job. While it may be clear that you need good business and management chops in the new music business, it's sometimes hard to know how to get them.

Plus, business-related questions come fast and furious to the music startup. Do I trademark my band or business name now or wait? Do I need equipment insurance, and if so, where can I find a fair deal? What about taxes? Do I have to pay quarterly or yearly as a self-employed musician? Do I need a special license to perform the work of a booking agent or artist manager? These and other questions are part and parcel of "doing business." And a lot of business success lies in having the right and timely answers to those questions.

In chapter 1, we looked outward to changes and trends in the entertainment industry. Now, we turn inward and look at the skills and mindset required to develop a successful twenty-first century music career.

WANT TO GET RICH?
According to the book *The Millionaire Next Door*, by Thomas J. Stanley and William D. Danko, the best way to make a million is to become self-employed. They learned that about two-thirds of the millionaires who still worked were entrepreneurs. They report, "Self-employed people are four times more likely to be millionaires than people who work for others."

THE ENTREPRENEURIAL REVOLUTION

Fortunately, today presents a great climate for entrepreneurs. In the same way that independent record labels have been the R&D (research and development) labs for larger record companies (taking the risk, discovering talent, developing product, and pre-testing the marketplace), so have small businesses been the life-blood of the larger economy. They are the creative "labs" in which innovative products and services are born.

And while the economic downturn is forcing entrepreneurs to handle their operations more efficiently, there continues to be an unabated explosion of business startups. The Trendwatching Institute dubs this trend the "Rise of the Minipreneurs"—a vast army of consumers turning entrepreneurs, including small and micro businesses, freelancers, side businesses, weekend entrepreneurs, Web-driven entrepreneurs, part-timers, free agents, cottage businesses, seniorpreneurs, co-creators, mompreneurs, crowdpreneurs, pro-ams (professional-amateurs), solopreneurs, eBay traders, advertising-sponsored bloggers, and so on.

The combination of cheap digital technology, global reach, and tremendous support networks is spawning a true entrepreneurial revolution, and you can be part of it.

THE MUSICIAN AND BUSINESS

Speaking of entrepreneurship, unlike the civil servant and invest-ment banker, musicians are self-contained business entities with all the responsibilities and obligations that are part of all business activity. Since most musical work falls into a "do-it-yourself" approach, it's important to understand that the "it" you will be doing, for the most part, is business. Whether it's booking a gig, negotiating a contract, or organizing a promotion plan for your CD, the fact is you are exercising a variety of skills to grow a business: You, Inc.

The trick is figuring out what you're good at and then translating those skills into "profit-centers" or revenue streams. Most musicians wear a number of different "hats." In any one week, you may wear a performer's hat, an educator's hat, an agent's hat, an arranger's hat, and a songwriter's hat. Sometimes, you will wear all these hats in a single day! Each "hat" is a potential revenue stream and activity center that can be strategically managed to expand your customer audience. And each stream you choose to develop requires it own smaller plan within your larger plan.

The challenges loom large. You probably went into music because you didn't necessarily want to do business. Perhaps you watched your parents or relatives chafe under the constraints of business jobs. Maybe you cling to an antimaterialism that scorns and fears the pursuit of profit, and that casts "art" and "commerce" as hopeless opposites. We can add to this the fact that few of us ever received real-world strategies for developing successful careers from our schools and homes.

But whatever the poison, the effect is this has kept many musicians ignorant of how to go about creating success for themselves in the world. This is often the reason for all that erratic progress— those fits and starts in musicians' lives. Even when the goals are clear, the best paths to those goals remain a mystery.

In addition, creating your own personal music career map sometimes means clearing out previous experiences that may be holding you back. I call this clearing process "emotional bushwhacking." All of us carry around excess baggage and psychic trash that burdens our journey. This stuff has the effect of weighing us down and blurring our sight. The world is mediated to us through a lens created over the years of our lives, through our family experiences, our schooling, and the choices (both good and bad) we've made. Someone once said we don't see things as they are, we see things as we are, and I believe this is true.

As a professional musician, you will need all the resources and energy you can gather for your career journey. The key lies in understanding yourself enough to become aware of those things that tend to derail your efforts and short-circuit your progress.

Perhaps the most honest indicator of our emotional fitness is our relationships. You'd do well to look at these closely. Why? Because the music business is one of the most relationship-driven businesses on the planet. Your ongoing success will be determined, largely, by the quality and quantity of the relationships you build over time. Clearing out the emotional weeds that choke our actions and attitudes is an extremely important ingredient of the journey to your goals.

It takes great courage to look these things square in the eye, and many of us will need help sorting it all out. Fortunately, there are people who specialize in helping people become emotionally fit. Seek a referral from friends or from your school for a counselor who specializes in personal development. Many have "sliding scales" and will adjust charges based on your ability to pay.

CHECKING YOUR BUSINESS READINESS

Artist-entrepreneurs (aka, professional musicians) may not necessarily have set out to start a business. Their main focus is on developing their own craft, but they soon face a need to come to terms with a commercial environment in order to be able to make enough money to continue their artistic work, or they see the commercial market as a means of communicating with a larger audience. From this, then, evolves developing the necessary management and organizational skills to facilitate the performance and promotion of their work (e.g., organizing a tour production, writing business plans, understanding copyright and contractual issues, etc.). Of course, this is quite familiar to musicians. Most music-related work is of a freelance nature, requiring personal success skills like organization, self-promotion, and management. This has a long history. Even Beethoven worked hard securing gigs, hanging flyers, and negotiating his fees.

In the world of the freelancer, you control your own career and orchestrate your own work according to your own goals and objectives. And it's a good idea to take a look at what you bring to the business table in terms of skills, traits, and motivations.

Here's a "Entrepreneurial Self Quiz" from the SBA (Small Business Administration). I think it's a useful tool for discerning your own entrepreneurial instincts. See how you do. Under each question, check the answer that says what you feel, or comes closest to it. There are no right or wrong answers, but honesty is key.

Here we go:

ENTREPRENEURIAL SELF QUIZ

Are you a self-starter?

❑ 1. I do things on my own; nobody has to tell me to get going.

❑ 2. If something gets me started, I keep going all right.

❑ 3. Easy does it. I don't put myself out until I have to.

How do you feel about other people?

❑ 1. I like people. I can get along with just about anybody.

❑ 2. I have plenty of friends. I don't need anyone else.

❑ 3. Most people irritate me.

Can you lead others?

❑ 1. I can get most people to go along when I start something.

❑ 2. I can give the orders if someone tells me what we should do.

❑ 3. I let someone else get things moving. I go along if I feel like it.

Can you take responsibility?

❑ 1. I like to take charge of things and see them through.

❑ 2. I'll take over if I have to, but I'd rather let someone else be responsible.

❑ 3. There's always some eager beaver around wanting to show how smart he or she is. I say, let him/her.

How good of an organizer are you?

❑ 1. I like to have a plan before I start. I'm usually the one to get things lined up when the group wants to do something.

❑ 2. I do alright unless things get too confusing. Then I quit.

❑ 3. I get all set and then something comes along and presents too many problems. So I take things as they come.

How good of a worker are you?

- ❑ 1. I can keep going as long as I need to. I don't mind working hard for something I want.
- ❑ 2. I'll work hard for a while, but when I've had enough, that's it.
- ❑ 3. I can't see that hard work gets you anywhere.

Can you make decisions?

- ❑ 1. I can make up my mind in a hurry if I have to. It usually turns out okay, too.
- ❑ 2. I can if I have plenty of time. If I have to make up my mind fast, I tend to think I should have decided the other way.
- ❑ 3. I don't like to be the one who has to decide things.

Can people trust what you say?

- ❑ 1. You bet they can. I don't say things I don't mean.
- ❑ 2. I try to be on the level most of the time, but sometimes I just say what's easiest.
- ❑ 3. Why bother if the other person doesn't know the difference.

Can you stick with it?

- ❑ 1. If I make up my mind to do something, I don't let anything stop me.
- ❑ 2. I usually finish what I start—if it goes well.
- ❑ 3. If it doesn't go right immediately, I quit. Why beat your brains out?

How good is your health?

- ❑ 1. I never run down.
- ❑ 2. I have enough energy for most things I want to do.
- ❑ 3. I run out of energy sooner than most of my friends seem to.

Now count the checks you made besides the answer to each question.

How many checks are beside the 1st answer?_____

How many checks are beside the 2nd answer?_____

How many checks are beside the 3rd answer?_____

How did you do? If most of your checks are beside the first answers, you probably have what it takes to run a business. If not, you're likely to have more trouble than you can handle by yourself; better find a partner who is strong on the points in which you're weak. If many checks are beside the third answer, you should probably plan on getting a regular job and try being an *intrapreneur* (acting entrepreneurial within employment).

ENTREPRENEUR SUCCESS TRAITS

Behaviors	Attitudes	Skills
Taking the initiative	Achievement orientation and ambition	Creative problem solving
Solving problems creatively	Self-confidence and self-esteem	Negotiating
Managing autonomously	Tolerance for ambiguity	Management
Networking effectively to manage independence	Preference for learning by doing	Strategic thinking
Putting things together creatively	Adaptability/ Flexibility	Intuitive decision making in uncertainty
Using judgment to take calculated risk	Creativity/ Innovation	Social networking

Fig. 2.1. Entrepreneur Success Traits

INFORMATION IS YOUR FRIEND

Entrepreneurs need good information to function and, today, career and business-planning information is hyperabundant and readily available, if you know where to look. The "minipreneur" trend has hatched an entire industry focused on entrepreneurs and what they need. Books, blogs, magazines, software, websites, podcasts, and cable television and radio shows designed for micro-businesses are popping up everywhere and feeding the flame of entrepreneurship.

What kinds of information do you need for your career and business? In general you'll need:

- information about your industry
- information about key players and "tastemakers" in that industry
- information about a specific market
- information about competitors in that market
- information about legal requirements for your business idea
- information about startup costs in your line of business
- information about taxes and other financial requirements.

The music industry is a fairly complex industry, and you really need as much industry knowledge as you can get. By that, I mean that you have some understanding of issues such as these: Are there slow and busy times within the industry? What professional organizations are important to belong to? How is your profession or industry structured? What divisions exist for entry level, mid career, and advanced levels? What happens during the normal course of business? For instance, if your focus is recorded music, what happens in order for a song to be published? Can you name all the steps? Which steps would a customer expect you to perform, and which would be referred elsewhere? What is the jargon used in your industry or profession? What words will you need to know in order to communicate with people while doing your work? How is the industry segmented? What rules govern your profession? What licensing is required? Which government agencies regulate the industry/profession?

Besides information, you'll also need guidelines for the ever-growing variety of business demands that you will face. What's the best office setup for your needs? How do you hire help and where do you find it? What's the most effective use of your time? How much should you spend on promoting your music service or product?

Where can you find the answers to these questions without having to enroll in an MBA program?

To start, check out the Small Business Administration. The United States Small Business Administration (SBA) is one of those quiet government programs in which pearls lie hidden. This is the best return on your taxes you'll ever get, so listen up. Congress created the SBA in 1953 to encourage the formation of new enterprises and to nurture their growth. It exists to serve small businesses by providing information and financial backing and speaking on their behalf in the corridors of Capital Hill.

The SBA's mandate is very broad. The agency's definition of "small business"—service companies and retailers with annual revenues of $3.5 million or less, manufacturers with fewer than 500 employees, wholesalers employing fewer than 100 workers—embraces over 98 percent of the companies in the United States.

The SBA's staff is 4,000 nationwide, organized in 110 offices. So, taking advantage of the SBA requires learning what it's equipped to offer, and then discovering how to tap into its abundant resources. Here are two you can take advantage of today:

❏ **SBDCs (Small Business Development Centers).** When I was starting my publishing/consulting company (Music Business Solutions) in 1992, I contacted an SBA program called the Small Business Development Center (SBDC) in Salem, Massachusetts. SBDCs operate out of over 900 delivery points across the country, providing management training and other startup assistance to emerging businesses.

I was matched with a small business advisor who reviewed my business plan, provided me with my first software training, and offered suggestions and ideas galore for making Music Business Solutions a success.

Though untutored in the music business, my advisor was very experienced in the ways of general business management and marketing. Together, we forged a plan to launch and grow my business. In addition, he demystified the computer for me and introduced me to a whole new world of software resources I never knew existed.

To find the SBDC nearest you, contact your local SBA office. You can find their number in the U.S. Government section of your phone book. You can also find a list of all SBDCs in the U.S. at: www.sba.gov. Click on "Local Assistance."

❏ **SCORE (The Service Corps of Retired Executives).** If you don't live near a SBDC, you generally won't be able to take advantage of their services. That's where the online service of the Service Corps of Retired Executives (SCORE) comes in. SCORE complements the work of SBDCs. In fact, many SCORE representatives work out of SBDCs. Some 12,000 volunteers are available to consult, without charge, on topics ranging from writing a business plan to exporting your product.

Through in-depth counseling, SCORE volunteers help business owners and managers identify basic management problems, determine their problems' causes, and help them become better business managers. SCORE also offers "prebusiness" workshops nationwide to current and prospective small business entrepreneurs, covering a vast range of pertinent topics.

Almost any small independent business not dominant in its field can get help from SCORE. The approach is confidential and personal. Clients don't even need to have a business— consultation and counseling before a business startup takes off is an important part of the service too. And you can get counseling via e-mail. Visit the SCORE Website at www.score .org to be matched with an appropriate adviser.

Musicians and music-related businesses requiring guidelines on starting and developing a successful enterprise should make the SBA their first stop on the business trail. It won't necessarily provide you with music industry insights, but insofar as you're a business in a particular state, it could help you immensely.

ALTERNATIVE APPROACHES

Business advice may also come from unusual places. Boston band Two Ton Shoe realized early on that they'd move their project along faster with an organized plan. To help the process, they posted announcements at the Harvard Business School saying they were looking for management consulting for launching their own record label. This resulted in them teaming up with a trio of HBS students who succeeded in getting class credit for developing an independent study project with the band as the focus. This was similar to a typical SBI project but a little less formal.

The students spent their spring semester working with the act to develop a comprehensive business plan, including a section on industry trends and local factors. "Needless to say, this was a big bonus for us, and free!" says Two Ton Shoe guitarist Jake Shapiro. "Two years down the road, we've maintained relationships with the HBS grads, and it's quite possible that we will form a management team with one or more of them as our label and band grow."

THE ENTREPRENEURIAL MINDSET

The times we are living in are very supportive of entrepreneurship and working as a freelancer. But these fertile conditions must be accompanied by a certain attitude and approach so things grow in their optimal way. In my own work with hundreds of artists over the years, I have noticed a certain "mind-set" that goes along with the successful orchestration of work and relationships in thriving careers. The successful music entrepreneur does three things well: clears away obstacles, sets goals, and makes plans.

1. Clearing Obstacles

By obstacles, I'm talking about the internal environment where we think and feel our way through life. The poet Robert Frost once observed, "Something we were withholding made us weak, until we found out that it was ourselves."

It's true; we can easily end up our own worst enemies. Whether legacies of family dysfunction or just negative self-talk, we are merciless in finding ways to beat ourselves up.

Tracing the roots of this self-destruction (ultimately, that is what it is) may be a painful journey, but a necessary one. Until we do, we'll be hunched over with the weight of the world, not seeing straight, short-circuiting our happiness and poisoning our relationships. Sometimes, the only way to address this is through counseling or psychotherapy. If you think you need to, you're probably right. I did, found it, and it changed my life.

The times are ripe for liberated minds. We're finally beginning to accept we will never return to the more static, less opportunity-rich but also more comforting world in which most of us were raised. The changes we're living through are both permanent and dynamic. As Charles Handy wrote in *The Age of Reason*, "The real social revolution of the last thirty years is the switch from a life that is largely organized for us to a world in which we are all forced to be in charge of our own destiny."

That presents us with an exciting opportunity, but also a pressing challenge.

Today, we all have the chance to compose our own lives. It's a liberating prospect, but also daunting, because it requires a high degree of self-knowledge. If we don't start at the core—if we instead accept reflexive, inherited, or half-thought-out definitions of who we are and what we have to contribute—we run the risk of being overwhelmed by the possibilities that we face.

I call clearing the obstacles "emotional bushwhacking." We need to take a scythe to the overgrowth in order to see our true path. To break through to those other parts of ourselves that sit submerged beneath our everyday consciousness demands courage. But there is nothing more brave than filtering out the chatter that tells you to be someone you're not, and nothing more genuine than breaking away from the chorus to learn the sound of your own voice.

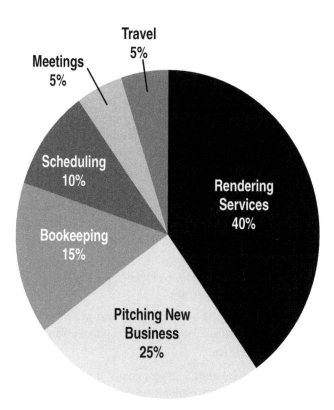

Fig. 2.2. How Entrepreneurs Divide Their Time

2. Setting Goals

If you're going to be on your own, you won't have a boss setting agendas and assigning projects. You will be the chart setter. You will be the time organizer. You will be the gig creator.

This means planning, and planning means first setting goals. Some people absolutely love this part of freelancing. They're planners at heart. They enjoy describing themselves as "goal oriented." They live by lists and relish crossing off items as things get done.

Others resist goals like the plague. To them, goals chain progress and limit horizons. They see them as "anti-art." We've all met these types. Some are just lucky, having fallen into good fortune with little or no planning. Others are propped up by trust funds and chronic parental bailouts. Still others are spinning their wheels, two months behind on car payments, and not really getting anywhere, fast.

Most of us, however, simply pay little or no attention to goals. In fact, we probably spend more time planning our vacations than setting goals and planning our careers.

You can make excuses or discount goal setting as being too rigid and linear for the creative person, or you can get with the program and finally start making some real progress toward achieving your dreams! Quite simply, you can't get to where you are going until you know where that is. Similarly, you can't hit a target you can't see.

But a list of projects is only as good as the larger goals that frame them.

We've heard lots of goal definitions. A goal is a thing aimed at; a goal is a destination; goals are dreams with deadlines. How you define "goals" doesn't really matter. What matters is making goals a value in your life. Goals focus effort, activate purpose, and strengthen resolve. Here are some general goal development tips you can put to use right now.

1. **Own them.** Be sure the goals and activities that you are working for are yours and that you really want and desire to achieve them.

2. **Keep them real.** Setting a goal you believe is unattainable will result in frustration. Strike that delicate balance between vision and realism.

3. **Give them form.** Write down your goals and post them in a place you can see them every day. Make a painting or drawing of them and hang it where you can see it every day. The mind tends to follow what's in front of it. Plus, there's a certain magic to taking your goals out of your head and materializing them in ink or image (more on this in chapter 3).

4. **Knit them to the now.** Once you set your long-range goals, try reflecting them in things you do every day. This way, you are always moving towards them. Success is not *someday*, success is *every day*. Decide what you should be accomplishing and then stick to your knitting. Every step along the way to achieving a goal is just as important as the last step.

5. **Revise as needed.** Rewrite your list of "Things To Do" daily after first reviewing your desired goals.

6. **Time and tempo.** Create a timeline or matrix chart on which you display your goals visually and the dates when you will have them accomplished.

And, of course, you've heard the saying, "the journey is the goal." That's true. It is not the achieving of a goal that is so important, it is what you become in the process.

MUSICIAN SKILLS THAT FAVOR ENTREPRENEURSHIP
Ability to handle rejection
Teamwork
Coalition building
Collaboration
Ability to strike compromise among diverse individuals
Engaging fans
Packaging a service
Creativity
Improvisation
Perseverance
Comfort level with multi-tasking
Ability to handle unpredictable outcomes
Discipline of practice
Public performance
Listening skills

Fig. 2.3. Musician Skills That Favor Entrepreneurship

3. Practical Planning

Of all the challenges that freelancers face, nothing matches in difficulty the *everydayness* of business ownership. It exists from the moment you wake up until the moment you collapse in exhaustion at the end of the day. It's exhilarating, terrifying…and constant.

What keeps this relentless routine from taking undue toll on you is the management systems you put in place. As already mentioned, good planning places you in the driver's seat rather than under the wheels. So far, you've cleared obstacles and set some goals. The first clears the way for creative thinking, and the second gives you something to aim at.

This third part looks at turning those goals into operational strategies, which means planning and management. Planning is a lot like map making. In fact, I like to think of career and business planning as a sort of cartography; it lays out the best way to the destinations you've set.

Planning is also the most difficult part of freelancing because it inevitably brings us face to face with our own management challenges. Most businesses (and most careers) fail, not because they have an inferior product or service, and not because they lack a market for their product or service. Most fail because of *management incompetence.*

So, when talking about planning, we are really talking about management of your self, your time, your team, and your knowledge. The ways you manage yourself, the approach you take to managing other people, and the ways you manage time, money, and information will be the primary reasons you're creative work succeeds (or fails) in the long run.

Try out these general management tips as foundation practices for bringing order to the normal chaos of freelance life. I've been using them successfully for over twenty-five years:

1. **Do only what you set out to do.** Focus on your specified project. Resist the urge to be distracted by what your eyes see. Instead, like a boomerang, let your brain keep guiding you back to achieving your immediate goal. Put other reminders in an action file, and do them when you're finished with this task.

2. **Do the best task at the best time.** After selecting the most productive task, do it at a time when you can accomplish it most effectively. Do tasks physically or mentally difficult for you at your own peak energy times; this includes making tough decisions. Do jobs you enjoy most (even if others consider them hard work) at low-ebb times. Don't try to do difficult work against all odds when you know you'll have lots of interruptions. Maximize your biorhythms.

3. **Get rid of "stuff."** Paper, publications, and possessions require maintenance; maintenance costs time, energy, space, and money. How long do you really need to keep

your old project files, seminar flyers, reference materials, conference materials, and association or business journals? Dispose of seldom- or never-used items. Ask yourself, "What will happen if I let this go?" If the answer is "Nothing," then get rid of it! Keeping it requires the same decisions over and over. Remember: It's okay to make a few mistakes; that's a small price for the contentment of having less "stuff."

4. **Touch it once! (Or, at least, try to.).** Be decisive: If at all possible, handle mail only once, and move on. If later action is needed, put it in an action file. Indecision is organizational death, yet most people aren't even aware of their inability to make decisions. Don't shuffle papers with the vague "I-don't-know-what-to-do-with-this-so-I'll-put-it-here-for-now" syndrome. Use the simple DRAFT technique: Delegate, Read, Act, File, or Toss. DRAFT spells death to ever-growing clutter.

5. **Think before acquiring more.** Evaluate before buying/accepting new items. Get off mailing lists that serve no purpose; drop subscriptions to periodicals you seldom read. Ask yourself if you really need this item, or are you simply acquiring it because it looks interesting, because someone passed it on to you, or because "it might come in handy sometime." Where will you store it? Items must do something more than collect dust. Accept as few papers and possessions as possible. For each item you do acquire, purge two!

6. **Use the 80/20 rule.** The 80/20 rule suggests that 80 percent of your accomplishments come from only 20 percent of your efforts. In a business context, the 80/20 rule reminds us that the relationship between input and output is not balanced. It's an interesting concept. The trick, of course, is to figure out what makes that 20 percent so productive. Then, devote more of your time to these productive activities, and reduce the time spent on unproductive work.

A caution: Whatever map you come up with to help you arrive at your business destinations, remember that the map is not the territory. Maps are provisional abstracts of the actual terrain you'll be traversing. They do, of course, provide lots of help along the way: pointing out hills and valleys, warning of dense scrub, and introducing you to various bridges and shortcuts. But maps can't reveal all the nuance and detail on the actual road in real time. This is the "X factor" in planning. No planning will be able to encompass all possibilities and variables.

We'll look at planning in more detail in chapter 3 when we explore writing your career/business plan.

CHAPTER 3

Plan Your Work, Work Your Plan

Consider these four common scenarios:

Scenario 1: A talented band wants a record deal, but their gig schedule is erratic, and members' day jobs keep sucking their energies, so there's not much left for anything else.

Scenario 2: A terrific songwriter keeps churning out tunes weekly, but they just sit in her notebook while she dreams of someday recording them.

Scenario 3: A singer and producer team up and record two cuts for release but then realize all the cash has gone to recording and manufacturing with none left for promotion and marketing.

Scenario 4: A music-school graduate with great promise sits in his insurance job cubicle and wonders, "What went wrong?"

Sound familiar? After twenty-five years of working in artist development, I've become painfully aware of a tremendous amount of musically gifted talent being squandered. Some musicians progress in fits and starts—one step forward, two back; two steps forward, one back...and so on. Others are just spinning their wheels, stalled. Still others are going in circles. A few, perhaps the most tragic, are spinning their wheels *and* going in circles.

What accounts for all this misguided effort? It could be many things: a lack of talent, drug abuse, laziness, etc. But, more often than not, musicians tend to get nowhere because of the absence of a map. A map is a plan that points to your destination and lays out the best routes to get there. Maps give us the "bird's-eye view"—the lay of the land, so to speak, so that our journey toward our destination is discernible and deliberate, rather than haphazard and blind.

Singer-songwriter Kelly Pardekooper of Iowa City put it this way: "The bottom line for me is that until I had a plan written down in black and white, I was just swimming in the dark, I had no anchor for my boat, no Felix for my Oscar."

A good music business plan is the map to the fulfillment of your goals. Whether you're a band, soloist, production house, or some other business, a plan can turn foggy notions into operational strategies, hunches into actions, dreams into reality.

MAPPING OUT YOUR MUSIC DESTINATIONS

Dreams. This is where it all begins isn't it? For this reason, I like to think of one's business plan as a "vision/mission." It starts with vision. Before your first gig, you envisioned yourself playing it. Remember? Vision precedes mission and fuels it with the necessary energy to go the distance. Mission implements vision and provides the vehicle that moves you towards your goal. Together, they're unstoppable!

"Success" can be defined as the progressive realization of a worthwhile goal. If you are doing the things that are moving you toward the attainment of your goal today, then you are "successful," even if you are not there yet. It's the goal that starts the whole journey. An illuminating study on goal setting sponsored by the Ford Foundation found that:

- 23 percent of the population have no idea what they want from life, and as a result, they don't have much.

- 67 percent of the population have a general idea of what they want, but they don't have any plans for how to get it.

- Only 10 percent of the population have specific, well-defined goals, but even then, seven out of the ten of those people reach their goals only half the time.

- The top 3 percent, however, achieved their goals 89 percent of the time—a .890 batting average!

What accounts for the dramatic difference between that top 3 percent and the others? Are you ready? The top 3 percent wrote down their goals. Are you laughing yet? It can't be that simple! Or can it? Dreams and wishes are not goals until they are written as specific end results on paper. In some very real sense, writing them down materializes them. Goals have been described as "dreams with a deadline." Written, specific goals provide direction and focus to our activities. They become a roadmap to follow. And the mind tends to follow what's in front of it.

MUSIC-RELATED BUSINESS OPPORTUNITIES	
Acoustic Consultant	Music Journalist
Artist/Personal Manager	Music Publicist
Audio Forensic Specialist	Music Publisher
Booking Agent	Music Supervisor
Commercial Music Producer	Music Therapist
Concert Promoter	Music Widget Maker
Digital Marketing Specialist	New Media PR Agent
DJ Service Coordinator	Online Editor
Film Scorer	Online Music Retailer
Game Music Supervisor	Podcast Producer
Instrument Repairman	Private Music Instructor
Jingle Writer	Project Studio Owner
Macro & Micro Blogger	Record Label Executive
Mobile Music Marketing Manager	Social Media Consultant
Music & Brands Consultant	Virtual Worlds Developer
Music Copyist	

Fig. 3.1. Music Related Business Opportunities

So, what is your dream goal? Is it to be the most in-demand session player on the East Coast? To be the next Jason Mraz? To get your song cast with a multiplatinum-selling recording artist? To start a company that creates soundtracks for videogames and commercials? Or is it to simply earn extra income playing music while holding down a successful nonmusic day job? Each one of these requires a specific map.

Are you even aware of your options? Music careers today are being rewritten as traditionally separate industries converge and spawn new opportunities for those familiar with audio in its manifold expressions. For example, did you know that book publishers are establishing music divisions, as they "repurpose" their titles onto CD-ROMS and other multimedia formats? As mentioned in chapter 1, music initiatives of all kinds are popping up in non-music companies. Think about where music is used today, and an explosion of possible paths will present themselves.

Knowing your options and establishing clear goals is your first step. Start with filling out the chart in figure 3.2.

Long-range goals are what you see yourself achieving, say, ten to fifteen years out. Think long and hard about these. Consider what you want your performance experience to be, your market visibility, your notoriety, what you want for your life personally as well as careerwise. Be specific.

Medium-range goals (five years out) should naturally grow from your short-range goals and naturally feed into your long-range goals. For example, I want to cast one of my songs with a top country artist; I want to perform in Japan; I want to score an EA videogame. Come up with your own, and be specific.

Your *short-range goals* (one to two years out) are goals you can see on the near horizon. For example, in light of the above medium-range goals, I'll hone my songwriting craft through cowriting with better songwriters; I'll network with booking agents and bands in the Asian markets; I'll score a video game for a student in a new media program near Boston. Come up with your own, and be specific.

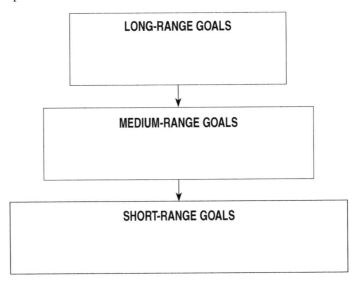

Fig. 3.2. Goals

The first two letters of the word *goal* are *go*. So, release the emergency brake, and put your goal in gear by taking that all-important first step. Once you have written down your goals, the question then becomes, "How do I get there?" It's time to start mapping out your career. I like to think of this as your Music Opportunity Plan.

NO NEED TO REINVENT THE WHEEL!

- Mozart borrowed from Bach to compose concertos.
- Seventeenth-century French musicians borrowed from military music of ancient Greece and Turkey.
- Paul Simon borrowed from South African musicians to create *Graceland*.
- The Rolling Stones borrowed from Muddy Water, B.B. King, and Solomon Burke.

In all creative fields, borrowing brings bounty.

HOW TO STRUCTURE A MUSIC OPPORTUNITY PLAN

Your music business/career plan will have six major components. They are:

I.   **Summary Statement.** What is the need you fill or problem you solve?

II. **Detailed Description of Your Business/Career Path.** How will you differentiate yourself from what is already out there?

III. **Marketing Plan.** Who are you selling to?

IV. **Operations Plan.** How will you manage things?

V.   **Project Timeline.** What are your action steps?

VI. **Financial Plan.** How will you make money?

We will look at each in turn. You may want to make a rough outline for your own plan as you read this chapter. Don't be surprised, however, if the complete plan ends up thirty or more pages long! That's about right.

Would you like some free help drafting your plan? Then contact your local SBDC (Small Business Development Center). As discussed in chapter 2, this is a federal program sponsored by the SBA (Small Business Administration) designed to provide small business owners with counsel and resources. These centers work out of colleges and universities, and offer free small business counseling and training, usually through another program called SCORE (the Service Corps of Retired Executives).

Okay, it's time to flesh out the different parts of your plan.

I. Summary Statement

The summary statement is often written last because so much gets sharpened in the writing of the plan that it needs to be rewritten anyway. For now, try to write down a draft that sums up your business and career plan as best you understand it.

You'll want to define the business you're starting, the type of products/services it will offer, and its role in the context of the overall music industry—particularly how your business concept is unique in that context. Be clear, be concise. Here are a couple of examples:

Revolver Records

> "The purpose of Revolver Records is to find the best, upcoming dance-music artists in the world, form strategic partnerships with them, fund their recording and development, and then use both traditional and new media outlets to promote their "brand" to the world. Complementary to promoting the artist is promoting the Revolver Records brand as an exciting source of new dance sounds."

Jeannie Deva Voice Studios

> "To provide singers around the world with a simple, direct method of voice training that is physiologically factual and nonstyle specific. To develop the full functionality, health, and expressivity of a singer's voice while maintaining and enhancing the unique identity of each vocal artist. To empower singers of all genres and styles with confidence in their instrument and their own vocal identity in live and studio performance. To raise

the bar on vocal excellence within the world music commu-
nity, thereby contributing to a planetary artistic renaissance
elevating the culture."

The summary should close with mention of anything that differentiates your project from all other similar ones. Try to keep your
summary statement to fewer than two hundred words.

CHOOSING A NAME FOR YOUR COMPANY

If you're like most business owners, your business means a lot to you.
In some ways, you consider it like your child. You have planned for it
since its conception, have nurtured it from birth, have given it tender
loving care, and have great hope for its future. It makes sense, then,
to consider naming your business with the same intelligence and
care that you would exercise in naming a child. Your business name
will be your number one asset, so take care in choosing one!

Here are four guidelines to help you name your company for the
long-term:

❑ **Make the name meaningful.** Since your company name is
   often the first thing someone knows about your business,
   consider it an important marketing tool (e.g., "Delicious Vinyl,"
   "Infectious Records," etc.).

❑ **Make sure the name is easy to pronounce and remember**
   (e.g., "Mountain Records" rolls off the tongue easily;
   "Stanhope House Records" does not).

❑ **Make sure it's available.** You want to ensure your company
   name is not being used by anyone else. Trademark your name
   and logo. The U.S. Patent and Trademark Office (uspto.gov)
   oversees trade and service marks. Make sure no one else
   owns the rights to your name and/or logo. If not, be sure to
   register it. It may be your only way to prevent someone from
   claiming he or she owned the name first, or from claiming to
   be you later. Registrations can be made in different "classes,"
   to cover recordings, live performances, merchandise, and
   other classes, so make sure you cover the bases. Registration
   costs can add up in a hurry, but a band or artist name and
   brand may become one of your biggest assets, so it's well
   worth it to protect it early.

❑ **Choose a name that you can live and grow with.** Be forward thinking in your choice of a business name, so that it can expand as you do. Some newer music companies choose to avoid the use of words like "records" and even "music" in their names, and instead, go with terms like "productions" or "media" instead to reflect changing technology and to allow the expansion of their company into other areas of entertainment and media.

II. Detailed Description of Your Business/Career Path

This section begins to flesh out the summary statement.

1. **Begin first with the history and background of your project.** This provides the overall context in which to view your current enterprise. List all data that pertains to the various facets of your present business. Don't pad it with your whole life story, just the pertinent highlights that have brought you to the present moment.

2. **A management description** should follow next. How is your business project organized? What does the leadership (it's style and command chain) look like? How are decisions made and facilitated? What kind of staffing (full-time, part-time, contractors, interns) will be necessary to operate the business? What ongoing business meeting schedule will be followed to ensure smooth operation? It's sometimes helpful to create a visual team flow chart (see section IV) to illustrate company functions.

3. **Describe the business structure you will use** (i.e. sole proprietorship, partnership, corporation, etc.) and why you chose that particular form. The chart on the next page provides a bird's-eye look at your options with some of the pros and cons of each. Your answer to this question has many legal and tax implications, varies greatly from state to state, and from time to time. Again, seek the advice of your small business advisor at your local SBDC office, your attorney, or your accountant if you have any nagging questions.

Comparing Legal Structures for Your Business

(+ positive; – negative)

Sole Proprietorship

+ Controlled by owner	– Personal liability for business debts
+ All profits to owner	– Limited resources
+ Little regulation	– Potential increased risk of IRS audit
+ Earning taxes at personal level	– Likelihood of no continuity at retirement/death

General Partnership

+ Joint ownership and responsibility	– Conflict of authority
+ Access to more money and skills	– Partners liable for actions of others
+ Earnings taxed at personal level	– Profits divided
	– Possible end of business at retirement or death of one partner

Limited Partnership

+ General partner(s) runs business	– Limited partners have no say in the business
+ Limited (silent) partners have no liability beyond invested money	– General partners have a personal liability for business debts
+ Earnings taxed at personal level	– More regulations than general partnerships

Limited Liability Company

+ Limited personal liability	– Relatively new entity with untested legal issues
+ Unlimited number of shareholders	– Costly to form and maintain
+ Profits and losses taxed at personal level	– Closely regulated by the state and IRS

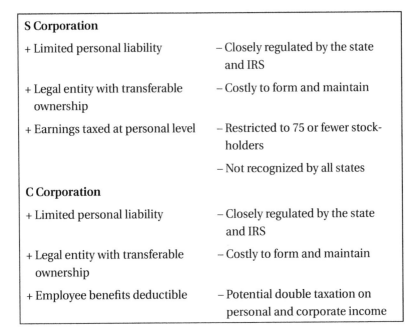

S Corporation

+ Limited personal liability	– Closely regulated by the state and IRS
+ Legal entity with transferable ownership	– Costly to form and maintain
+ Earnings taxed at personal level	– Restricted to 75 or fewer stock-holders
	– Not recognized by all states

C Corporation

+ Limited personal liability	– Closely regulated by the state and IRS
+ Legal entity with transferable ownership	– Costly to form and maintain
+ Employee benefits deductible	– Potential double taxation on personal and corporate income

Fig. 3.3. Comparing Legal Structures for Your Business

DRAFT AN AGREEMENT BETWEEN BAND MEMBERS

In the glow of the creative process, it's easy to forget to put things in writing. Write out an agreement in case issues come up at a later time (and they often do). The agreement should address the rights and responsibilities of the band members, including who owns what percentage of the business, what property is owned or controlled by the business (including the band name, website, and equipment), and who funds the bands and looks after its finances. Break out the percentage of ownership rights of each track. Who wrote it? How will you split royalties? Discuss what will happen if band members depart or new members join. Again, we suggest you consult a qualified attorney, to see if and when incorporation or a formal partnership would be recommended to help protect your assets. At any stage, it's important to have some kind of written agreement in place.

III. Marketing Plan

Now we are getting into the essence of what your company is uniquely about. Marketing ultimately results in *selling*, and it is an absolute truth that unless a startup business can sell its offerings, it will not survive. Getting orders—selling or licensing your products and services to paying customers—is of fundamental importance to a new business. This part of your plan is your opportunity to demonstrate how it will happen.

The marketing section of your plan breaks down as follows:

1. **Description of the Market for Your Product/Service.** In chapter 5, you will explore the details of your target market. You will draw on this information for this part of your plan. That research helps you correctly position your product in your primary and secondary markets and find your own unique niche within them. You will also include here what referral markets might be relevant and useful for your product or service. More on that in a moment. Like all of your planning, market research should be viewed as an ongoing process.

2. **Primary Market Description/Data.** Your primary market can be very broad, but you'll obviously need to narrow it down in order to describe it effectively. Who or what does the business provide these services or products to? Are there specific industries or geographic locations services are provided to, or are they offered internationally? Is the entity business-to-business, business-to-consumer, or both? Are you planning to sell mainly through retail? Your website? Others' websites?

   Here you will want to ask: What part of this larger market do I fit into? In other words, who are my *specific* customers? You might say "all musicians" or "every recording artist", but that's obviously too broad to be useful. "All musicians" may be your primary market, but you'll want to focus on the most relevant segment of the musician market for the most effective marketing strategy, like "musicians over forty years old" or "formally trained musicians in the Dallas-Fort Worth region."

   Provide a detailed description of your ideal customer. This doesn't mean that you cannot have customers who don't fit this description, but you should have a good sense now of who your *primary* target customer is.

If you can see a number of markets for what you're planning to sell, then list them all and give each a general description. For each one, try and get a sense of what makes that market 'tick' – what it values, where it feeds mediawise, what motivates it, and how it matches to what you are offering.

3. **Secondary Market Description/Data.** You will probably have more than one target customer (or market segment), and it is important to provide details of each. For instance, as a music publicist you might provide services to individual clients as well as to large record labels. Or, say you're a commercial music producer. Your primary market may be ad agencies and your secondary markets may be corporate video producers, college AV departments, and radio stations. Include as many secondary markets as make sense.

4. **Referral Markets.** These are complementary businesses that can *refer* customers to your business (and that you can refer your customers to when appropriate). For example, a college music teacher you know refers parents of young kids to your local private music instruction service. Or a Drum Circle workshop leader you know refers attendees to your percussion instrument store. Referral markets are endless but are only as valuable as the relationships they're built on. Online marketing strategies like "link exchanges" and "affiliate marketing" arrangements are the digital complements to traditional referral marketing.

5. **Competition Profiles.** In addition to your customers you'll also want to describe your competition. Be as specific as possible. Gather research on your three or four most pertinent competitors, assess the relative strengths and weaknesses of each, and compare your product or service with similar ones in terms of price, promotion, distribution, and customer satisfaction. Try filling out the "Mission Worksheet" in figure 3.4. It will help you identify and put into words your own special distinction.

Remember, information is readily available if you know where to look. The Web will be your key resource. But you should also visit retail stores if possible and speak with buyers in your particular category of music product or service, study relevant trade magazines, or see who listens to your company's genre of music, check statistics from RIAA and SoundScan, go to public libraries and tap into the skills of a reference librarian; even call the company you want to become or be similar to.

STATING YOUR MISSION WORKSHEET
In a sentence, how do you describe what your company does?
In a phrase, what product or service do you offer?
In a phrase, what group of people do you serve?
What benefits or positive outcome do you promise to those you serve?
When thinking about your offerings compared to your competitors' offerings, what words describe how yours are different or better?

Mission Statement Framework

[Name of your business] provides [description of the product or service your business offers] for [describe the group of people you serve] who seek [define the positive benefit you deliver] and who prefer our solution over available alternatives because we [describe your point of difference; what differentiates you].

Fig. 3.4. Mission Worksheet

6. **Marketing (Branding) Strategy.** Now that you've gathered information on your primary and secondary/referral markets, and your competitors, you're now ready to develop your marketing strategy or implementation plan. This too can be broken down into several component parts.

   a. **Positioning Statement.** "Positioning" is related to finding your market "niche," filling the gap you've discerned through studying your market and your competition. It establishes the desired perception of the way you want your target market to perceive, think, and feel about your services compared with the alternatives.

   Here are a couple positioning statements drawn from sample business plans at Bplans.com.

MusicWest

First, is from a music instrument shop in Albuquerque, NM:

For our target clientele, including those who feel abandoned by the local retailers, MusicWest will provide a complete one stop shopping experience that will address all the needs of the aspiring musician. By offering repairs and unique marketing programs such as our "You play, we pay" and our "100% of purchase price trade up policy," we can exceed the local client base's expectations of what a music store can be. Unlike the vast majority of our competitors, MusicWest will more selectively stock products with value in mind and not just the lowest price, and we will always strive to provide the highest level of attention to our customers in order to gain their trust and purchasing power.

Gamehenge Tapers Co-op

And another from a nonprofit music-related co-op:

Gamehenge Tapers Co-op is a not-for-profit organization that was created to serve the Portland tapers community. The tapers community is a hobby-based community that trades live recordings for personal use, never for commercial gain. The Co-op will provide this community with the equipment needed to further the taping of shows which in effect supports the trading community as well (people who trade these live shows for personal consumption only). The Co-op sells the recording equipment at wholesale prices plus a low overhead percentage. By offering the members heavily discounted rates, it encourages them to become more active tapers. Because the organization, is a not-for-profit co-op, members are willing to volunteer their time to help the organization, allowing it to become successful. The organization, exists to support the trading community.

No matter what products or services you provide, you can carve out a niche for them based on your experience, skills, resources, and interests and deepen that niche as you work to serve it. Ask yourself questions like: Who needs what I'm offering the most? Where can I provide that product or service that will give me a chance to expand what I do to utilize my other interests? What do I have to offer that is special or unique? The answers to these questions will help you "position" yourself to most effectively promote what you're selling. Ultimately, the place you want to position yourself is in *your customers' minds.* It's a matter of how your market "sees" you in its mind's eye that ultimately matters.

b.   **Marketing Mix.** As we will see in chapter 6, the particular combination of marketing methods you choose for your marketing campaign is referred to as your "marketing mix." Methods can include news releases, sponsorships, social media, personal contact, publicity flyers, contests and giveaways, classified ads, trade shows, radio spots, charitable donations, and literally hundreds more.

When making your selection, keep in mind this fundamental rule of successful marketing: The measure of a successful marketing campaign is the extent to which it reaches—at the lowest possible cost—the greatest number of people who can and will buy your product or service.

Generally speaking, the more of your time a marketing activity requires, the less money it costs you, and vice-versa. For example, networking costs almost nothing in money but lots in time. On the other hand, advertising in a city newspaper costs a bundle while requiring relatively little in time.

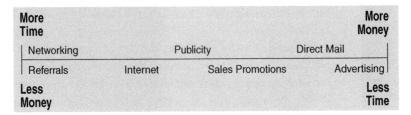

Fig. 3.5. Activities Requiring More/Less Time vs. Money

    c. **Pricing Philosophy.** How much you charge for your product or service will depend on many factors. Here is where the research about your competitors comes in especially handy.

        Undercutting your competition is one common way to gain market share. But there is another approach. Research has shown that buyers, when making a purchase decision, select what they consider to be the best *value*, all things considered—the benefits they perceive divided by the price. *Price, therefore, is only one part of the purchase decision process.* For example, the label Accurate Records of Cambridge, Massachusetts has routinely sold its CD releases for $4-5 *above* average retail price. It has been able to do so because of the high-quality, unique music its founder, Russ Gershon, signs and produces.

        If you want to increase your customers' perceived value of your product, you can do so by either increasing the benefits or decreasing the price. It is almost always preferable to work on the benefits—both tangible and intangible, both rational and emotional, both large and small—that will make it possible to sell at a higher price.

    d. **Method(s) of Sales/Distribution.** This, of course, is related to your marketing mix and details the methods you will employ in implementing the various parts of your mix. Methods can include direct marketing, retail consignment, or working through brokers, sales agents, or wholesalers. Also known as "sales channels," these methods need not only distribute goods. (For example, a record label might make use of a regional distributor as a sales channel.) They can also distribute "awareness" of your company and its offerings. Say you invented a unique guitar strap, and you placed it in a national mail-order catalog targeted to musicians. That catalog would be distributing awareness of your company towards making sales.

It's helpful to analyze the distribution channels of your competitors before deciding whether to use the same type of channel or an alternative that may provide you with a strategic advantage.

e. **Customer Service Policy.** As we saw in chapter 1, one of the clearest market developments of the past twenty years is the increasing power of the consumer to drive production and the marketplace. It's a buyer's market, and customers are demanding more and more from businesses. This has forced companies to give increasing attention to developing their customer service standards.

Meeting the needs and expectations of fans and customers requires that you know them as individuals. That means consistently collecting their input, removing barriers to communicate with them, and taking steps to foster a long-term relationship with them, rather than just a limited, transactional one.

See if you can translate elements of this customer dynamic into your own customer service policy. Write down your customer philosophy, and then list all applications you can imagine related to your business. Clear, straightforward, customer-friendly policies should accompany your vision. Think of ways to build rapport with customers, how you can show appreciation to them, and ways you can make a lasting impression. Consider how you can go the extra mile with your fans. Find ways of distinguishing yourself from your competitors in this area, and you will ensure a faithful clientele for years to come.

When considering customer service, it is always useful to ask yourself why *you* continue to frequent certain businesses. More than price, more than product quality, you will often return again and again to these businesses because you feel taken care of. The people of those businesses go the all-important "extra mile" to make you feel special. They anticipate your needs and provide for them in the various ways they deal with you.

IV. Operations Plan

Operations has to do with the overall physical and logistical operations of your company. How are you actually going to run your business? The operations section of your plan is where you begin to explain the day-to-day functions of your company. As such, this section becomes the preamble to your company's "Operations Manual." This eventual manual should describe the specific details of the processes by which you produce, distribute, maintain, and manage your products and services.

Examining your basic operation is particularly important for internal planning. A capable manager does not take any activity in the business process for granted. Each step is worthy of evaluation and improvement. In fact, a little bit of extra planning in the operational area can mean marked improvements in profit margin.

The operations section of your plan typically has four parts to it: facilities and equipment, organizational dynamics, expansion plans, and risk assessments.

1. **Facilities and Equipment** will encompass such things as your location, office space, studio facility, computer technology, instruments, gear, sound and light equipment, and vehicles you use to haul it all around. "Creating Your Workspace" (page 67) provides much greater detail on these matters and you may want to scan it for ideas to help with the operations section of your business plan.

    In this section, you'll answer these three questions:

    - Where is the business located? How much space is rented/owned/allocated?

    - What relevant equipment do you own, and what remains to be purchased?

    - What arrangements have been or need to be made with other businesses in order to provide the products and/or services offered by your business?

    When evaluating your *facilities*, examine those aspects most important for your particular business. Do you need a prestigious address in a downtown office building? Do you need to be close to key suppliers for your manufacturing processes? Do you need access to transportation resources? When record label distributor Jay Andreozzi looked for a spot to set up shop, he made sure he found one near Boston's Logan Airport in order to expedite shipments to his international customers.

What aspects of your facilities are most likely to affect your company's success? Are you near your target market? Are you in a convenient location? Does your lease have particularly favorable terms? Will you be able to grow in these facilities without moving?

If you're a home-based business, how will that affect the company's bottom line and image? What is your neighborhood like? Are there special amenities nearby? Is there something you wish were close by but isn't? How does that affect your business? Finally, describe *where* your office will be located within your home.

In this section of the plan, list what *equipment* your business will need and whether you currently own or must purchase that equipment. Also in this section, describe the necessary supplies you'll use in your business. Imagine the complete cycle of meeting your ideal customer, convincing her to hire you, performing work for her, and getting paid. What supplies do you need at each step? What about software? Beyond word processing and spreadsheets, you will probably need software to store and manage client information, invoices, and orders. What about music production software like Pro Tools, Logic, or Ableton Live, and hardware like outboard gear and computers? A brief note on equipment *insurance* should also be included here, if relevant.

Investors and lenders also appreciate seeing the founders of a company have a cash investment in the business, in addition to "sweat equity," so a mention of what you yourself will be bringing to the business in terms of hardware, software, and other assets would be appropriate to mention.

We will cover office setup and equipment in chapter 4. For now, just identify and generally describe the location of your business and the essential equipment you will need to launch it. Draw from the startup budget you created earlier in this chapter for the equipment inventory.

Organizational Dynamics. How is the company set up to ensure smooth, efficient operations (that is, "nonmoney/time/energy-wasting")? Every manufacturing business has a production process—the way it goes about fabricating a raw or component material and creating an item with greater usefulness or desirability. But even if yours is a service or retail business, you have a method of "producing" something of value for your customers, whether it's music lessons, media visibility, better-sounding recording studios, or successful music performances.

Take time to evaluate and assess your production plan to see if you can enhance efficiencies, improve the quality of the finished product/service, and in the long run, increase your profit margin. Look at the various stages involved in creating your product or service. Can these stages be shortened? If so, you will be able to produce more and sell more in less time.

Examine also how you plan to organize and orchestrate your workforce. What role does each worker have in this process? Do you use a team approach, with one group of workers responsible for a job, from start to finish? Or, do you use a production-line approach, with a worker doing the same portion of each job and then passing it along to someone else?

Increasingly, companies are using *variable labor* in addition to permanent employees, as an integral part of their workforce. Variable labor—employees hired to perform a specific task for a specified period of time—is particularly useful for seasonal work or unusually large or special orders. Temp workers are a form of variable labor, as are interns and subcontractors.

Sometimes it helps to draw an organizational chart that graphically represents workflow and structure, like the staff chart below for a mid-size indie record label.

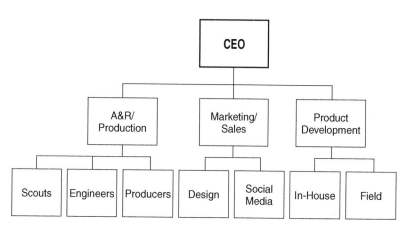

Fig. 3.6. Organizational Chart for a Record Label

2. **Expansion Plans.** Here is where you project some of your general goals into the future. Where do you want to go? What do you want your business to look like in three, five, or seven years? What will you need when you progress from local to regional success? Regional to national? National to international? Do you even want to go national or international?

In founder-led and small companies, the personal goals of the entrepreneur and the goals of the business should reasonably relate to one another. Otherwise, the inherent tensions will undermine the success of the business. Jimmy Buffett is best known as a successful singer/songwriter with several gold and platinum records and sold-out concert tours, but he is also a best-selling author, owns two Margaritaville restaurants, a recording studio, his own record label, a profitable mail-order business, and a newsletter, as well as interests in several minor-league baseball teams. He hasn't had a hit record since 1977 and yet is one of the highest-earning entertainers each year, according to *Forbes* magazine.

Perhaps you'll want to develop other divisions within your primary company. Maybe a publishing wing, or a video division, or possibly branch out into an entirely new market. Maybe you aspire to be a niche leader, carving out a narrow place in the market that your company can dominate; or perhaps your goal is to be an innovator in your business category.

Whatever the goal, in the course of your planning process you will find it useful to establish *markers*—milestones—to keep you on track. By developing specific objectives, you have signposts to measure progress along the way. Think it through as clearly and completely as possible, and leave some flexibility built in for creative surprises.

3. **Risk Assessments.** Not only does risk assessment show you're being open and honest with your financing source, but it forces you to consider and assess alternative strategies in the event your original assumptions do not materialize.

    List possible *external* events that might occur to hamper your success: a recession, new competition, shifts in customer demand, unfavorable industry trends, problems with suppliers, or changes in legislation. Also, identify potential *internal* challenges such as income projections not realized, long-term illness, or serious injury. Then generate a contingency plan to counteract the most significant risks. Think them through.

V. Project Timeline

In the project timeline, you want to lay out the schedule for your business goals, both short range (e.g., producing a CD, licensing a track, setting up an internship program, launching a new business division, procuring distribution, etc.) and long range (e.g., signing a joint-venture deal, licensing your catalog to an Asian record company, expanding into a new city, etc.). This is also a good place to schedule the unfolding of your marketing plan. Think through the essential steps needed for the attainment of each goal and then estimate how much time each will take.

Your project timeline can also list your future milestones. A milestone list allows you to see what you specifically plan to accomplish, and it sets out clearly delineated objectives. For example: Initial Financing Secured, Product Design Completed, European Band Contacts Established, First Products Shipped, etc.

VI. Financial Plan

People in business usually fall into one of two categories: those who are fascinated by numbers, or those who are frightened by them. If you're in the first category, you're probably delighted to have finally gotten to this section. If you are one of those in the second category, however, you're probably intimidated by the very prospect of having to touch financial matters.

Take heart: Numbers are neither magical, mysterious, nor menacing. They merely reflect other decisions you have made previously in your business planning. Every business decision leads to a number, and taken together, these numbers form the basis of your financial forms.

After defining your product or service, market, and operations, you need to address the real backbone of the business plan: the financial information. No matter how wonderful your plan is, it isn't going anywhere without capital investment, whether it's yours or someone else's. Most business plans will have four separate financial forms or spreadsheets: *Startup Expenses, Income Statement* (shows whether your company is making a profit), *Cash-Flow Projection* (shows whether the company has the cash to pay its bills), and *Balance Sheet* (shows how much the company is worth overall). In this chapter, you'll create only the first two, and your income statement will cover three years. The additional forms are very helpful in an already functioning business, but in this book, we are concerned with an entrepreneurial startup, and so the financial information is simpler and also more concrete.

Next to your competitive differentiation, this is the part of the plan potential investors and lenders will concentrate on the most. If you will be using your plan to secure a loan or to attract investors, you'll need to approach the financials in more depth. This is where a SCORE or SBDC advisor can prove indispensable.

Some guidelines for preparing your financial forms (or, how *not* to act like the Wall St. "giants"):

- Be conservative: avoid the rosy picture.

- Be honest: expect to be asked to justify your numbers.

- Don't be creative: use standard formats and financial terms.

- Be consistent.

1. **Startup Costs.** You have already worked out your startup expenses earlier in this chapter, so draw on that information. Of course, for both sections you want to create spreadsheets to hold and display the financial data.

1.	**Legal Costs** (incorporation, trademark clearance, etc.)	$
2.	**Fees and Licenses**	$
3.	**Design** (logos, letterhead, etc.)	$
4.	**Printing**	$
5.	**Fixing Up/Equipping the Office, etc.**	$
6.	**Hardware/Software Expenses**	$
7.	**Rent before Startup**	$
8.	**Insurance before Startup**	$
9.	**Office Supplies**	$
10.	**P.O. Box Rental Fee**	$
11.	**Website Development/Maintenance**	$
12.	**Industry Expenses** (subscriptions, travel, etc.)	$

Fig. 3.7. Expense Worksheet

2. **Three-Year Income Projection.** Financial projections provide your team with an idea of where you plan to take the business. Perhaps more importantly, they tell a lot about your intrinsic good sense and understanding of the difficulties your company faces.

    It "normally" takes a well-run business with a marketable product or service about three years to turn a profit. So, to start with, think through all the possible expenses you'll have over a 36-month period. These are "the costs of doing business."

    They will include:

    - All *startup* costs (e.g., licenses, trademark, office equipment, etc.)

    - All *operating* costs (e.g., rent, utilities, insurance, marketing, etc.)

    - All *production* costs (e.g., studio time, engineers, manufacturing, etc.).

No need to break each year down into monthly projections; just make three annual columns with side itemizations of projected revenues and costs. The first column will also contain your startup costs for the first year.

The spreadsheet in figure 3.8 illustrates the financial cash flow and three-year projections of the fictional jam band, Ping.

THREE YEAR CASH FLOW

	Year 1 (2007)	Year 2 (2008)	Year 3 (2009)
Revenues			
Record Sales	40,000	90,900	204,525
Merchandising	47,000	100,000	225,000
Personal Appearances	42,000	85,000	191,250
Sponsorship	0	15,000	35,000
Licensing (Music Publishing)	2,700	5,400	12,150
Recording Studio	12,000	18,000	402,500
Total Revenues	**143,700**	**314,300**	**708,425**
Cost of Sales			
Record Sales (Manufacturing)	8,800	19,998	44,995
Merchandising (Purchasing Inventory)	10,340	22,000	49,500
Personal Appearances	9,240	18,700	42,075
Sponsorship	0	0	0
Licensing (Music Publishing)	594	1,188	2,673
Recording Studio	2,640	3,960	8,910
Total Cost of Goods Sold	**31,614**	**65,846**	**148,153**
Gross Profit			
Operating Expenses			
Record Production	5,500	8,000	9,000
Postproduction	700	1,200	1,500
Digital Distribution Costs	60	20	20
Overhead	21,130	28,487	29,911
Total Opearing Expenses	**33,390**	**37,707**	**40,431**
Selling General & Administrative Expenses (Touring & Promotional Costs)	**41,950**	**51,268**	**62,556**
NET INCOME	36,746	159,479	457,285

Fig. 3.8. Three-Year Cash Flow

Whatever you decide you need financially, make sure it's based on a hardheaded assessment of the true costs of achieving your goals. A basic rule of thumb in estimating costs is to always add 15 percent onto whatever figure you come up with. This covers all those additional "hidden" and unexpected costs that inevitably arise. Also, it doesn't take a boatload of money to start most businesses. Rhino Records was started with three dollars (that's not a misprint). The founders turned a three-dollar pile of used records into a $70-million business selling collections of novelty tunes and past hits. It you have a good idea, the requisite skills, and the drive, then you're more than halfway there.

STAYING FLEXIBLE

Don't worry if you feel a bit overwhelmed by the avalanche of detail your business and career plan requires. Who wouldn't? Give yourself time. It's helpful to set yourself a goal for completing the first draft of your plan—say, three months from now.

Begin with one section at a time, and meet periodically with your small business adviser to review your plan's development. He or she will be able to discern blind spots as well as affirm the plan's overall direction. When performing songwriter Gilli Moon began working on her own business plan, it went from one version to another over a long period of time. "In fact," she says, "I'd sit with my mentor once a month and revise it, for about four years. Now I do it once a year."

Remember, too, that your business plan is just a provisional guide that will evolve over time. It is never really "finished." Co-founder of Nimbit, Patrick Faucher, states unequivocally, "One thing is for sure, whatever plan you write, it is imperfect and will always change over time." This is no reason, however, to not write your plan, says Faucher. "It's a valuable tool to help you focus effort and measure against what you set out to do. I can't imagine starting a business without one, because it causes you to define what success is for the project."

If you're thinking of foregoing the effort altogether and just "winging" it, remember that no planning inevitably leads to wasted time, money, and energy—all three in short supply for startup businesses! Remember, too, that your plan is *primarily for you*. It's an opportunity to direct your passions and energy. This is also how Panos Panay, founder of Sonicbids, sees it: "I don't think that you should write a plan necessarily for raising money; you should write it as a roadmap for you." A map is a good metaphor and your plan should be designed to get you to your destination (business goal) in the most effective and efficient way possible.

CHAPTER 4

Smart Management for the Professional Musician

According to the Small Business Administration (SBA), the number one reason for small business failures in the United States is a lack of effective management. Seven out of ten new businesses fail in their first three years due to management incompetence, not a lack of business.

The same can be said about bands and other independent music projects. Musicians come together, decide to form a band, woodshed for months in basements and garages, land their first gig, perform it, and go back to the basement.

A few months later they land their second gig and then, in another couple of months, a third. In between gigs, they're practicing, practicing, practicing. Some start to feel stir-crazy. Soon, a band member gets discouraged and quits. It takes three months to find a replacement, and the cycle begins again. One step forward, two back. Sound familiar?

Now, some musicians might not mind this. They're content to play when they feel like it and don't entertain goals beyond the garage. But for those trying to build a professional career, they had better heed the SBA's findings: Most businesses fail because of management incompetence. The way you manage yourself, the approach you take to managing other people, and the ways you manage time, money, and information will be the primary reasons your company succeeds (or fails) in the long run.

This is both good news and bad news for musicians. The bad news is that top-notch managers are extremely hard to find. An effective artist manager is reluctant to take on unproven talent. Yet how can talent prove itself without good management? It's a classic Catch-22.

The good news is that you can learn how to manage your own career. Daunting, you say? Perhaps at first, but what's the alternative? Staring at those same four walls months at a time, or worse, letting disillusionment sap every last vestige of musical inspiration from your soul? It happens. Eventually, you will want someone else to do the heavy lifting of management, but for now, it's up to you, until you can attract that expertise.

Self-management need not be daunting. In fact, most bands are already managing themselves to a greater or lesser degree. With a few basic skills and a working knowledge of some powerful resources, you can raise your music project to the next level of success. Effective management begins with *you*.

THE SELF-MANAGED MUSICIAN

So, what is management? Well, it includes lots of things: organizing, planning, staffing, supervising, controlling, coordinating, and innovating. Essentially, it is making something planned happen within a specific time through the smart use of available resources.

That definition encompasses planning, goals, intelligence, and resourcefulness. Management is essentially "conducting" your business and "orchestra" to "perform" the strategic "composition" (your career) magnificently. Your success as a manager comes down to the difference between managing your work and letting your work manage you. Therefore, like the maestro, the most important ingredient to your company's success (besides you) will be *smart, creative, and resourceful conducting (i.e., management) of your business.*

Figure 4.1 illustrates the many dimensions of management you will be conducting. As you can see, management puts a lot on your plate.

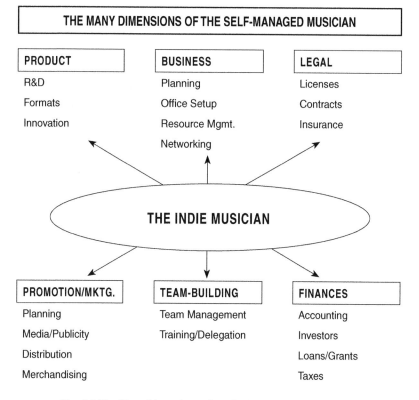

Fig. 4.1. The Many Dimensions of the Self-Managed Musician

THE BASICS OF GOOD MANAGEMENT

What are the required skills for effective career and business management?

1. **Organization.** Numero uno is organization. Management and organization are closely linked. Music management involves continual organization of people, equipment, time, money, information, and long- and short-range goals. Organization is the foundation on which all successful management rests.

   Organization is closely related to planning. Plans are like maps helping you get to your destination quicker and to avoid dead ends in the process (see chapter 3). To be an effective planner, you need: a knowledge of how your busi-

ness works, an understanding of the marketplace, an awareness of the specific tasks needed to complete your goal,
information about external conditions that may effect your
business, an understanding of what obstacles you are likely
to encounter, a knowledge of how fast you work, a familiarity
with people and services you may require, and a knowledge
of how to go about getting the information you lack.

That's a tall order.

You're going to invest some time gathering the information that will turn you into an effective planner, but it is an
investment that pays high dividends. Time efficiency expert
Robert Moskowitz calls planning "the mechanism that lets
you get out of the crush and constant flow of events . . . Good
planning puts you in the driver's seat instead of under the
rear wheels."

2. **Oversight.** This means keeping the whole project in full view.
    A music career has many dimensions and the self-managed
    musician endeavors to keep an eye on every one of them
    simultaneously (see figure 4.1). These dimensions include:

    - musicianship: writing, practice, rehearsing, and
      repertoire

    - business: licenses, legalities, taxes, and accounting

    - recording: studio research, choice of producer, engi-
      neer, and masterer, and manufacturer

    - performance: booking, stage show, sound and lights,
      and touring

    - promotion and marketing: publicity, radio, reviews,
      distribution, merchandising, and video.

    Being organized helps to facilitate the oversight of this
    multidimensional project so that no single area is neglected
    in the overall progress of your business and career. Keeping
    a handle on each of these dimensions and learning how
    to balance them is the key to success. This is why good
    management is like conducting: you don't need to be able to
    play every instrument perfectly, but you do need to have the
    whole score in mind as you conduct your business.

3. **Communication.** The self-managed musician is in constant communication with a myriad of people in an effort to promote his or her music career. This communication takes many forms: emails, letters, tweets, phone calls, flyers, blog posts, business cards, EPKs, etc.

   - Effective management communication means grammatically correct writing, articulate speaking, and creative use of graphic design. This word brigade represents you and your music to the world. The saying, "You never get a second chance to make a first impression" is particularly apt in the music business. A misspelled word or grainy image can banish your project to oblivion in an industry driven by state-of-the-art communications. High-quality communications insure a hearing and ranks you with the winners.

   - Well-managed communication also happens in-house in the form of planning meetings among group and support team members. Don't ever assume everyone in your band or on your team knows what you're thinking. Tell them your ideas and plans, and welcome feedback. Many bands and music projects have suffered because of chronic miscommunications.

   - It's good to remember too that "marketing" in its essence is communication. It is communicating so well that people want to know more about you. More on this later.

4. **Networking.** Successful music management depends on contacts and other support resources. "Networking" is where communications and contacts meet. It's the process of building strategic alliances with those who can help further your career. And, after the music, nothing is more important than who you know in the music industry, and who knows you.

   - Establishing music-industry contacts assumes, of course, a certain level of interpersonal and relationship-building skills. In my work with artists over the years, I have noticed that, as a group, they tend to be of a more solitary and contemplative nature. Introversion rather than extroversion tends to characterize musicians. And this is appropriate in light of the work they do.

- But too much isolation can lead to difficulty in forming friendships, intimate relationships, and social contacts. As a result, artists sometimes find themselves painfully unprepared for the ways of the world. This is a key reason, I believe, why artists have such a hard time with the *business* of music. Doing business, making contacts, and networking all involve a high level of social interaction. The successful self-managed artist will learn to strike a balance between art and business, creativity and commerce, and isolation and interaction. We'll explore the practice and challenges of networking in greater depth in chapter 5.

- Organization, oversight, communications, and contact building are the four primary skills needed to successfully manage your band or music career. How do you measure up? If you're a solo artist without a manager, you'll need to develop these skills on your own. In a band, the managerial responsibilities can be shared among all the members, and they should be. One member might be good with social media, another with graphic design, still another with making new connections.

- Sit down with the above list of required skills and together assess what you can and cannot handle in-house. The places you find "gaps" can be filled by using outside help.

CREATING YOUR WORKSPACE

Did you know corporate executives waste an average of forty-five minutes a day looking for things they can't find? If the primary reason for business failure is management incompetence, and if organization is the primary ingredient for good management, then it is crucial for you to set your workspace up in a way that will keep you organized and efficient. A helpful way to do this is setting up separate "work centers" focused on specific tasks. No matter where you finally decide to set up, you will need to equip and organize your workspace to maximize your production and minimize distractions.

While business today is decentralizing through the use of mobile technologies, you will still need a center of operations with print-based copies of important documents, just in case your hard drive crashes. And with everything going virtual, it helps keep things real by having an organized space in which to carry on your business. There are, minimally, four work centers most small businesses need:

- ❑ **Telephone work center.** Where you keep your card file of names and addresses, answering or voice-mail machine, and all phone messages.

- ❑ **Mail center.** Where you process all your mail. Have bins or boxes in which to place incoming and outgoing mail. Keep stationery, envelopes, stamps, cards, publicity materials, and anything else you need to send out regularly. You might also want to keep a postage scale, overnight and priority shipping envelopes, and a paper cutter at hand.

- ❑ **Money-processing center.** If you want to make sure you have enough money, you have to mind your money. That means having a time and space for processing your financial transactions, such as making deposits, invoicing, bill paying, balancing your checkbook, and keeping bank records.

- ❑ **Filing center.** If you have a place for each file and a file for each type of written material you need to keep, you'll have no need for piles. The key is organizing your information early on in your business and staying on top of it. To keep your desk and other surfaces clear and still have quick access to what you need, create three filing areas:

    - *Immediate:* files you refer to daily or are working on currently; these can be kept on your desk

    - *Current:* files that you use on a weekly or monthly basis; these can be kept in a filing *cabinet*

    - *Archives:* info materials that you are keeping for reference or for purposes of documentation can be kept in a remote location.

Of course, all of these "work centers" revolve around "Grand Central"—your computer, the single most important piece of equipment for your business. Here's a look at a well-organized home office space:

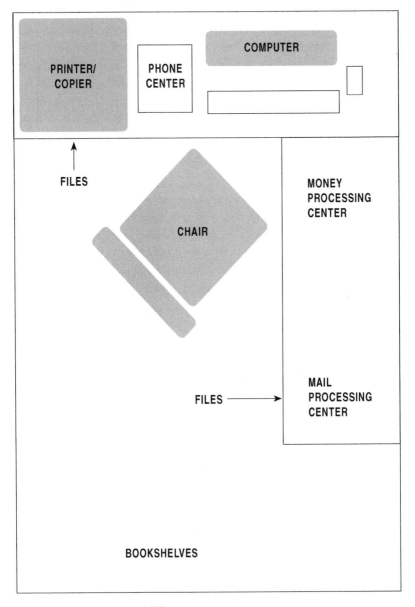

Fig. 4.2. L-Shaped Office

Optimizing Your Workspace

Here are several "best practices" you can apply to the physical organization of your workspace:

❑ **Keep the most frequently used objects**, tools, and supplies closest at hand. The L-shaped workspace is recommended for this purpose and is illustrated on the previous page.

❑ **Avoid built-in desks or other fixtures.** Use adjustable shelving. Buy a pair of two-drawer file cabinets rather than a four-drawer unit. Think modular, not fixed.

❑ **Pay attention to lighting.** Poor lighting can lead to eyestrain, headaches, irritability, and overall lower efficiency. Two types of lighting are necessary: *ambient light* (a blend of natural light and artificial light, usually provided by a ceiling fixture or halogen pole lamp), and *task lighting* (provided by lamps at each work area).

❑ **It's easier to look down than up**. If you are using a computer, always position it so that the center of your monitor is about seventeen inches in front and about six inches lower than your eye level, or square with your chin, when you are sitting in your normal work chair.

❑ **When using a telephone**, try to find a way to keep your hands free. This enables better production and minimizes neck strain. Good telephone headsets are available for about $30. (Plantronics is a good brand.)

❑ **Be health conscious.** Avoid the coffee-to-get-up, alcohol-to-come-down syndrome. This can set your body and mind on a roller coaster. Good health requires that you stand up and move around often. After reviewing your work area, can you honestly say that this is the most functional, comfortable, safest, and logical way to set up the area? Or, do certain tasks or pieces of furniture and equipment stand out as awkward, difficult, even painful to use? Use your common sense to eliminate the barriers to performance that you find. *Ergonomics* (literally, *work economics*) is the science of designing the job, equipment, and workplace to fit the worker. The science of ergonomics addresses the many ways office workstations can be optimized for ideal comfort and productivity.

Ergonomic chairs, desks, and computers are important, as are fresh air, visual diversion, and control of noise levels.

Dealing with the Necessary Paperwork

All businesses must interact with various levels of paperwork in order to function professionally. Some require more paperwork than others. For example, a solo eBay retailer can probably get by with just a simple DBA (doing business as) license. A record label with three employees and two independent contractors, on the other hand, must have all the basic licenses, permits, insurance, and tax regulations required of all businesses with employees, *plus* a rack of additional specialized documents like artist contracts, copyright forms, licensing agreements, distributor one-sheets, and more.

It takes a good deal of persistence and resolve to stay on top of all this paperwork. It's easy to ignore the need for licenses and permits, especially when you're embroiled in all the excitement of starting a new business. But failing to do so—often, from the beginning—is one of the most common (and costly) mistakes entrepreneurs make. Yes, it's a red-tape jungle. But think of it as an obstacle course set up to test the intensity of your desire and your willingness to go the extra mile to make your company happen.

Fortunately, for most independent musicians, the requirements are relatively painless. Let's look at what paperwork you will need to launch and grow your business and where to get it.

Basic Business Licenses

❑ **General Business License.** Contact your city's business license department to find out about getting a general business license, which grants you the right (after paying a fee, of course) to operate in that city. When you file your license application, the city planning or zoning department will check to make sure your area is zoned for the purpose you want to use it for and that there are enough parking spaces to meet the codes. We'll look more closely at zoning issues in a moment.

❏ **Fictitious Name (DBA).** When a business goes by any name other than the owner's real name, the business is being operated under a "fictitious name" or DBA (Doing Business As). "Mack's Music," "Sound Mirror Mastering," and "Geffen Records" are all examples of fictitious names. In some cases, this license may be required by your bank for you to open business checking and savings accounts.

How to Obtain: Call the licensing bureau of the city in which you plan to operate and find out their licensing requirements and application procedure. Some states require you to place an ad in the local newspaper for a certain amount of time, announcing the opening of your business. Expect to pay anywhere between $50 and $100.

❏ **Seller's Permit or Resale Certificate.** A Seller's Permit may exempt you as a business from paying sales tax to your vendors (i.e., suppliers, printer, CD duplicator, photographer, etc.) since you are considered a wholesaler. To get this exemption (only on business purchases), you need to be authorized to do so from your state. You'll need to apply for a State Sales Tax Vendor ID/Certificate of Authority at your state's department of taxation, and you'll be given a sales tax vendor ID number which identifies you as a manufacturer/wholesaler.

The point to remember is that your business is exempt from paying sales tax on *resale* items—elements that are part of the raw materials in your product for sale. But the tax is not eliminated, just deferred. You will need to submit the sales tax you do collect from customers to your state department of revenue each year.

This certificate authorizes you also to collect sales tax on retail sales, that is, sales directly to the public. As a small business, you will probably only have to file this once per year. Keep good records! If you operate a service-based business (like a music licensing company, music instruction service, or booking agency), your activities may or may not be subject to sales tax, depending on your state regulations, and so this permit will not be necessary. This is when contacting a SCORE representative (see chapter 2) in your state can be very helpful.

❏ **Other Possible Licenses and Permits.** Always check with
your local town or city hall for other licensing requirements.
Depending on your business, other requirements may
include:

- *Liquor, Wine, and Beer License.* Allows you to sell
  alcohol products.

- *Health Department Permit.* If you plan to sell food,
  either directly to customers or as a wholesaler to
  other retailers, you will need a county health department permit.

- *Fire Department Permit.* If your business uses flam-
  mable materials or if your business will house large
  numbers of the public, you may need this.

- *Air and Water Pollution Control Permit.* If you burn
  or discharge anything into the sewers or use gas-
  producing products (e.g., paint sprayers), this will be
  required.

- *Agent License.* Required in some states for representing artists as an agent and/or personal manager.

- *Noise Permit.* If you use amplified sound, you'll
  usually run into "residential noise limits" requiring a
  certain time restriction and decibel limit.

- *Sign Permit.* Some cities and suburbs have sign ordinances that restrict the size, location, and sometimes
  the lighting and type of sign you can use outside your
  business.

Working within Zoning Laws

Zoning has to do with the way the governments control the physical
development of land and the kinds of uses to which each individual
property may be put. While many communities have modernized
their zoning ordinances, some states still have zoning laws *against*
home-based businesses. These often date back to the early 1900s
and were designed to protect against "sweat shop" conditions for
work-at-home textile employees. In recent years, larger recording
studios in metropolitan areas have taken to reporting home project
studios in residential areas to local zoning boards. If you operate

a music production business out of your residence, and there are zoning restrictions in your state against home-based businesses, you could get fined (and even shut down).

When it comes to zoning, be in the know. Before you sign a lease, check with the local zoning department to make sure the building is zoned for your use. Find out about any special requirements, such as off-street parking or sign limitations. Don't rely on the landlord for this information. Just because a similar business previously occupied the same building without zoning problems, it is no guarantee you'll have no problems. The old business may have been there before current zoning laws were in effect (called "grandfathering"), or maybe they had a special arrangement or variance that may or may not be transferred to you.

A call to your municipal clerk's office will get you started. After that, a big part of staying out of trouble with zoning problems is common sense and common courtesy. Here are some guidelines:

❏ **Be a good neighbor.** Keep your business out of sight, and it will be out of mind.

❏ **Be sensitive to the traffic you create.**

❏ **Keep parking accessible for neighbors.** If you have interns or employees, or operate a business that requires customers to visit your home, make sure that you plan for adequate parking.

❏ **Consider obtaining a P.O. box for your business mail.** Or you may consider using one of the numerous mail service centers that have sprung up around the country; they offer mailbox rentals, shipping, photocopying, faxing, and other support services for small businesses.

PROTECTING YOUR INTELLECTUAL PROPERTY: TRADEMARKS AND COPYRIGHTS

Ideas may be your greatest asset. When you begin to transfer them into names, inventions, product designs, logos, music, writings, or other forms, they become intellectual property. Just as you would protect your *physical* property against theft and damage, you should also protect your *intellectual* property from the same. In this age of digital copying and rampant piracy, it's important to understand what intellectual property is and how to best protect it.

There are three types of intellectual property protection: patent, trademark, and copyright. They serve different purposes and shouldn't be confused with one another. A *patent* is granted to the inventor of a new or useful idea. It's a grant of property rights that excludes others from making, using, or selling the same invention, and it expires after a number of years, depending on the type of invention patented. For more on patents please visit the U.S. Patents and Trademarks Office (uspto.gov), since we won't be addressing that topic in detail here.

Trademarks and *copyrights* are the two forms of intellectual property most musicians have to deal with, and we'll look at each one in turn.

Trademarks

Unlike patents and copyrights, trademarks affect *all* businesses. When you use the name of your business publicly, you are using it as a trademark. When you sell products using a brand name, you are using that brand name as a trademark. If you are providing a service, the brand name for that service is a *service mark* or, essentially, a trademark for services. A trademark or service mark may consist of letters, words, graphics, or any combination of these elements. A trademark *distinguishes* the goods and services of one company from those of another.

For the sake of convenience, I will use the words "trademark" and "service mark" interchangeably.

Both the federal government, through the United States Patent and Trademark Office (USPTO), and state governments have the power to grant trademarks and service marks. Federal law requires marks to be used in interstate commerce (i.e., doing verifiable business between two or more states). The ® symbol means the USPTO has reviewed and registered the mark. A "TM" or "SM" symbol, on the other hand, indicates that the word, phrase, or design is being used and claimed as a trademark or service mark but is not yet federally registered. Many states do not have any review process associated with the registration of marks.

Next to you, *your company name* is your number-one asset, so it's crucial to select it carefully and protect it relentlessly. You automatically have some protection for your trademark if you were the first person to use that trademark in commerce, even if you did not formerly register your trademark with the USPTO. For example, when PBS television launched the series *Nova*, the show's producers failed to register the trademark with the USPTO. Several years later, a gentleman started a science fiction magazine called *NOVA* and proceeded to register the name with the USPTO in Washington. He was granted the mark and then sued PBS for trademark infringement. But he lost. Even though he had the formal trademark, PBS had been *using* it for several years on a national and international basis. *Use* superseded *formal registration*, and the magazine owner had to relinquish the mark.

Notwithstanding, it is usually easier to prove an infringement case and collect damages, if the mark has been formally registered.

Also, an entrepreneur may lose the exclusive right to a trademark if the mark loses its unique character and becomes a generic name. *Aspirin, escalator, thermos, brassiere, super glue, yo-yo,* and *cellophane* all were once enforceable trademarks that have since become common words in the English language. These generic terms can no longer be licensed as trademarks.

Trademarks are granted for twenty years and may be renewed indefinitely if a firm continues to protect its brand name. If a company allows the name to lapse into common usage, it may lose protection. Common usage takes effect if a company seeks no action against those who fail to acknowledge its trademark. Recently, for example, the popular brand-name sailboard Windsurfer lost its trademark. Like yo-yo and thermos, *windsurfer* has become the common term for the product and can now be used by any sailboard company.

Finally, some marks are ineligible for federal registration. The USPTO won't register any marks that contain:

❑ Names of living persons without their consent

❑ The U.S. flag

❑ Other federal and local governmental insignias

❑ The name or likeness of a deceased U.S. President without his widow's consent

❑ Words or symbols that disparage living or deceased persons, institutions, beliefs, or national symbols, or

❑ Marks that are judged immoral, deceptive, or scandalous.

A NOTE ON PROTECTING ARTIST/BAND NAMES

To make sure artist and band names are free to use before signing any contracts, you should search some of the online artist and band directories, like the Ultimate Band List (www.ubl.com) and the All-Music Guide (www.allmusic.com).

Doing Your Own Trademark Search

You hopefully decided on a business name back in chapter 3, when setting out to draft your plan. Now you need to know if the trademark you've chosen is available. You can do your own trademark search for free on the Internet by visiting the U.S. Patent and Trademark Office's website at www.uspto.gov. Or you can visit one of the Patent and Trademark Depository Libraries, available in every state. These libraries offer a combination of hardcover directories of federally registered marks and an *online* database of both registered marks and marks for which a registration application is pending. Most of these libraries also have step-by-step instructions for searching registered and pending marks.

In addition to searching for registered or pending marks, you can employ less formal methods of searching. For example, you may also use product guides and other materials available in these libraries to search for possibly conflicting marks that haven't been registered. This can be important because an existing mark, even if it's unregistered, would preclude you from registering the same or confusingly similar mark in your own name, and using the mark in any part of the country or commercial transaction where customers might be confused.

To find the Patent and Trademark Depository Library nearest you, see PTO's list at www.uspto.gov/go/ptdl.

Use the Web; it is a ready-made source of business names. Any of the top search engines (e.g., Google) will let you type in the name and search for it on all the indexed Web pages of that engine. Because no search engine is 100 percent complete, a thorough search will necessarily include several additional search engines.

A good place to find domain names being used by Web-based businesses is the dotcom directory at whois.net. Simply type in the domain you're looking for. The site then lets you know if that name is available.

Formal Trademark Registration

Again, rights to a business name come through use, not a formal registration with the USPTO in D.C. But registering with the USPTO can have several benefits. Formal registration:

- provides notice to everyone that you have exclusive rights to use the mark

- entitles holder of mark to sue in federal court for infringement

- establishes incontestable rights regarding use of the mark for commerce

- entitles you to use the trademark registration symbol ® as opposed to simply ™

- provides a basis for filing trademark application in foreign countries.

The trademark registration process is fully explained at the USPTO website (www.uspto.gov). You can either register electronically or print out a form and mail in your registration. The current cost (c. 2013) for trademark or service mark registration in the U.S. is $375 (or $325 if you file electronically).

To register a trademark with the USPTO, the mark's owner must first put it into use "in commerce that Congress may regulate." This means the mark must be used on a product or service that crosses state, national, or territorial lines or that affects commerce crossing such lines—for example, a record label selling CDs in other states, or a touring band providing performances in other states.

Once the USPTO receives a trademark registration application, the office must answer the following questions satisfactorily:

- Is the trademark the same as or similar to an existing mark used on similar or related goods or services?

- Is the trademark on the list of prohibited or reserved names?

- Is the trademark generic—that is, does the mark describe the product itself rather than its source?

- Is the trademark too descriptive (not distinctive enough) to qualify for protection?

If the answer to each question is "no," the trademark is eligible for registration and the USPTO will continue to process the application. You can expect to receive a "Filing Receipt" within eight weeks. After that you will receive a notice that your band or business name will be published in a government publication known as *The Trademark Gazette*. If there is no opposition to your mark, your registration will be issued. The whole process may take anywhere between twelve and eighteen months.

Your intent to establish a mark can be shown by affixing the letters TM or SM next to your company name or logo. Once the registration is complete, you may begin using the ® symbol.

Copyrights

Items protected by copyright include books, magazines, software, advertising copy, newspapers, music compositions, movies, audio recordings, and artwork. Items not protected by copyrights include concepts or ideas, titles, names, and brands.

In its most basic sense, "copyright" means "the right to make copies". In fact, a copyright is actually a bundle of rights, each of which can be copyrighted independently and sold, assigned, leased, and/or licensed separately.

In the U.S., copyright protection *automatically* extends to any material once fixed in a form. This is the case whether you file for a copyright notice or not. So, through *creation*, a work is copyrighted, not through any formal registration process. Copyrights extend to creators for their entire lives and to their estates for seventy years thereafter.

Formal registration of copyrights, however, is recommended as it provides some extra insurance and a "path" to the work's creator, if someone wants to make contact. It also makes infringement cases move more quickly through the courts.

Where to Register Your Copyrights

The U.S. Copyright Office website (www.copyright.gov) is the right place to register. Remember, the Copyright Office receives and registers copyright claims; *it doesn't evaluate them or make decisions about whether a song has already been copyrighted by someone else.* If ten songs with the same title come in, they'll all get registered. It's up to you to take responsibility for not infringing on copyrights and monitoring your own copyrights.

As your business grows, your copyright registrations may become increasingly frequent, along with the number of checks you cut for the filing fees (currently $50–65 per registration; $35 per online). If you make at least twelve filings a year, however, the Copyright Office will accept a $250 advance payment. The payment gets deposited into an account, the fees for future registrations are deducted, and statements are sent to you for your records. This saves time and streamlines the payment process.

The Copyright Office was mandated several years to simplify its processes, and so it is currently phasing out the multiform system it has used for years (i.e., Forms TX, VA, SR, PA, and SE), for a new, single one called the eCO (electronic copyright office) Form. Learn more at copyright.gov/help/faq.

Who Owns the Copyright?

As an independent contractor or freelancer, you usually own the rights to what you create unless you sign a contract giving the rights to your client. If ownership is not stipulated in a contract (often done so with the phrase, "work for hire"), the creator owns the copyright to the work.

Before you sign any contract, be sure you know who will own the work you create during your employment. Oftentimes, the entity paying you will try to lay claim to all work, not just what you were hired to create, during the term of the contract, *so be on the lookout for this type of clause in all contracts!*

If you hire someone to create a work for your business and you want to own it—public relations material or ad copy, for example–you will want to have the agency or individual sign an agreement assigning rights to you.

You may have heard the term *fair use*. This rule says that portions of works may be reproduced for educational purposes, news, commentary, parody, or research without infringement under some circumstances. Fair use is decided on a case-by-case basis using the following criteria:

- purpose of use—for example, whether it is commercial or for nonprofit, educational purposes

- the nature of the copyrighted work

- the effect of the use upon the potential value of or market for the work
- how much of the entire body of the work is used.

When You're Planning on Using Other Peoples' Music...

If you are using someone else's copyrighted recorded composition(s), you need to obtain a mechanical license in writing. A mechanical license cannot be denied (it is a statutory right, set by Congress), but it can be a cumbersome process. There are three ways to get one.

First, find out who owns the copyright on the composition by contacting BMI (212-586-2000 or www.bmi.com), ASCAP (212-621-6160 or www.ascap.com) or SESAC (800-826-9996 or www.sesac.com). Search their online databases. Armed with this info, you can contact the publisher and negotiate your own rates.

If you don't want to negotiate your own rates, **contact the Harry Fox Agency** (212-370-5330 or www.harryfox.com) who is authorized to issue mechanical licenses at the statutory rate of 9.10 cents per song up to five minutes. Songs over five minutes are calculated at 1.75 cents per minute, per song. To figure out your royalty fee, multiply the cost per song by the number of units manufactured. For example, one 7 minute song on 1,000 CDs would cost 1,000 x (7 x $0.0175) = $122.50.

There are additional separate rates for Permanent Digital Downloads and Master Ringtones. Statutory rates change every two years. You can find them listed at: www.harryfox.com/public/licenseeRateCurrent.jsp.

If you're a community group, religious organization, school/university, or individual, and not an existing Harry Fox customer, and would like to obtain a license to make and distribute within the U.S. 2,500 or less recordings, you can now get an HFA mechanical license at SongFile.com. This would apply to most artists or artist-owned labels in the U.S.

If you can't afford the standard fee, contact a group like the Volunteer Lawyers for the Arts (go to vlany.org to find the chapter nearest you). They can often help negotiate reduced royalties for schools and nonprofit groups.

You can find an excellent FAQ on mechanical licensing at the Harry Fox Agency website: www.harryfox.com/public/FAQ.jsp.

Copyright Infringement

Infringement of copyright happens when works—paintings, books, computer software, films, and music—are reproduced without permission from the copyright owners. Infringement can also occur when works such as plays and films are performed, screened, or made public in other ways without permission from the copyright owner. A person who sells infringing versions of a work, even if somebody else made them, is also in breach of copyright, as is a person who authorizes someone else to make an infringement. If a work is very distinctive and original, reproducing part of it may be a breach of copyright.

There are many different ways copyright owners may find their copyright has been infringed upon. For example, infringing activities include:

- **Bootlegging,** where illegal recordings are made of live performances;

- **Piracy,** the illegal copying of music products that have been released without permission from the copyright owner. Common ways this is done are by uploading tracks to file-sharing services like Limewire or Bitorrent, copying CDs onto cassettes, or copying them onto other CDs using a CD burner. Pirate products are not necessarily packaged in the same way as the original, whereas;

- **Counterfeiting** involves duplication of both the music product and of its packaging. For this reason, unwitting buyers are less able to recognize counterfeit copies than is the case with some pirate copies.

- **Sampling** is the practice of digitally copying or transferring snippets or portions of a preexisting (copyrighted) master to make a new composition. An artist will take a piece of a preexisting recording and use that piece (i.e., "sample") to create a new recording. Sampling exists mostly in rap, hip-hop, street, or dance records.

A person doing any of the above can be sued, as can most parties involved in the manufacture, distribution, sale, and performance of such works. If you are a record company and your artist is using the copyrighted song, you as the record label are at risk. Copyright infringement is a federal offense, so beware!

Your intellectual property is the product of your skills and experience, a constitutional right, and worth protecting.

Other Paperwork You May Need

❑ **Barcodes.** If you plan on selling recordings and you would like those sales to show up in SoundScan reports and other tracking systems, you will need to obtain a Universal Product Code (UPC), which is kind of like a barcoded social security number for your products. A UPC consists of twelve digits: The first six numbers uniquely identify your organization, the next four (which *you* choose) specify the release, the following number corresponds to the format (CD or single track), and the last number is used to check that the scanner read the product correctly.

Most retailers no longer carry non-UPC products (because they can't scan them at the cash register), and major label A&R departments conduct much of their market research on unsigned bands and indie labels by checking SoundScan sales on the retail level.

"Hard data helps get more attention. The more data you can give to a potential label, manager, agent, talent buyer, venue, etc., the better," says Lou Plaia, founder of ReverbNation. "If you can show all these people that you are selling a lot of your music in markets where you play, it proves you have fans willing to buy something from you."

SoundScan now also accepts live-show CD sales reports—the place, after all, where most indie artist sales happen. However, only labels, distribution companies, and retailers can report these sales directly to SoundScan. Individual bands and artists can use an intermediary service like Indiehitmaker.com (for a fee, of course) to get their data submitted.

If you'd like to receive an application for a UPC or need more information, contact GS1 (formerly, The Uniform Code Council) online at www.gs1us.org. (GS1 is a nonprofit organization dedicated to standards development and maintenance for automated product identification and electronic data.) The fee is determined by the number of products you need to identify and your company's gross sales revenue.

A less expensive (and easier to follow) barcode service is provided by Buyabarcode.com. It has a one-time registration and setup fee, and the code lasts a lifetime. CDBaby.com and most other online music storefronts and services will also set you up with a barcode for very little cost.

❏ **ISRC (International Standard Recording Code).** The ISRC is the international identification system for sound recordings and music DVDs. Each ISRC is a unique and permanent identifier for a specific recording, to help identify recordings for royalty payments. It is assigned *per track*, not per CD. It's smart to identify your recordings this way. They are embedded in the metadata of your CD during the mastering phase. For further information on ISRCs go to: usisrc.org.

MONEY, MONEY, MONEY

Creative, right-brained people are usually not driven by money, don't manage it very well, and have some funny beliefs about it. For instance, there are artists who believe that they must starve to do real art, that they can't have a juicy income and remain honest and true to their vision, and that somehow accepting money for one's art is selling out and giving up some of one's independence.

Books on entrepreneurship, especially those written by MBAs, put a tremendous emphasis on the financial aspects of new companies. Of course, money *is* crucial to keeping the business afloat. But too much emphasis on financials can blind one to the simplicity of small business money management.

"Business is very simple," exclaims ultrasuccessful new media composer Norihiko Hibino. "Cash in and cash out. Between those two will be profit. People sometimes get confused by too many parameters in the balance sheet. But remember, you can only make money between those differences."

Quite simply, accounting tells you if you are making money. If you create a profit and loss statement each month, you can ascertain your position quickly. If you are losing money, you can make changes in your operations, such as increasing prices or reducing expenses, to correct the situation long before the year's end and ensure that your overall year will still be profitable.

Being clueless about money is unaffordable, so put some time into learning about how it works. Money is a big topic, so I will concentrate on just two areas for now: setting your fees and taxes. You can find some additional great, easy-to-access resources in the appendix.

Guidelines for Setting Your Price and Your Fee

Setting your price can be a tricky thing. The determination must be based on a broad, thoughtful basis and requires a basic under-standing of both your financial and business goals. "But this is definitely an art, not a science," writes Sara Horowitz in *The Free-lancer's Bible.* "Run your numbers, talk to your peers, trust your gut, and learn from experience. Everyone else does. If there were set formulas for pricing, it would be illegal and called price fixing."

Follow these six tips for setting your price:

❑ **Keep your prices realistic.** Set your prices based on your own financial goals, not those of your competitors' alone.

❑ **Cover all your costs.** A successful pricing strategy is one that results in the most dollars after all your costs are met.

❑ **Check your price against inflation.** If you maintain your prices despite inflation, you will erode your profit margin.

❑ **Include in your pricing the value of your time,** as well as the other benefits your business brings to customers. Avoid committing the mistake of not including a salary for yourself, particularly if you are operating a service business.

❑ **Price low, but smart.** Pricing low is a common strategy, espe-cially for startups. But be careful! Low price can also signal low quality, and it becomes difficult to raise prices later once customers are accustomed to your low prices.

❑ **Use discounts with care.** Discounts are good for encouraging repeat/bulk orders, bundling sales, and early payment of customers. Discounts are also used to clear out merchandise that has become outdated.

Related to price, of course, is your own fee. The following table illustrates how to determine your fees if you are a service-oriented business (that is, the bulk of your sales come as a result of providing a service—like music instruction or performing—rather than through selling a product, such as a CD).

The chart below is based on a forty-hour workweek, which leaves a maximum of twenty-five billable hours per week. Since overhead varies greatly from one business to another, it isn't included in this breakdown.

DETERMINING YOUR FEE Time/Income Factor Analysis				
One Year	= 365 days – 104 days (weekends)			
	= 261 days – 8 days (holidays)			
	= 253 days – 10 days (health)			
	= 243 days – 10 days (vacation)			
	= 233 days x 8 hours per day			
	= 1,864 hours per year			
	– 30% (promotion, operations, professional development)			
	= approximately 1,300 hours			
	= approximately 25 billable hours per week			
Annual Income*	50%	70%	90%	100%
	12.5 hrs/week (650 hours)	17.5 hrs/week (910 hrs)	22.5 hrs/week (1,170 hrs)	25 hrs/week (1,300 hrs)
$25,000	38.50	27.50	21.50	19.25
$30,000	46.00	33.00	25.75	23.00
$35,000	54.00	38.50	30.00	27.00
$40,000	61.50	44.00	34.00	31.00
$50,000	77.00	55.00	42.75	38.50
$60,000	92.00	66.00	51.25	46.00
$75,000	115.50	82.50	64.00	58.00
$100,000	154.00	110.00	85.50	77.00
* Does not include allowance for overhead and taxes				

Fig. 4.3. Determining Your Fee

Here's how to understand figure 4.3. Let's say that you want to earn $35,000 this year before taxes. If you plan on working 50 percent (billing 12.5 hours per week), then you need to charge $54 per hour. If you think you will be able to work 90 percent (bill 22.5 hours per week), then you only need to charge $30 per hour. BUT, you also must include the costs in running your business.

Imagine that your fixed costs are $10,000 per year plus $6 per session. So, at a 50 percent workload, you need to cover $35,000 income, $10,000 fixed expenses, and $3900 per session cost (650 sessions), which equals $48,900. Look at the chart, and you will find that to bring in gross revenues of $50,000, you need to charge approximately $76 per hour. Yet, if you plan on billing 90 percent, then you need to cover $35,000 income, $10,000 fixed expenses, and $7020 per session cost (1,170 sessions), which equals $52,020. Check the chart and you will discover that you will only need to charge about $44 per hour.

Use that chart along with an online rate calculator such as the one at freelanceswitch.com (see Resource Directory), as guides for determining the best way to price your service.

GETTING PAID IN THE PARKING LOT: CHEATING BY HIDING INCOME

Under the table. In the parking lot. Off the books. Of course, it's income. And yes, you must report it on your tax return.

Miles Mingus plays a regular gig at Jazzy Jack's Pub. Jazzy Jack has a cash business; all his barflies pay for their drinks with hard currency—no plastic or checks, thank you. And Jack pays Miles the same way: in cash, which he takes from an envelope in his desk in the back office. Nobody's claiming a lot of the income and nobody's paying a lot of the taxes—until Jack gets audited.

The IRS is not a morality agency, it is a monetary agency. It doesn't care what you do for a living as long as you pay taxes on the income you make doing it. If you make your living as a hit man or a lady of the night or a drug dealer, be sure to pay the IRS its fair share. Remember the Chicago mobster Al Capone? He wasn't sent to prison for murder, bootlegging, or racketeering; he was convicted of tax evasion for not reporting the money he earned in his self-employed endeavors.

When the IRS calls for an audit, its only purpose is to collect more tax money with some interest and penalty to boot. Criminal activity is not suspected. But if you are caught in outright cheating—particularly in deliberately failing to report a significant amount of income—the IRS will not hesitate to prosecute you.

TAX GUIDELINES FOR THE SELF-MANAGED MUSICIAN

For simplicity's sake, I am going to assume in this section that you are running a sole proprietorship (an unincorporated business of one) as opposed to a partnership, corporation, LLC, or any other business entity. If you're not a sole proprietor, some of the advice in this section may not directly apply to you.

The Anti-Hobby Rule

The IRS keeps a watchful eye out for individuals who consistently run businesses at a loss just to amass valuable deductions. Their guidelines state that a business must make a profit three years out of five, or else the enterprise is considered a hobby, which lowers or eliminates possible deductions. There have been exceptions to this, however. By showing good records and a business plan, small enterprises *have* convinced the IRS that they at least are *intending* to be profitable.

The following list will help you determine if you're doing whatever you're doing to make a buck. No single item on the list settles or resolves the issue, nor is this a complete list used by the IRS in making a decision, but these are the items normally taken into account. The IRS considers all the facts surrounding an activity in determining if the activity is engaged in for profit.

1. **Carrying on the activity in a businesslike manner.**

   - Are your books and records kept completely and accurately?

   - Is your activity carried on like similar businesses that operate at a profit?

   - If methods you used proved unprofitable, did you change your methods or adopt new techniques in an attempt to improve profitability?

2. **Expertise of the taxpayer or his advisors.**

   - Have you prepared to enter this business by studying the accepted managerial and technological practices of those already in the field?

- Are your business practices similar to others in your profession? If not, are you attempting to develop new or superior techniques that may result in future profits?

3. **Time and effort expended.**

- Do you put more time into marketing your business than you put into watching television?

- Do you employ someone with the expertise you may not have or who puts in the time you are not able to?

- Did you leave another job to devote more time to this activity?

4. **Success in carrying on similar or dissimilar activities.**

- Have you taken a similar activity and converted it from an unprofitable to a profitable enterprise?

- Have you had general success in running other kinds of businesses?

5. **History of income or losses with respect to the activity.**

- Losses early in the history of a business are common. Are your losses due to heavy early expenses or have they extended beyond the normal time for this kind of activity to begin making a profit?

6. **Amount of occasional profits.**

- There may be a disparity in the amount of profits that you make in relation to the losses you incur or in the amount of money spent on assets used in your activity. The purchase of a $3,000 Gibson guitar, but not one paid gig, may tell the IRS it's a hobby. Do you have an opportunity to make a substantial ultimate profit in a highly speculative activity?

- A software developer may work on a project for years before it is viable. Is your business the type that will have an occasional large profit but small operating losses over many years?

RETAINING RECORDS MADE SIMPLE

❑ Keep tax returns (not records, but actual returns) forever. Label a box "My Tax Returns" and put them in there.

❑ Keep every year-end summary of your pension forever. Label a box "Pensions" and make a folder for each year you have. Put that plan's year-end statement in the folder and close the box.

❑ Keep everything else for seven years from the last time it had any impact on your financial life. Label a box "2014 Tax Records: OK to throw out 12/31/2021."

Note: Be extra careful of the next two.

7. **Financial status of the taxpayer.**

- If this is your only source of income, then you must be in it to make a profit.

- If, on the other hand, you've got large income from other sources and this activity generates substantial tax benefits, this could indicate to the IRS that the activity is not carried on for profit but as a home-made tax shelter.

8. **Elements of personal pleasure or recreation.**

- The IRS says "elements of personal pleasure or recreation" may indicate the lack of profit motive. Does this mean your business can't be pleasurable too? Hmm.

INCOME TAX + SELF-EMPLOYMENT TAX = A LOT OF TAX!

Here's an eye-opener about a solo entrepreneur's self-employment (SE) tax liabilities:

A $10,000 net profit for a self-employed at a 15% tax bracket means that $1,500 must go for federal income tax and another approximately $1,500 for SE tax. Add them up: 15% plus 15% equals 30%. Depending upon state and city, the indie owner may owe another 5% to 10%, or $500 to $1,000, for state and city income taxes. That could bring the figure up to 40% of net profit going toward taxes, or approximately $4,000 of every $10,000 net income. And remember, 15% is one of the lower tax brackets. For some, the government takes an even bigger bite. How about at a 35% federal rate! That would change the above total income going for taxes to 60% (35% plus 15% plus 10%).

Independent Contractor Status

As a musician, you will often be hired as an "independent contractor" (IC). This is a classification different from "employment" because in this case, *you* are fully responsible for your taxes rather than the employer. As such, you will receive from the payer, form W-9 that you fill out with your name, address, and social security number.

In a payer/contractor relationship, payers are required to file information returns to report certain types of payments made to independent contractors during the year. For example, Form 1099-MISC, Miscellaneous Income, is filed with the IRS to report payments of $600 or more to persons not treated as employees (e.g., ICs) for services performed for the payer's trade or business.

ICs report their income and expenses on the Schedule C, "Profit or Loss from Business" or C-EZ, "Profit from Business" (Form 1040). Since an independent contractor does not have taxes deducted from client checks, you must pay estimated taxes on a quarterly basis if your tax liability for the year will be more than $1,000. If you omit to do this, the IRS may penalize you. The due dates for quarterly taxes are usually the fifteenth of the month in January, April,

June, and September each year. Check with the IRS for the exact dates each year. You can e-Pay your estimated tax payments using the Electronic Federal Tax Payment System or EFTPS. This allows you to schedule and make your payments either over the phone or on the Internet and they will automatically be withdrawn from your account.

Deductions

To be deductible, a business expense must be both ordinary and necessary. An *ordinary expense* is one that is common and accepted in your field of business. A *necessary expense* is one that is appropriate and helpful for your business. An expense does not have to be indispensable to be considered necessary.

Section 179 of the tax code states that up to $18,000 in expenses for capital assets (like a computer or PA system) may be deducted per year. However, that deduction is limited by item cost and taxable income. This means that if you earned only $2000 you can take only a $2000 deduction even if the item costs more.

In order to qualify for a 179 deduction, you must fill out Form 4562 and attach it to your tax return. Of course, you want to also take a deduction if your business is run from your home or apartment. Three rules apply to the *Home Office Deduction*:

Rule 1: Exclusive Use. The part of your home used for business must be used exclusively for business.

Rule 2: Used on a Regular Basis. The part of your home used for business must be used on a regular basis for business.

Rule 3: Principal Place of Business. Your home office or studio or workshop must be your principal place of business.

SMALL BUSINESS TAX WRITE-OFFS

Music business expenses that are deductible may include:

1. Advertising Costs
- Materials
- Services
- Labor
- Transportation

2. Amortized Costs
- Record production
  - → Studio Rent
  - → Producer
  - → Engineer
  - → Sidemen (Women)
  - → Arrangers
  - → Copyists
  - → Services
  - → Equipment Rentals
  - → General Labor
  - → Supplies

3. Bad Debts

4. Bank Charges

5. Books (that aid or update your education with respect to your business, where required by law)

6. Car or Other Vehicle's Business Operating Expenses
- Gas
- Oil
- Tires
- Parts
- Labor
- Accident Repair
- Painting

7. Commissions, Percentages, and Other Fees Paid Out
- Agent Fees
- Audit Fees
- Bookkeeping Fees
- Business Administration Fees
- Catalog Management Fees
- Contractor Fees
- Copyright Assignment Fees
- Attorney Commissions and Fees
- Publishing Fees
- Copyright Registration Fees
- Copyright Search Fees
- Licensor Fees
  - → Print Licensor
  - → Synch Licensor
  - → Mechanical Licensor
  - → Performance Licensor
  - → Transcription Licensor
  - → Copyright Licensor
  - → Patent
- Patent Attorney or Agent Fees
  - → Patent Search Fees

8. Depreciations
- Buildings
- Copyrights
- Musical Instruments
- Patents
- Furnishings
- Office Equipment
- Recording Studio Equipment
- Transportation Vehicles

9. Employee Benefit Program

10. Freight and Other Cartage

11. General Expenses for Expendables
(or purchases with a useful life of less than one year)
- Costumes
- Mic and Guitar Cords
- Strings
- Picks
- Rosin
- Capo
- Instrument Cleaner and Polish
- Small Office Equipment

12. Gifts

13. Insurance
- Property
- Fire
- Theft
- Casualty
- Liability
  - → Malpractice

14. Interest on Business Debts

15. Keogh Plan Contributions

16. Laundry and Cleaning

17. Live Performance Expenses
- Concert Hall Rent
- Equipment
- Services
- Road Crew Wages and Expenses
- Sidemen (Women)
- Security
- Promotion and Advertisement
- Publicists
- Stage Wardrobe
- Makeup

18. Maintenance Costs

19. Manufacturing and Production Costs

20. Office Equipment

21. Pension and Profit Sharing Plan

22. Postage

23. Rent on Business Property
    * Buildings
    * Equipment
    * Transportation Vehicles
    * Office Furniture and Equipment
    * Rehearsal Studio

24. Repairs and Maintenance of Business Property

25. Salaries and Bonuses Paid Out

26. Services
    * Legal
    * Tax
    * Accounting and Bookkeeping
    * Auditing
    * Secretarial
    * Consulting

* Promotion
* Publicity
* Advertising
* Publishing
* Agent
* Instrument Tutor
* Voice Tutor
* Mobile Recording
* Concert Security
* Sound and Lighting
* Engineering
* Janitorial
* Demo
* Sidemen (Women)
* Dubbing
* Copying
* Printing

27. Supplies for Manufacturing

28. Travel and Entertainment Expenses

29. Utilities
    * Phone
    * Gas
    * Electric

30. Wages Paid Out

NOTE: Since the IRS is innocent until proven guilty when they disallow deductions, records of business transactions are imperative in order to minimize any disallowances.

Fig. 4.4. Small Business Tax Deductions

Write Off "Dead" Inventory for Tax Savings

Do you have boxes of unsold merchandise lying around? No need to take a loss on it when you have the option of donating them.

Here's what's so cool about this write-off: Regular C corporations can deduct the full cost of the inventory donated, plus half the difference between cost and fair market value, up to twice the cost. S corporations, partnerships, and sole proprietorships earn a straight cost deduction. Four nonprofit organizations that can handle your donations are the National Association for the Exchange of Industrial Resources (800-562-0955), the National Cristina Foundation (800-274-7846), the Gift-in-Kind Clearing House (704-892-7228), and Educational Assistance Limited (708-690-0010). Donated items are redistributed to thousands of qualified schools and charities across the United States.

How might this apply to you? Have any unsold CDs, instruments or gear lying around?

Sales Tax Issues

If you close your business or never get it off the ground after you have already procured a tax ID number, make sure you notify the department of taxation. If you don't, you will continue to get computer-generated estimated bills and fines! Also, if you buy a home-based business from someone else, make sure you have a bulk "Sales Tax Clearance Dome," which is an okay from the tax people that there are no liens on the business.

INCOME TAX AND BUSINESS TAX DEDUCTION

For most people, this will amount to about 35 percent of your income. So for every $100 you earn, $35 goes to pay taxes. The more you earn the more you pay.

For example:

Since you pay about 35 percent of your income in taxes, when you take a business tax deduction, you're essentially saving 35 percent of the cost of the expenses you incurred.

So if I buy a desk, chair, filing cabinet, computer, printer, and software for $3000 to set up my office, how much will it ultimately cost me?

$3,000

x .35

= $1,050 (3000 − 1050 = 1950)

The $1,050 comes right off your taxable income, reducing the amount that can be taxed.

But ONLY if you save EVERY receipt and keep good records (write down what the exact item is on every receipt).

MANAGING THE MANAGER

Entrepreneurs face lots of self-management challenges. First, a one-person business has to rely on self-starting energy, which usually is abundant, except when things go wrong on an emotional level. For example, the breakup of a relationship or a soured or mean-spirited customer can knock you out of your equilibrium. Too, only part of your business has immediate and direct rewards. A week's worth of work may not issue in anything substantial for a month or more. Entrepreneurs will also find that so much of their time is spent on "administrivia," which keeps them from focusing on their core mission. Entrepreneurial life can be lonely. Because the support that used to come from an extended family, clan, or community isn't always present, and you yourself must figure out how to nurture your own support network.

So, effectively managing yourself is the foundation upon which all your career success lies. While there is an undeniable reality that technology has ratcheted up the pace at which we are expected to respond to business and career demands, you still can, and *should*, set limits on your work life. Consider the following steps to help yourself control the amount of time you work.

❑ **Learn to determine what is not urgent.** There's a tendency in the technology-laden business world to believe that everything has to be done *immediately* because the technology exists to transmit things without delay. Because of this, people tend to treat everything as urgent rather than determining what is truly urgent and what can wait. To learn to do this, begin asking questions about projects before you agree to "get something right out." This applies to requests from partners and customers. As long as you are conscientious, people will respect you for setting limits on what you can accomplish in a given time frame.

❑ **Have a set beginning and ending time for your day, as if you still work in the office full-time.** Just because you *can* work 24/7 because of technology, doesn't mean you *should*. There is always more work to complete, but that does not mean you should exhaust yourself working just because you have all of your work tools at your fingertips. There will be times you will need to work long hours, but in general, you should set strict beginning and ending times for your workdays to avoid burnout.

❑ **Designate a time each day when you are not reachable.**
If you are always wondering if the phone will ring, you will
never be able to relax completely. For that reason, get into the
habit of choosing when you will allow the phone to intrude
and when you will not. This means turning the ringer off
sometimes. It will be difficult to do this the first few time you
try, but eventually you will wonder why you haven't done it
before. Start by turning it off for just an hour and work your
way up to more time.

❑ **Give your home and cell number to a very few business
contacts.** It is confusing for people to have too many numbers
for you, and stressful for you to be reachable everywhere you
go. Provide the majority of people with only your voice mail
number, and check it frequently. Email may also be your pref-
erable gateway.

❑ **Establish a clear idea of what is expected of you.** A large
portion of the energy that people expend in work is spent
on the wrong tasks. When you take on a project, ask as many
questions as are necessary to obtain a clear picture of what is
expected. This will help you cut down on overwork by limiting
the time you waste on unnecessary work.

❑ **Learn to say no.** If you consistently say "yes" to things that
you later wish you had declined, set up a mechanism for
helping yourself to say "no." When you are faced with a
request, ask people if you can call them back in a few minutes.
Take that time to think carefully about how you should
respond. If you decide not to, you can work up your resolve to
say "no" before returning the call.

❑ **Stop and think before you make a phone call, write a letter,
send a fax, or have a conversation,** and evaluate whether
you should be spending time on that activity. Ask yourself
what would happen if you didn't do it. If you can live with the
consequences, do not complete the task. This streamlining is
essential to gaining control of your schedule.

❑ **Take yourself away from your work environment.** People
who work in virtual offices particularly need regular breaks
from work. A break can be a day on the weekend spent hiking
or driving in the country, or any change in your environment.

Have at least one full day a week during which you do not check your messages or do any work.

Successful career management creatively combines internal skills with external tools. Making all the parts and people in your enterprise work in concert toward common goals is indeed a task worthy of a maestro. Marketing and finance have to harmonize together; company goals and ongoing programs need to keep the same tempo. Think of the maestro conducting an orchestra: coordinating, timing, scheduling, prompting, and keeping all performers focused on the same score. That's you.

This doesn't mean that you have to do all the work alone. The modern credo DIY (do it yourself) is actually a perfect recipe for burnout. The key is learning how to manage your work in the context of others, connecting with people who can help with the heavy lifting and cooperate with you to fulfill mutually satisfying goals. This is what we will explore next.

PART II

Go Forward

CHAPTER 5

Networking in the New Music Economy

It has long been said that success lies not so much in *what* you know as in *who* you know. Relationships have been the catalysts of business practice forever. After all, it's not record companies that relate to each other, but *people* within these companies. Likewise, corporations don't hold conversations; people do.

This is good news for all ye who seek success in music. Your mouth is your most valuable marketing tool! No longer do we live in a society where one's set of acquaintances is fixed by one's family upbringing or education. In today's information-intensive world, you can contact virtually anyone you need to through networking.

"Networking" is the process of building a connecting system of people working in the industry who know your talents, skills, and goals. These connections will alert and lead you to opportunities in your goal area.

Networking is not about making superficial contacts just to meet your immediate need. It's about cultivating relationships. And like all relationships, the most successful networking bonds benefit both parties. When you approach networking from the perspective of giving, you make small but regular deposits in your social capital account, steadily increasing its value. You treat *all* members of your community generously—for example, by giving them new career leads, pointing them to resources that they might find useful, and helping them solve business problems.

Music is perhaps the most relationship driven business on the planet. It's a "who-you-know/who-knows-you" kind of business. The quality and quantity of your relationships will be the primary engines of your progress. So, what are you doing to strengthen and expand your web of relationships? Before looking at strategy, let's address some of the challenges people face in the networking arena.

NETWORKING CHALLENGES

Networking presents more of a challenge to some than to others. Those endowed with the gift of gab network with ease but not everyone is gifted with a golden tongue. What follows are some of the most common obstacles people face when seeking to network.

1. **Introversion.** Those of a more shy and introverted nature have the most trouble with networking. In general, introverts are quiet, reflective, and reserved. They recharge alone and prefer one-on-one conversation to the crowd.

    If this is you, then accept that this is your nature, and set some snack-sized goals to help you build your relationships. Approach networking opportunities somewhat strategically, creating a meaningful connection with one to two people, going off to recharge, then jumping in the fray once again.

    Fortunately, even the shyest person has access to myriad contacts. Your old teachers or professors, colleagues at places where you used to work, friends from all phases of your life, acquaintances, members of your church or synagogue, neighbors, contacts on your friends list at Facebook or LinkedIn, and people that you run into in your regular daily life are all networking contacts. These are not really strangers at all. They're people you can talk to.

2. **Time.** Time constraints are another barrier to networking. Networking is a high time, low-money marketing strategy, and there are no shortcuts to building strong, trusting relationships. That's why it's important to set realistic networking goals.

    I suggest trying to meet and interact with just two new people a week. This can mean anything from talking to a booking agent on the phone, to visiting a recording studio for a tour, or writing a promotional letter to a music publisher. The music industry is huge. There are no lack of contact opportunities. Two contacts a week is manageable for most. Making two contacts a week will result in over one hundred solid contacts a year. If two, three, or four band members each do this, your contacts will multiply dramatically.

3. **Space.** You may be living in an area where there isn't much music or industry activity. Here's where the brave new world of social networking can really help you out by giving you

access to information and people. Working your blog or even email messages allow you to connect to like-minded people. Find ways to connect using your passion and creativity. Have things you only want to share with a small group of people? Just create a group on Facebook, add friends, and start sharing. Once you have your group, you can post updates, poll the group, chat with everyone at once, and more. You can do a similar thing on LinkedIn and most every other social networking service. After all, that's what they're all about!

Also, don't overlook your local Chamber of Commerce. These organizations usually consist of the most prominent business people and represent generations of business partnerships. Even if you don't get any solid leads from the members themselves, you will get the scoop on everything and everyone in the community (and this can mean early entry into potential deals). Sometimes, the most promising opportunities are found in your own backyard!

4. **Emotional Barriers.** Relationships involve emotions, and it's important to bring a healthy emotional intelligence to your networking activities. This harkens back to the discussion in chapter 2 on performing the "emotional bushwhacking" necessary to break through to a healthier mindset. We are all the result of choices (both good and bad) we have made and the socialization we received from family, schools, and other groups we have been part of. If our own emotional needs weren't properly met when we were children, then it will be hard bringing the kind of developed emotions required for healthy, thriving adult relationships.

The first thing to do is shed the useless negative self-talk. ("You have nothing to offer," "You'll make a fool of yourself," "You can't, you can't, you can't....") If you want to really evolve, then accept the fact adulthood is mainly about *deprogramming/reprogramming yourself.* This may mean seeing someone (a counselor, for example) who can help you achieve these breakthroughs by illuminating the roots of your fears.

Whether you think you can or you think you can't, you're right. As Wayne Dyer is wont to say, "When you change the way you look at things, the things you look at change." Truer words have never been spoken. Get help if you need it.

Use the Student Advantage

What's the student advantage? Informational interviews. If you are a student you can get access to people in order to pick their brains on a certain subject or project you're working on. Professionals are usually willing to give fifteen or twenty minutes to help a student, and that encounter could lead to additional encounters. Always ask at the close of the interview: Would it be alright if I follow up with additional questions or if I need clarification on a certain point? Always try to leave the door open.

Clear these barriers and you're on your way to a strong relationship network.

STARTING WITH WHAT YOU HAVE

When you stop and think about it, you are a member of a number of communities. These may include:

- church, synagogue, mosque, or ashram
- volunteer organizations
- neighborhood watch group
- gym, swim club, tennis club
- political party or activist group
- college or alumni association
- friends of your family and families of your friends
- social networks.

Let's flesh out some of the possible groups you already have contacts in, or in which you can begin to expand your relationship network.

- **Business Associates.** As you move from job to job, you come in contact with colleagues who are moving around as well.

- **Professional Associations.** Don't just join them. Become an active member, by serving on committees, so your colleagues can see you in action.

- **Friends and Family.** Your brother-in-law's uncle's cousin may be a recruiter in your field. Keep your family and friends apprised of your career goals.

- **Former Professors and Instructors.** Your former professors and instructors were most likely professionals in your field. Some probably still are.

- **Former Classmates.** College friends are now colleagues. Also, check out the alumni directory of your college (and of your fraternity or sorority, if it applies) for a wider range of contacts.

- **Clergy.** Think of how many different types of people clergy know and the wide variety of fields and industries they represent.

- **Politicians and Their Staffs.** No matter where you live, you have access to politicians who represent you locally, at the state level, and even at the national level. A quick phone call or email to a politician or one of his or her staff members can easily result in one or more solid leads.

- **Newspaper, Magazine, and Television Reporters.** Every day, reporters interview a variety of people to gather the news. After you read interesting articles or see something intriguing on your local television news, contact the reporter responsible, congratulate them on their work, and ask if they can recommend any potential networking leads.

- **Online Contacts.** Your social networks are an ever-expanding treasure chest of contacts for your career.

Since it's difficult keeping all these names organized in your head, I suggest writing them down on paper or in a computer file. All of them. Once you write them down, you then want look at your list for patterns and connections between people you may not have noticed before. You also want to see where they fit in your relationship circles. Let's look at this next.

STAGES OF RELATIONSHIP GROWTH

Relationships tend to grow in stages—five stages that represent the growing trust the people in your life have in each other (see figure 5.1).

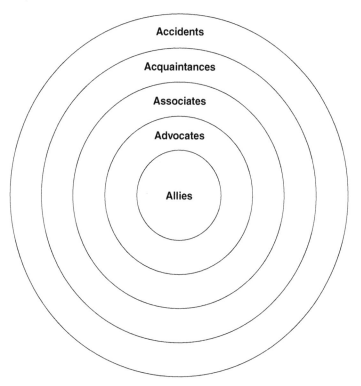

Fig. 5.1. Relationship Circles

Accidents float around outside the five concentric circles. For example, you're on a plane in seat 14A. Next to you, in 14B, is an "accident." An accident is a person you have no regular way of seeing. You might have a perfectly delightful conversation, but nothing will happen in the future, unless you make it happen.

Inside the outermost circle of the bulls-eye are *acquaintances.* These are people you could find again if you had to because you know someone in common. Think of the videographer you met at your cousin's wedding. Because you don't have regular contact, it's more challenging to build the relationship, but you could find her again through your cousin.

Inside the next circle are *associates*. If you are in school, all of your classmates, ensemble members, and sports teammates are associates because they've joined the same group: your school. At meetings and rehearsals, they see each other repeatedly. In general, it takes six contacts—six good conversations—before two people know and trust in each other enough to go out on a limb, put their good names on the line, or go to bat for each other. So, your challenge is to help people make the most of those repeated contacts. Just because people are associates doesn't mean they have a relationship. Until they begin to act as resources for each other, they won't join each other's inner circle. People who trust each other are an inner circle.

Once trust is established, your members become *advocates* for each other. An advocate says, "Jackson would be great for the awards committee." Or "Let's ask Ellen to produce the show." Or "Get Juanita to introduce the keynoter. She's so comfortable in front of a crowd." An advocate knows her contact so well that when she sees an opportunity or a resource that would appeal to that person, she takes action. Advocates trust in each other's character and competence so completely that they will unhesitatingly pass each other's names along and bring each other into their circles. Advocates can give vivid examples of each other in action: serving a client, saving the day, or solving a problem.

Finally, in the center circle, your members will have a few *allies*. Allies are on their "personal board of directors." Allies will do all they can to help each other reach their goals. They will seek opportunities for each other. They'll celebrate when things go well and commiserate when things go wrong. Allies experience a high degree of confidentiality and always tell each other the truth.

So, with these five circles in mind, return to your relationship inventory. Where does each person fit? Try organizing this list accordingly, and you'll have a better sense of who you can reach out to for help and connection.

HOW TO MAKE SMALL TALK

- **Practice.** Converse with everyone you come across: cashiers, waiters, people you're in line with, neighbors, coworkers, and kids. Chat with folks unlike yourself, from seniors to teens to tourists.

- **Smile**, be the first to say "hello," and always look people in the eye.

- **Stay focused** on your conversation partner by actively listening and giving feedback. Maintain eye contact. Never glance around the room while they are talking to you.

- Start with **common topics**. Listen more than you talk. Avoid anything religious, philosophical, political, and controversial— at least during a first encounter.

- Have a few **exit lines** ready, so that you can both gracefully move on. For example, "I need to check in with a client over there," "I skipped lunch today, so I need to visit the buffet," or you can offer to refresh their drink.

WHERE TO NETWORK

Here are some simple ways you can begin networking and increase your music industry contacts. Remember, though the digital revolution enables connections, there's still nothing like face-to-face contact.

- **Become involved in a scene.** Whether it's a musical genre (rap, metal, folk, etc.) or a political movement (Rock the Vote, National Association Against Censorship, etc.), immersing yourself in a particular musical community will enable you to meet and become known to others.

- **Read publications related to your scene.** Keep up with current events, people, and issues. Read the music section of your local paper. You'll pick up what clubs, labels, and bands are hot in your area of interest.

- **Go to clubs and musical events.** A show is a magnet for different people working in a genre/community. Other people at the show will have similar interest and goals to your own. Get to know them.

- **Ask questions.** People love to talk about themselves and their work. Expressing a common interest will create a bond.

- **Don't only try to meet the head of the company.** Avoid the natural tendency to handicap your contact lists. You may want to concentrate on powerful people, or people in certain industries, but frankly, you need to write down everyone you can think of. You're more likely to strike a friendship with a peer who works in the company who may call when they hear of an opportunity.

- **Attend conventions.** (CMJ Music Marathon, NAMM, South-by-Southwest, etc.). They offer a wealth of opportunities to meet and mingle with people working in all areas of the industry. Hit the booths and exhibit halls; you'll have a captive audience. Most conventions have volunteer programs that allow you to work in exchange for a free registration. Many people working in the industry will be volunteering alongside you, giving you an extra networking advantage.

- **Give and get business cards.** Hand them out whenever you have the opportunity. Most people keep the business cards they collect and will know where to find you when the time comes. Keep a record of those you give cards to so you can send them updates when they occur.

- **Follow up.** When you are given a business card, or make an impression with someone in a position to help/hire you, follow up the meeting with a letter and promotional materials.

- **Join clubs and associations that assist and address people with your interests.** There are songwriter organizations, producer associations, and others that provide opportunities for connecting. Many organizations have regular meetings that nonmembers can attend. See "Trade Associations as Networking Centers" on the next page for more on this.

- **Consider getting involved in your local music school or college music department.** You can take classes or work with student programs. School radio stations, social networking forums, student organizations, and newspapers can be very tuned in to local music scenes.

TRADE ASSOCIATIONS AS NETWORKING CENTERS

Trade associations act as "grand central stations" of people and information specific to a particular kind of business or trade. There is one (or more) for just about every category of business. Some of the more well-known music-related associations are:

- A2IM (Association of Independent Music)

- AES (Audio Engineering Society)

- AMC (American Music Conference)

- CMA (Chamber Music America)

- ESTA (The Entertainment Services & Technology Association)

- FMC (Future of Music Coalition)

- NAMM (National Association of Music Merchants)

- NAPAMA (National Association of Performing Arts Managers & Agents)

- NARAS (National Academy of Recording Arts & Sciences)

- NARM (National Association of Record Merchandisers)

- MENC (Music Educators National Conference)

- MPA (Music Publishers Association)

- RIAA (Recording Industry Association of America)

- TEIA (Touring Entertainment Industry Association).

Associations regularly publish directories for their members, and the better ones publish statistical information tracking industry sales, profits, ratios, economic trends, and other valuable data. If you don't know which trade associations apply to your industry, find out by asking business owners in your segment.

REFERRAL NETWORKING AND THE JOB SEARCH

Most professional musicians live a freelance life. Their work style involves multiple short-term projects which they cobble together for their support revenue. But an early stage career musician will also have to work at a regular job to make ends meet. As with freelance work, so with regular jobs, most opportunities are landed through relationships.

According to the site CareerBuilder.com, about 75 percent of all jobs are found through networking. I would agree. People gain three things through networking: private information that is not found anywhere else, influence in wider arenas, and access to diverse skill sets to help them get things done. The first (information) is probably the one most helpful in your job search.

Networking is about information, not power. You don't need a rich uncle or a best friend whose wife is in charge of hiring in order to network. Janitors and secretaries and junior salespeople are great networking contacts. So, stop looking for powerful connections, and start viewing *everyone* you can come into contact with as a potential referral source. Assume everyone has some information that will be useful to you somehow.

Also, focus on your acquaintance circle. Why? The reason is simple. Unusual connections are the norm in a job search. Your allies and advocates tend to travel in the same circles (pun intended) as you, so it's more productive to look beyond your closest relationships.

With this in mind, the next thing to do is make your "Top 50 Companies List." These are the places you respect and can see yourself working at. Write them all down and begin studying them. Research gives you more confidence. The more you know, the less you stress. Absorb all the information you can, and then go with your gut. Let your instincts be your guide. Make informed decisions about how much you want to earn, whom you will work with, what tools and talents you need to master, the hours, the environment, the stress level. Then you can move forward with a sound decision about what you want to do. You can avoid quite a few pitfalls this way.

Read the company's website, especially current news items, and try to focus on the areas of the company that interest you. It may be tech support, marketing, or just general administration. With this information you can now start leveraging your contact network.

Where do you start with your inquiries? When you can't talk to someone in the normal course of your day, use email. Email has replaced the telephone entirely for networking queries.

Here are my favorite networking questions. When you want to gain access to a particular employer, ask everyone you know: "Who do you know at _____ organization?"

When you want to get advice and counsel, ask for it! "Who do you know who would know anything about _____?"

If you ask fifty people in a row, it's the same as standing up in a crowded auditorium and asking, "Who in this room would know anything about opportunities to serve as an intern at Apple's Music Division?" By using email and starting with well-established relationships, even a shy person can get access to the same information without having to actually speak to anybody, let alone a group of complete strangers.

Assume all companies are hiring at all times, because they are. Ask for referrals to people at any level in the industries that are of interest to you. Ask for permission before using someone's name. "May I use your name when I contact that person?" If you've been polite and to the point, and you didn't ask for a job, in your communiqués with Person A, she'll be much more comfortable giving you an email for Person B.

Provide a résumé only when requested. Otherwise, don't send it. When people see a résumé, they are programmed to delete it or send it on to Human Resources, which amounts to the same thing. Also, when people see a résumé, they assume you want a job in their company. This forces them into that uncomfortable role of telling you they can't help you. What you want is information, and the power of information is independent of the power of the source of that information, because information is mostly free. In most cases, it does not require much of an introduction to get information. In short, the front door may be locked, but your most casual acquaintance may be able to walk you right in through the side door.

For people who don't know you well, you will want to condense your situation into a one-paragraph narrative that can be used in an email or said aloud in a telephone call or even a social setting. The classic version of this piece of personal branding is known as an *elevator speech*. Suppose you stepped onto an elevator and glanced over at the ID badge of the person next to you, and it read "VIP." Maybe the person is the CEO of the company you work for, or want to work for. What could you say in the brief time you are together that could change your life, and hers? That's an elevator speech.

Explain (a) who you are, (b) how you know them, (c) why you're contacting them, and (d) what you want to happen next. Be straightforward, be direct, and remember to push hard for referrals—people you can talk to next. Broken down, here is the skeleton of a typical script for a thirty-second introduction: "Hello, ___. My name is___. I was referred to you by ___. I'm interested in learning more about ___. I wonder if you would have a moment to share with me any advice, ideas, leads, and referrals."

Your goal is to eventually ask this question of the person you have been referred to: "After what I've learned from you, and my other research, I'd be very interested in applying for a job with your company in _____. Who would I talk to about that?"

Then, with your refocused résumé and your referral's introduction, you can skip that pile of 200 to 20,000 applicants. This is the power of your referral network.

"NO" MEANS NEXT!

Rejection is part of life, especially in the entertainment industry....
When George Lucas told studio executives that he wanted to have two robots star in his movie, they said he was nuts. Theodore Geisel's first book was rejected by twenty-three publishers, but his Dr. Seuss books went on to sell half a billion copies. Fred Smith was told by a professor in graduate school that his business proposal for a package delivery company would never get off the ground. It almost didn't. He was turned down a hundred times before he got the money to start Federal Express. Both Alanis Morissette and Christina Aguilera went down to defeat on the eighties show *Star Search*. Jimmy Buffett was turned down by every record label in Nashville before he finally got a deal. If you get a "no," just move on to your next prospect.

Networking Action Steps

- Have one conversation today (and every day, if possible) with someone you don't know—a friend of a friend, the barista at Starbucks, a teaching assistant, your mail carrier, anyone. Get into the habit of talking to people everywhere you go.

- Challenge yourself to call or email one person in your immediate network at least once a week to ask for their career advice or help introducing you to people in their networks who might be willing to speak with you.

- This week, contact at least one person who works in a field that interests you and invite that person out for coffee. Bring a notebook and write down all the advice you receive. If this whole process sounds a bit daunting, practice an informational interview with a career services staff person, family member, or friend.

CHAPTER 6

Essentials of Music Promotion and Marketing

How many times have you thought this: "I'm just not cut out to be a salesman," "I don't like promoting myself," and "I'm too busy to spend my time marketing"? When it comes to talking about your career or business, would you rather lay low than toot your own horn? Many musicians would rather let their creative work speak for itself than actively spread the work about what they do. Unfortunately, this means they limit their exposure to potential customers, which in turn can stunt the growth of their careers.

You may be a rocking guitarist or jingle writer, or you may build the most cool-looking hand drums, but if the right people don't know about the amazing work you have to offer, then how are they going to buy it? Marketing yourself, your songs, your products, your services, or your live shows is imperative in this dense media market we inhabit. But getting your signal through all the noise often seems like a herculean task, leaving us feeling paralyzed or powerless.

At one time or another, we've all shared these feelings.

Fortunately, to get the business you need, you don't have to have a "sales personality," or try to become someone you're not, or grit your teeth to do things that you find offensive.

It is true that until you become visible in the music marketplace and sought after (that is, "in demand"), you *will* need to find ways to "toot your own horn" that you're comfortable with—ways that will produce the results you want.

The way you *think* about this will have a great deal to do with how much business you get and how easy (or difficult) it is for you to get it.

If marketing feels like a burden or toil you'd rather not do, it will be difficult, if not impossible, for you to communicate the kind of enthusiasm and excitement that will draw fans and customers to you.

Or, if marketing is something you only think about when you're desperately in need of business, and you must force yourself to do it begrudgingly, you'll have a hard time developing a creative and effective plan for getting the business you need. This is why it is so important to develop the right kinds of marketing mind-set.

DEVELOPING A MARKETING MIND-SET

I've found that people who have plenty of business don't think about marketing as a drag. Whether they're shy and retiring or outgoing and effervescent, they're so excited about what they have to offer that they want to make sure people know about it. In fact, they feel eager—almost compelled—to reach out and make contact in whatever ways come naturally to them so people will know about their products and services.

So, even if you have no marketing or business background, even if you're starting out in a brand-new community without any existing relationships, even if you're competent but not yet outstanding at your work, you can develop a positive marketing mind-set that will enable you to create effective and affordable ways to attract business. You might have to make some mental shifts in order to think about getting business in these ways, but if you do, you too, can project a positive mind-set and make getting business easier and infinitely more enjoyable.

1. **Think opportunity, not obligation.** Instead of thinking about what a drag it is to have to get business or how difficult, unpleasant, time-consuming, and costly it is to market yourself, shift your attention instead to how eager you are to let others know about what you offer. If you've chosen the right business niche for yourself, you obviously like your work and think it's important. You know it's needed and that it improves the lives or the businesses of your customers. Your work is more than a good idea or a way to make some money; it's a benefit to those you serve. Focus on that.

   Without the funds to pay for elaborate marketing efforts and the ability to hire top-notch professionals, your own compelling sense of passion for your work will be the most essential element in attracting business to you. This kind of passion is contagious. It will come through in all your spoken and written communication whether you're introducing yourself or have created a classified ad. So, start to think about marketing as a way to share your enthusiasm for what you do.

2. **Think contact, not activity.** Marketing is about making contact with people who need what you offer. It's not about keeping busy. If you're offering a product or service that addresses an unmet need or solves a problem, you probably have a pool of potential customers who need what you have to offer right at this very minute. But chances are, they all don't know about you, and you don't know about all of them. Somehow, you need to find each other. And that's what marketing is about.

    Often people ask, "What's the best way for me to market what I do?" They're looking for the *one* steady, reliable way they can count on for making contact with clients and customers. But there is no single business-getting route that's guaranteed to reach everyone. There are probably a wealth of activities that will work well for you and your business. Finding the ones that work best is an experiment. In fact, marketing is about experimentation and not an exact science. People who are motivated to make contact with those who need them are always experimenting with new possibilities to get their message out.

3. **Think communication, not manipulation.** Often people think marketing is about being cute and clever, and creating a lot of hype or sizzle, especially in the entertainment biz. Worse, they fear it's about being manipulative. Sizzling, cute and clever hype may attract attention, but it doesn't build trust, respect, or value.

    Marketing is, essentially, *communication.* Every word you choose, the font that expresses it, the tone of your phone message, the colors on your liner notes, and the way you shake hands at a networking event are *communicating,* marketing, always, incessantly.

But it's a particular kind of communication. Marketing is communicating with your market so well that it wants to know more about you.

So, instead of worrying about being cute and clever or manipulative, think about getting your message across. Shift your attention to what it is about what you do that's important to your customers and audience. Think about how you can communicate your message to them in terms they'll understand. Think about how you can help them see the benefits of what you offer.

IT'S ALL IN THE WAY YOU SAY IT
Make words work for you.

A school in Virginia couldn't get kids signed up for a course called "Home Economics for Boys," so they put themselves in the shoes of the students and changed the name of the class to "Bachelor Living." Ta-da. It worked.

BUILDING YOUR DATABASE OF CONNECTIONS: THE LIFEBLOOD OF YOUR MARKETING

What is your basic marketing goal? Answer: To make John and Jane Public know that you exist and that they should find out more about you. The way to achieve this is through *targeted* marketing and promotion. A targeted strategy insures maximization of resources. Untargeted promotion, or "shot gunning," can waste gobs of time, money, and effort.

There are thousands of companies out there promoting their services and products, but only a handful are doing it effectively. It's the difference between hanging fifty posters that hundreds read and displaying one poster that thousands read.

Targeting makes all the difference. So how does one go about it?

The first step is to get organized by compiling your key contact lists and continuing to add and delete from these lists throughout your company's history. They are the "Grand Central Stations" (a phrase you'll see again and again in this book) of all your marketing and promotion, and will allow you to feed the networking that is so crucial for business success today.

There are three separate databases you'll want to develop: one for media, one for customers/fans, and one for industry. Let's look at each.

Media

Newspapers, magazines, radio programs, television, and online media are all driven by common needs: To fill time and space with information of value to their readers, viewers, and listeners. They're eager for this information and quite willing, at their own expense, to publish or air it. They need your news.

Begin your media database with the local scene, and then branch out regionally, nationally, and even internationally, depending on your marketing goals. A good public library is your key resource here. Tell the reference librarian what you're looking for, and you'll be guided to the media directories you need. Several good ones are listed in the Resource Directory appendix. You can find most local media information in the *Yellow Pages*. Pay attention also to writers, bloggers, and radio DJs who have helped break ground for other independent musicians and music companies. When the time is right, you can contact them with your promo.

Fans/Customers

This is your grassroots support network. The best ways to compile a fan database is at your gigs. Make it as easy as possible for people to join your fan list. Have pens and attractive cards on every table to capture this information. Make them visible by announcing their existence throughout the night. Designate someone in the band or crew as the "Fan List Manager." Use your website for the same purpose. Capture names at every connection.

As with all lists, the best way to store them is on a computer with a "contact management" program. One that has been developed with the indie musician in mind is *Indie Band Manager* (www. indiebandmanager.com). *Outlook* (Microsoft) and *Act!* (Sage Software) are two excellent programs as well. *FileMaker Pro* and other database programs can also serve you well here.

If you are selling from your website, there are some wonderful and robust shopping cart software products that can help manage your database along with many other marketing activities like order tracking, sales reporting, newsletter management, affiliate selling, and more. Three I recommend are Mal's e-Commerce (www.mals-e.com), Nimbit.com, and Corecommerce.com. The first two are very good and inexpensive; the latter is remarkable and a bit pricey. There are literally dozens of services like these out there.

Industry

Your industry database will be composed of people and organizations that can promote your music, hire you, use your songs, or book performances for you. This will include club owners, promoters, booking agents, managers of groups who might invite you to be their warm-up act, blog gurus, music supervisors, music department heads at companies like Apple and Electronic Arts, artist and repertoire (A&R) executives at record companies, publishers, producers interested in buying new songs, and others from within as well as beyond the music space.

If you're a music production house or a record label, you'll want separate industry databases for such categories as music publishers, ad agencies, manufacturers, recording studios, music libraries, music supervisors, instrument rental services, and other vendors. See the Resource Directory in the appendix for recommended industry directories.

I recommend working at least thirty minutes every day on your contact databases. Review them, study them, add to them, and continue increasing their value. Once you've built a strong database of contacts your next step is to begin *communicating* with them, that is, actively *market* and *promote*.

IMPRESSIVE PRESENTATIONS

First impressions are crucial in the music industry. Bands and solo artists are made or broken on the basis of their first impressions. Though this may seem unfair, the competitive nature of today's music business has resulted in an expectation of higher and higher standards from a band's presentation of itself. It may be true that we shouldn't judge a book by its cover, but the fact of the matter is, we do. The way your music services and products are packaged will often determine whether the message even gets "unwrapped."

Today, a band must grab attention and hold it. If you miss your first chance, you've blown it.

This is why creating impressive presentations is so important. Professional musicians will need several graphic ambassadors to help represent them to the various people they will meet: agents, music directors, media representatives, and a variety of clients who may be interested in what you have to offer. These "ambassadors" include websites, electronic press kits (or EPKs), business cards, photos, logos, and résumés. They also extend to album graphics, postcards, flyers, and anything else you use to convey your message, like email and even voice mail recordings.

"Packaging" is a message platform to channel your ideas to people fast. Make your package bold, a "fast storyteller" and reflective of your product's personality. From the moment people see your product, your catalog, your envelope, whatever—memory connections are built. And people have great memories, if the imagery you provide is consistent. The physical and electronic packaging you choose to use in your business conveys your image and engages your market.

Assembling Your Portfolio of Graphic Ambassadors

Every musician seeking to build a career ought to have the following, ready to go, on a flash drive that they carry with them or on their laptop, and which they should update continually. This information serves as a kind of portfolio of your career assets and as "ambassadors" that represent you to the industry at large. You never know when an opportunity will cross your path, and you want to be ready to go. Your website is also important and is a topic we'll explore further in chapter 10.

These "assets" would not all be used in every situation, but individually and collectively, they represent materials that are often required when working in music. Being ready, being able to provide these kinds of resources quickly, puts you in the game, and shows you in a good light.

Also, these items should always be proofread for grammar and spelling by one or more of your most literate associates. The spelling of the proper names, of musicians, venues, festivals, *everything*, should be carefully checked against the Web. *There is no excuse* for your materials, which represent you in the world of the music business, to be anything but great, and totally correct.

Here is what you need:

1. **Three or more strong photos that really show you to great effect.** One headshot and two performance/action shots are sufficient. You should have each of these at 72 dpi for the Web, and also at 300 dpi for print use. It's good to have examples of both horizontally and vertically oriented photos, to make it more likely your image can be used, depending on layout needs of the media. If it's a band photo, make sure there is a consistent look to the members. Dress and pose accordingly.

2. **Your 150- to 200-word bio.** Your bio (short biography) should be up to date, touching on the most salient, unique aspects of your story. The best artist bios read like a magazine article. Born on a houseboat? Is your mother a descendant of Gershwin? Perform before a Laker's game? Maybe you should put this in. Perhaps you can mix in interesting quotes from band members or comments made on behalf of the band. The key is to hook the reader with aspects of your story that appeal to the heart as well as the head.

   Writing a bio is a great exercise to go through. It helps you focus on what you have done and what is most representative of the artist you are and wish to be. No need to reinvent the wheel here. See how your favorite artist's bio is written at their website, and try to achieve a similar flow. Bios should also be revised *often*.

3. **A list of performances and recording credits.** This is a running inventory of every gig you play and recording session you participate in. Also updated often.

4. **A scan of your W-9 tax form.** As a freelancer or independent contractor, you will be hired for short term projects and the person hiring you will often request a W-9 form for tax purposes (see page 91 in chapter 4).

5. **At least two MP3 recordings.** This should be recent work, of which you are proud. Most musicians have their recordings available on cloud-based servers like Soundcloud.com or via their own websites.

   What about video? YouTube has made it very easy for artists to display a video presentation of their work with its ability to transcode anything and produce an easy-to-watch and easy-to-embed streaming flash movie. You simply upload a video you made on a digital camera or camcorder, and YouTube's computers turn it into a flash video. Producers, the public, wannabe actors, corporations out for publicity, and clip collectors all use YouTube. However, only use this format if you are ready to. There is a trove of half-baked "music performances" on YouTube which do no service to the artist so, if you're gong to link to your video, make sure it reflects the level of professionalism you aspire to.

Another "graphic ambassador" you may consider creating is a *logo*. As the saying goes, "a picture is worth a thousand words," and a good logo can provide a vehicle that can give you a lot of miles in terms of exposure and visibility. The challenge of logo design is to take an idea or concept and compress it down into a symbol or piece of typography.

It is recommended you hire a graphic designer to do your logo, if you or a bandmate don't have the necessary design skills to get it done. Ask around for referrals. You can also contact a local art college and get a graphic design student to take on your project for a very reasonable price. You can also find some great designers at sites like 99designs.com, musicbusinessmarketplace.com, or elance.com.

Creating Your EPK (Electronic Press Kit)

With such rich resources available today, in terms of printing and graphics, your creative packaging should be nothing less than a visual feast leading the recipient step-by-step to the audio feast— your music.

Musicians today are asking: "Which kind of press kit do I need, print or electronic?" The good news is you can get by today with just a digital version. Most people would much rather open a PDF than a large envelope with numerous objects. It is simply more convenient and easier for the recipient. This means creating an EPK (electronic press kit). While websites are more fan focused (see chapter 10), EPKs allow bookers to find exactly what they need to know about your band for booking purposes (i.e. what you sound like, where you've played, and what your "look" is).

EPKs come in various formats, such as PDF, PowerPoints, Word documents, DVDs, and online hosting (such as wix.com or Word Press). There are a number of services available that will provide you with EPK templates. Both SonicBids (sonicbids.com) and PressKit (presskit.to) will make up a snazzy EPK for you, for a fee.

EXAMPLES OF EPKS

presskit.to/bigd

www.lindsayloumusic.com/press-epk.html

www.rumsandbumbletons.com/RBepk.htm

www.reverbnation.com/DylanTaylorMusic

mikeevin.com/press/epk/

The EPK should be a tightly constructed sales pitch. There should be no confusion about what kind of band you are. Image must be crystal clear. It needs to shine through all the separate parts of the document, unifying text, graphic, and audio links. In fact, it is advisable that when creating your EPK, you begin with the photo. Use it as the tone-setter for the entire project.

A good thing to remember when assembling your presentations is that standout creativity is in short supply. The presentation of your image and message is a tremendous opportunity to express your uniqueness and pique the imagination of your audience.

So, what should go into your EPK? Looking back at the previous section, these are the 'career assets' you want to include:

1. Your name and logo

2. Several photos spread throughout the kit

3. Your bio

4. Any quotes from the media or industry about you and your music

5. Recent gig activity, with select, past high-profile performances (if any)

6. Links to your music

7. Complete contact info

How many pages should your EPK be? I've seen EPKs that were terrific one pagers and also amazing eight pagers. Length is up to you, though I would advise staying on the shorter end. Visit the examples in the box on the previous page to see how other artists are using the EPK format.

TARGETED PROMOTION

There is an expression in the world of marketing: *Never "shotgun." Target!* Sending your EPK to a random list pulled from a directory is both wasteful for you and annoying for the recipient. A record company that puts out country music does not want to hear avant-garde jazz. A club booker for a top-40 venue probably doesn't want to hear world music. Send your promotional messages only to those you have already researched and who have either expressed interest in your work or who have made themselves available for "unsolicited" submissions. Everything else is a waste of time and energy.

You'll be sending your EPK to three main groups of people that can help your career:

1. **Entertainment Buyers.** These will include club owners, booking agents, festival and fair coordinators, private party organizers, and student activities directors at schools and colleges.

2. **Media Contacts.** These will include music magazine editors and writers, entertainment editors in the mainstream press, radio station music directors and key DJs, and television, film, and video music buyers.

3. **Industry Contacts.** These will include A&R (Artist and Repertoire) representatives from record companies, music publishers, multimedia producers, entertainment lawyers, and record pool directors, as well as representatives associated with relevant music initiatives in any company you see an opportunity in (for example, Red Bull's Music Academy).

Each group will require a certain slant that can be conveyed effectively in your cover letter. Kits going to clubs and colleges will want to stress the group's following and its powerful stage show. Those aimed at record labels will want to underline the band's staying power, original sound, and success at building a fan base.

Those seeking sponsors and endorsers will stress number of followers, along with any other details about location, age, and economic and educational level of this group.

With these foundational pieces in place, you are now ready to start conquering the world.

Finding Gigs in All the Right Places: Tapping the Sources of Lesser-Known Music Work

BEYOND THE CLUB SCENE

When most musicians think of "getting a gig," nightclubs are what usually come to mind. After all, clubs provide local forums for you to sharpen your stage act and spark that grassroots buzz so crucial for moving up to the next level of success.

The lion's share of club profits is derived from bar receipts, and people today are drinking less alcohol. Related to this are the numerous drunk-driving laws and drinking-age requirements, which have further eroded club profits and kept people home.

The heightened awareness of alcohol-related dangers has also affected liability insurance requirements for club owners. My father, for example, had a live entertainment club in Arizona that was put out of business because the state legislature (albeit controlled by a conservative, ultrareligious majority) upped the liability requirement for all Arizona bars (to the tune, for my Dad, of $24,000 per year!). While it hasn't gotten this bad in most other states, liability insurance does account for a big chunk of a club's expenses—one most musicians rarely consider when negotiating fees.

Before we start pitying the clubs for trends they can't control, it is also important to acknowledge how little clubs provide in terms of comfort, adequate ventilation, respect for musicians, and general cleanliness. These too have kept potential patrons away. To battle shrinking profits, clubs have resorted to everything from mobile DJs to karaoke. These are some of the real factors affecting your attempts at securing club gigs. So what are musicians to do?

Clubs are important for performing musicians, and we will explore ways of getting more and better club dates in the next chapter. But, for now, if you like to perform but feel a bit jaded against the club scene, you're in luck. There are hundreds—probably thousands—of hidden gig opportunities awaiting your act's performance. Besides a chance to play, these jobs will usually pay you more than a club date and also allow you to reach audiences who probably wouldn't set foot in most clubs. It's time to enlarge your borders.

PROFESSIONALLY READY

A key requirement for getting these better gigs is *professionalism*. The way you present yourself on a gig is possibly the most important marketing tool you've got. This doesn't just mean being a pro at your skill. That part is a given. You need to present yourself in a professional manner throughout the job. You're aiming higher and dealing more with the "suit-and-tie crowd," so your presentation has to really shine.

What does "professionalism" look like? Many things. First, the person that books your act should be a good communicator—someone who can succinctly and effectively deliver your sales pitch over the phone or on paper, has a high-functioning answering machine and upbeat message, possesses "people skills," and is able to negotiate contracts and mediate between band members. With these skills, you'll make great headway. Without them, you're sunk.

Professionalism also means having all your "marketing communications" ready to go: website, EPK, sales letters, business cards, contracts, confirmation letters, photos, testimonials from previous clients, music demos, mailing labels, envelopes, etc. While we shouldn't judge a book (or, in this case, a band) by its cover, in reality, we do. First impressions stick, and they're very hard to unglue, especially in the world of business. Opt for the very best materials you can afford.

In this world, you may actually benefit from sending physical materials through the mail. A well-designed single sheet with a great logo, photo, bio, and testimonials, along with a DVD of your performance, may stand out among all the digital flotsam and jetsam. Today, you can save a lot of money in setup by designing your promo materials on a computer with design programs like *Photoshop* or *Picasa*. Be sure your materials have a clear theme and that all your contact information is clearly displayed on every component in the package. And keep good records!

Unlike club gigs, these opportunities will usually require written contracts between client and performer. In fact, you will find that some of these events will require two contracts—one from the client, and one from you. (See figure 7.2, "Performance Agreement," which you should feel free to adapt for your own needs.) We will look at the ins and outs of performance agreements later in this chapter.

The information you need in order to access these gigs won't be found in most gigging and club directories. Your public library will be the key resource in digging out these hidden opportunities. Libraries are repositories of useful information. Get to know the reference librarian. This person will be your guide through the many databases and directories you're likely to consult.

As you find potential clients for your services, add them to your own contact database.

WHERE TO LOOK AND WHAT TO DO

What follows is a list of gig possibilities with information on how to access them. It's not a complete list. Hopefully, you'll be able to add your own ideas to it as you brainstorm with your bandmates. The gigs I'll be discussing cover a wide spectrum and won't apply to every musician. Some will match your act perfectly, and others you'll want nothing to do with. A few may require more music than you have right now. But that doesn't mean you can't be preparing for them in the days ahead.

Package Out: _____ Follow-up Call: _____

Date: _____

Name of Club/Facility: _____

Address: _____

_____

Phone Number(s): _____

Fax: _____

Contact Name: _____

Musical Style Preference: _____

Set Structure: _____

Budget Information: _____

Booking Procedure: _____

Past Acts: _____

Room Capacity: _____

Stage Size: _____

Sound System: _____

Monitor System: _____

Sound Person Name: _____

Lights: _____

Dressing Room: _____

Standard Amenities for Bands: _____

Additional Notes: _____

_____

_____

_____

_____

_____

Fig. 7.1. Booking Research Worksheet

Associations. Check out the multivolume *Encyclopedia of Associations*, and you'll find over 25,000 associations (read, similar interest groups) in the United States. Start with topical associations that strike your interest: environmental, arts, religious, media, educational, computer, social service, science fiction, etc. Virtually every association sponsors state, regional, and national meetings and conventions, and many of them hold dinners, programs, dances, or fundraisers that need music.

Call or email them and ask for two things: first, request they send you information about their association with a calendar of the coming years' events, and second, get the name of the association's entertainment coordinator or chairperson of the entertainment committee. When you reach the entertainment person (after you've studied the information sent to you), be ready with a sales pitch tailored to his or her own special interests. The key is to create a "tie-in" with what they're all about. Begin with local associations and branch out.

Businesses of all kinds are great possibilities for a wide variety of music work. Though business events are often booked by entertainment agencies or public relations firms, many are open to outside suggestions. Businesses need music for any number of functions including groundbreaking ceremonies, grand openings, seasonal sales, trade shows, promotions and retirements, company milestones, Christmas and New Year's Eve parties, and fashion shows. I once played a reggae gig for a Caribbean travel agency at a bridal fashion show in the Providence Civic Center in Rhode Island. Our job was to provide background music to entice brides to choose the Caribbean as their honeymoon destination. We were literally put behind a curtain, out of sight. So, we just jammed some reggae grooves for two hours and walked away with $1,500! This, and a few other gigs like it, helped us finance a recording we were making at the time. Can your act fit in with any of these events? Businesses are everywhere. The Yellow Pages may be your best source for ideas. The possibilities are endless.

Nonprofit organizations sponsor all kinds of events that need music. Again, begin locally with a directory from your public library and scope out those organizations with which you resonate. There are as many nonprofits as there are associations, so it's a wide-open field. Don't forget civic orchestras, historical societies, health organizations, and foundations—all of which may sponsor dinners, dances, or shows to benefit a cause. Some of these will be nonpaying (basic freight and technical costs excluded), but what is lost in cash can be gained in publicity and important contacts. As with the business and association gigs, these jobs often lead to repeat business for your act.

Conventions make up one of the largest, fastest-growing markets in contemporary America. Just about every business, industry, government agency, social group, and professional association has, at the very least, an annual meeting or conference to discuss common interests, socialize with colleagues, make useful contacts, and plan for the coming year. And they all hire musicians for entertainment. Try to find out if there will be a particular theme for the convention, and then tie in your act with that theme. A singing group called the Chromatics, made up of astronomers, play guess where? Right: all conventions having to do with space exploration and astronomy!

The people to contact for these gigs are events planners. They specialize in organizing all the different components of a successful convention. Most of them work through entertainment companies, but isn't that what you are? Again, the way you present yourself makes all the difference. There's a great annual resource called *Meeting Professionals International Directory* (www.mpiweb.org) that will give you the contact info on these people. You should be able to find it in a large public library. See also the Yellow Pages under "Convention Services and Facilities."

Country clubs need lots of music for an astounding variety of occasions. They have regularly scheduled dinners, dances, parties, and athletic events, as well as more specialized "theme" parties, seasonal activities, and shows. When you think of "clubs," however, don't limit yourself to just the big country clubs. Include every organized group you can think of, and you'll expand your market to include all kinds of nonpublic but well-paying gigs. Since country clubs are often linked to golf courses, you can find a complete national list of them in a directory called *Golf Courses: The Complete Guide to over 14,000 Courses Nationwide.*

Park programs abound, and local government agencies are often in control. Begin with the "Recreation and Park Departments" in your region. If you want to check out parks programs outside your region, consult *The Municipal Executive Directory* to put you in touch with key people in parks and recreation departments. Other government-sponsored work can include inner-city festivals, cultural-enrichment programs, officers and NCO clubs, and even foreign tours. Some of this information can be found through the mayor's office in the city of your choice.

Cruise Lines. Want to spend the winter jammin' on the warm waters of the Caribbean? Then perhaps cruise line work is for you. According to the Cruise Lines International Association (CLIA), the cruise industry is one of the fastest growing categories in the entire leisure market. The industry has tripled in size every ten years! New employees are needed to support the growing cruise vacation business, and this includes a wide assortment of musicians. Cruise lines rely on entertainment agents such as Marcelo Productions out of Miami (305-854-2228) and Proship Entertainment out of Quebec (514-485-8823), who regularly hold auditions in various cities. Players should be able to read as well and have a wide musical repertoire to draw from. Salaries range from $350 to $500 per week and include food, lodging, and transportation to and from the ship. For inside information on this job option, see *How to Get a Job with a Cruise Line* by Mary Fallon Miller.

Hotels are a prime market for musicians and not just GB (general business) acts. Hotel-sponsored parties are frequent, and a variety of music is sought for them. Much of this work comes through word of mouth. If you have a good relationship with the catering or sales staff, you'll get these jobs. A full list of a particular city's hotels can be obtained from that city's Convention and Visitor's Bureau or Department of Tourism.

TESTIMONIALS

If the guests enjoyed the performance, then why not drop them a line a week later to thank them for a great event, and to say that you would be grateful for any comments they have on the band? These are really valuable and go straight on your website and EPK to help potential new customers have even more confidence in hiring you.

Private parties are another specialized but excellent market to pursue. Since many of these are held in well-to-do homes, it is important that you be able to relate socially as well as musically.

How do you find out who's throwing a party? One way is to contact party organizers and caterers. Send them your business cards, letting them know what you can offer their clients by way of music. Stay in touch. You never know what will turn up.

Public relations firms and advertising agencies can be good music clients because they are involved in creating and staging all kinds of events. A band I was playing with was approached by a PR rep for McDonald's to see if we'd be interested in performing at the grand opening of one of their restaurants. It's nice when they come to you, but you can also go to them. Whatever your musical specialty, you should let all the advertising and PR firms in your area know, so when they need your type of music, they'll know where you are. Remember, public relations and advertising people thrive on innovation and are open to suggestions for new or unusual uses of music. Therefore, when talking with these firms, let creativity rule. Make suggestions that are too unusual to present to other clients, and you'll be treated as a kindred spirit.

Schools offer a broad market for all kinds of music, whether elementary, high school, or college. Colleges, in particular, are rich with playing opportunities. They should be viewed as small cities with scores of events happening each week throughout the year. If you're serious about playing the college circuit, you should definitely check out the National Association of Campus Activities (NACA). NACA holds annual regional conferences (read: trade shows) where musical acts can exhibit their wares for the hundreds of college talent buyers passing through. Live showcase opportunities are also possible, and if you're liked, can result in "block bookings" along the college touring circuit. To book yourself at colleges, call the student activities office, and find out who is responsible for hiring entertainment at that school. Call that person, and inquire about specific events during the upcoming year that might be appropriate for your style of music.

These are just a few of the thousands of "hidden" gig opportunities available to musicians. Musical jobs are everywhere, and there's no reason you shouldn't enjoy the rewards of these less-common jobs. With the current conditions in the club scene and surplus of willing bands, these lesser-known jobs should be all the more attractive.

Just remember, most of these jobs will bring you in close contact with the professional business world. The musician who can communicate on the same professional level will be the one who gets the gig.

THIS CONTRACT for the personal services of musicians on the engagement described below, made this_____ day of_____, 20____, between the undersigned purchaser of music and musicians.

ARTIST _____

LOCATION _____ DATE _____ TIME_____

ARTIST FEE $ _____ DEPOSIT_____

TICKET PRICE _____

PAYMENT Cash/School Check/Certified Check   CAPACITY _____

PAY TO: _____   TYPE EVENT_____

SETS_____   ARRIVAL TIME _____

CONTACT PERSON_____   PHONE _____

FAX _____

REQUIREMENTS:

DRESSING ROOM One clean, well-lit room for ten persons   STAGE SIZE_____

SOUND Employer/Band provides   LIGHTS Employer/Band provides

FOOD/BEVERAGES_____

This agreement shall be governed by and interpreted in accordance with the laws of the Commonwealth of _____. This agreement constitutes the entire agreement between the parties relating to the subject matter hereof, and all previous understandings, whether oral or written, have been merged herein. No alteration, amendment, or modification hereof shall be binding unless in writing signed by all of the parties. Upon its execution, this Agreement shall take effect as a sealed instrument in accordance with the terms and provisions set forth above.

The Agreement of the Artist to perform is subjected to proven detention by sickness, strikes, adverse weather conditions, acts of God, or any other legitimate condition beyond control for which the Artist will not be held responsible for any loss incurred by Purchaser as result thereof.

Kindly return contracts within ten (10) days in order to ensure confirmation of date.

The Purchaser in signing this contract warrants that he/she is of legal age and has the right to enter into this contract.

If you have any questions regarding the Agreement, or if we can be of further assistance, please do not hesitate to call or write.

Thank you for allowing us to be of service, and best wishes for a successful show.

AGREED AND ACCEPTED

_____   _____
ARTIST REPRESENTATIVE   PURCHASER

DATE _____   DATE _____

Fig. 7.2. Performance Agreement

GET IT IN WRITING

The performance contract—an agreement between the band or its legal representatives and the venue operator or promoter—is the basic legal tool for staging a show.

The contract should be a written document. The problem with an oral agreement is that in the event of a dispute, it is difficult to prove the terms agreed to between the venue rep and the band. If the contract is written, then the agreed-to points are much easier to prove. A sample written performance contract is shown in figure 7.2. Feel free to copy and adapt this contract to your needs. It should also be noted that a contractual relationship with clubs or promoters (presenters) is only as good as the relationship between the owner or promoter and the group itself, and will rarely be formalized in a written agreement. You should therefore make a threshold determination of whether the owners of the club are people with whom you really wish to deal.

Do not accept a contract written by the presenter. You want to insure that the interests of your group are primary. Consequently, you should send out your own contract. If they require that their contract be used, insist that your own contract also be signed by the presenter and made part of the presenter's contract. As long as your terms are reasonable, there shouldn't be a problem with this arrangement.

Contract Essentials Checklist

Regardless of the type or size of performing group, there are a number of standard elements that all contracts should contain:

1. The date of the agreement.

2. The artist's name, address, phone and fax numbers, email address, and primary contact person representing the act.

3. The presenter (hereafter referred to as "employer") name, address, phone and fax numbers, email address, and primary contact person representing the event.

4. The date and time of the performance, including number and length of set(s) and duration of breaks between sets.

5. The location of the venue where your performance will take place.

6. The artist's fee, plus the time and manner of payment (check, cash, etc.), whether there is a deposit required, and a guarantee that there will be no taxes, union charges, or other surprise deductions from the fee when it is paid.

7. Any technical requirements regarding stage size, lighting, sound, and dressing room amenities.

8. Arrival time, setup time, and the time for sound checking.

9. An "Act of God" clause, which releases the artist from liability for failure to perform if such failure is caused by an event beyond their control. Such clauses are referred to as "boiler-plate" (standard legal clauses common to most time-sensitive agreements).

You will also be requested to sign a W-9 form for tax purposes (see page 91).

What's standard for bands may not be for presenters. They may want the contract to include other "essentials" (from their perspective) such as a clause about decibel levels or a "radius clause" wherein your group can't play within three or five miles of the venue within 30, 60, or 90 days. The latter, however, usually happens only when the venue is a nightclub and the group has a large following.

You might also want to find out if the hiring organization or venue is liable for any damage to your stage equipment by customers during your hours of employment (as stated in the contract) or any damage to the customers if, say, a speaker falls and injures one of them. If the organization or the venue isn't liable, you'll want to check your own insurance coverage. You are ultimately responsible for your own equipment.

Contract Riders

The above points are the essentials of a performance contract, also known as the "contract face." This should suffice for most gigs. Any additional requirements fall under the heading of "riders"—supplemental attachments to the standard contract face.

Contract riders can range from such simple requests as a meal and beverage for band members all the way to the picayune, like the removal of brown M&Ms from the mix (I kid you not)!

Riders are vital, unless you wish to exist solely on the presumed generosity of club owners and concert promoters. On the other hand, you can't expect a club or a promoter to provide what you need unless they know what that is. It's best to make the rider part of the contract so you have only one document to sign.

CHAPTER 8

Playing the Clubs: Getting Your Foot in the Door without Getting It Slammed

You've been calling a club for months, and you finally get the booker on the phone. Don't celebrate, yet; the real work is still ahead. That crucial conversation you're about to strike up is an art that requires skill. Luck and talent won't help you much on the phone.

What you say and how you say it is as important as what you shouldn't say. By understanding the needs of your market, you can anticipate a booking agent's response and turn a "no" into a future opportunity.

GETTING YOUR FOOT IN THE DOOR

As mentioned in the previous chapter, the current club scene is experiencing a bit of a slump owing to a smaller club-going population and some antidrinking legislation. Despite these woes, however, the clubs still provide a crucial outlet for bands to hone their performance skills and catalyze local, regional, and national followings. So, how does one go about getting club gigs?

Selling your band on the phone is a tough proposition. Try to realize the volume of calls clubs receive, then imagine the booker's frame of mind. You want exactly what a hundred other bands a day want. What makes *you* worthy of the coveted slot?

Before you call, do some market research. Make sure your music is compatible with the club's entertainment focus. Check the local entertainment guides for info on who's booked where. If possible, make a personal contact first. The music business, like most businesses, is *relationship*-driven. If you can meet someone eye to eye, you'll have a head start.

When you call, keep your tone friendly and relaxed. Get right to the point. Bookers are busy. They need to know exactly what you want right away. Get a feel for each person's style. Be very clear about the date you want, thank them for their time, and leave a number. It's important to specify a particular night. That way, if your date won't work, there's a chance to ask what date will.

Instead of too-frequent callbacks that can irritate the booker, tell him or her you'll call them back in a couple of weeks. Then use that promise to launch the next conversation. Don't vent your anger on the booking agent. Remember, they're in control and you're not. You're in a buyer's market. The only control you have is your following. If you're trying to develop a club following, incurring the wrath of a booker could be a terminal setback.

Even in music meccas like Los Angeles, New York, and Nashville, the club circuit is small. Bookers and managers know when a band can draw a crowd. When you get to that point, a club that turned you down six months ago might call you.

But, nine times out of ten, clubs won't call you back. Accept this as the way it is. Be persistent, however. Give them a few weeks to hear your material, then call at least once a week, depending on the response. If they say they haven't listened to your MP3s or received the CD by then, give a gentle reminder or send another. Even when a booker is curt and abrupt, make a point of ending on a polite, friendly note. Cultivate a calm, hang-tough approach.

GIG SWAPPING: PLAY TO PACKED ROOMS WHEN PERFORMING OUT OF TOWN

In this crazy Web world where every artist is just a blog post away from being hailed as the "Saviors of Music," it is increasingly difficult to make positive press actually mean something. Unless you're blessed with that perfect storm of hype, media saturation, and industry connections, chances are you'll have to earn your fans the old fashioned way, one at a time.

So, how do you make touring work for you in this kind of environment? Gig swapping! Sure, you can write promoters and club bookers directly. But even if you're lucky and they say "yes," you still might find yourself playing with a mismatched, under-promoted bill on an off night to an empty room. A better approach is to perform with a friend's band who lives in that town—a band that has the connections and fans in that market to pull off a great live event.

"But I don't have musician friends spread out across the country like that!" you might say. Well, with MySpace, Facebook, Twitter, and online touring networks springing up all over the place, modeled after CouchSurfing.com, a musical partnership is just a click away. Find a band that complements your style. Ask them to set up a show in their town where you get to open for them. Then, when they travel through your town, return the favor. It's a shared investment and pretty simple to set up. As with most things, the key is in establishing real human relationships. Oftentimes, these kinds of negotiations can lead to lasting friendships, too.

THE RIGHT APPROACH TO GETTING MORE AND BETTER GIGS

The key to getting more and better gigs is communicating the benefits your act will provide the venue. Approach this as a partnership proposal. Your job is to convince the booker that it would be to the club's advantage to have you play there. How do you do this?

- First, **emphasize the crowd you will draw.** Even if it's just fifteen people, let them know.

- **Stress the uniqueness of your music.** What makes it stand out from the rest? If you can't answer this question, then you're not ready to play live.

- **Get online footage of your band.** Presenting high-quality video footage of your band performing is highly valuable, as it allows potential customers to see (and get a feel) for the type of band they are hiring. It is worth hiring a professional photographer and video producer to get some good quality footage of your band performing on stage. It doesn't have to break the bank. Contact fans in your own network or a local film school or art college for potential videographers.

- **Try getting some media ink first.** While the Internet may not seem like a fast way to land a local gig, if you contact music weblogs specializing in the type of music your band produces, you may find the right kind of support. If you are an unusual or new sounding act, try indie blogs first. Sometimes a regional blog or the entertainment page of a city blog will get you published. These pages have built-in fans who are looking for new material. Some of the readers have connections. For more ideas on getting covered by media, see chapter 10.

- **Let the booker know about your promotional plan** for the show and all the *free* publicity the club will receive from your messaging, flyers, radio announcements, and newspaper calendar listings. Show them you are organized, professional, and thinking ahead. This alone will set you apart from other, less organized bands.

Remember, a club is a *business*. It has to make financial sense for them to give you a gig. Bands that haven't got any following yet should get some media mentions or college airplay in the vicinity of the clubs they want to play first. You have to respect the club's position; if no one's ever heard of you, how can they make money off the show?

Here are a few ideas for how you can work together with clubs to develop a successful gigging strategy and bring in larger crowds.

- **Link up with local promoters.** There are dozens of promoters that would love to promote a club once a month. Put your heads together to create an anticipated event. When you've found someone who wants to promote you, make sure you and the promoter understand what you need from each other. Get on the same page in terms of pay, load-in time, your estimated performance time slot, and set duration.

- **Call local** record labels, record stores (there are still a few left!), magazines, newspapers, and radio/television stations, and see if they want to have a night at the club. Lots of radio stations promote clubs to their listeners and are always looking for new venues to affiliate with. Labels are always renting clubs to showcase their bands to the local media. Make sure all of these people have a copy of your latest recording.

- **Call all the above people and talk to the promotion departments,** especially at radio stations. See if you can send them tickets to your show. Make it a habit of mailing them tickets. Seeing your name again and again lets them know you're serious and enduring.

- **Bundle your show into a package.** Team up with two other acts, come up with a theme, and then approach the booker with your ideas. Tell them each band has a mailing list of "x," and you're SMS-ing all your contacts, running a Facebook ad campaign, and that you have that guest spot on local radio to plug your show. The club gets a fully packaged night, along with the followings of each act and the revenue this brings. Done creatively, you can probably get your pick of the night, if done enough in advance.

- **Set up a contest with the club,** like a funny face contest, or during intermission announce, "The first person to the bar with red sneakers gets a free CD and a drink." Bands can donate CDs and vinyl; clubs can donate free drinks. The point is to give everyone a good feeling about that club and that band.

PUT QR CODES ON YOUR CONCERT POSTERS

Win new fans on the road before you even pull into town!

You've confirmed a string of out-of-town dates. Now what? Time to send tour posters to each venue with QR Codes on them!

Fig. 8.1. QR Code

QR Codes (Quick Response Codes), those little black-and-white checker-box images that you've probably seen on posters, signs, and boxes, allow people to check out your music simply by scanning the code with a scanning app on their iPhone, Android, or camera-enabled smartphone.

Where can you get a QR code?

There are numerous QR code creation tools online. Just Google QR Code, and you'll find a huge list. The QR code creation tool I used to create the code in our concert poster is called Kaywa. It was simple to use and free to create codes. URL shortener bit.ly also has a way to create a QR code that allows you to track links, so if you love to track your QR code scans, they might be your best bet.

So, now you're not just some random band on a random poster taped to the bathroom wall in some rock club in a faraway town. You're all of those things *with* the ability to turn a random passerby into a real fan!

Scanning the QR Code can initiate a number of functions on that potential fan's smartphone, leading them to your website, to a page that offers special content (live videos or music clips), free downloads, or to a service that offers discount ticketing to your show. The options are many. Use your imagination and convert the merely curious into concert attendees. Then, once you're in the same room as them, put on a great show and turn them into lifelong supporters of your music.

Source: CdBaby.com

- **Run co-op ads** in local magazines and newspapers advertising the show and the contest. Give the ads some pizzazz. Include coupons for free admission or a free drink with admission. This will make your ad a hundred times more effective and bring in a lot more people. Also, put up flyers advertising the gig near the venue.

- **Establish a residency.** These are steady gigs that go on the calendar in advance once you've built up a following in that venue. My band, Underwater Airport, secured a residency at a club in Salem, Massachusetts where we play every six weeks or so. That gives the band a chance to develop a scene in that space that fans can rely on.

The lesson is: *Don't start until you're ready.* Make sure your vocals are strong, your arrangements tight, your equipment adequate, and your promotion happening. Jumping the gun and taking gigs for which you're not ready can take months—even years—to repair.

This saying is true: "You never get a second chance to make a first impression." Prepare and come out *strong*.

WHEN THE CLUB DOESN'T PAY YOU

Most artists performing at performing arts centers, on college campuses, for government organizations, in schools, and sometimes at festivals, most often get paid by business check, government check, or certified check. When it comes to clubs, however, cash is king. The way you prefer to be paid should be prearranged with the club owner or booker when the show is originally booked.

There is nothing worse than coming off the stage after a smokin' gig only to find that the club owner or event coordinator has decided to delay your payment. What's a band to do?

If you are owed money by the club owner and the owner refuses to pay, you have recourse to the courts (and to your AFM local, if it's a union club, but that's a whole other story). This can be an expensive proposition, in terms of time, and is not one to be pursued lightly.

For example, Massachusetts law, in general, provides opportunity if the claim is no more than $2,000 or if you are willing to limit your claim to that amount. You can bring your own action in the small claims court in the county where you reside or where the club is located.

The procedure requires you to go to the county clerk for your local court system and pay a small fee for filing, stamping, and serving the complaint (usually $15 to $25). The sheriff then serves the complaint on the defendant, setting forth a date, time, and place for a hearing. The defendant can file a counterclaim within forty-eight hours of the hearing, but it has to be verified, or sworn to (yours does not). If you lose, you cannot appeal, and that is the end of the case.

Your cause will be greatly strengthened, however, if you can present a signed and dated contract to the judge. Of course, the "standard practice" in nightclubs is to work on a handshake, without a written contract. Similar small claims procedures are in effect in most states.

Getting Legal Help

The sample performance agreement in the previous chapter (figure 7.2) can be used as is or modified for your own purposes. If you are going to need some additional modifications for your own performance contract, you will need expert legal advice.

In many cities, you can find low-cost expertise through nearby Volunteer Lawyers for the Arts (VLA) groups. The VLA's stated purpose is to "provide legal assistance and educational programs to the artistic community, particularly those artists and arts organizations who are financially unable to obtain necessary legal services elsewhere." In order to access VLA services, it is necessary to fill out an application and pay a $50 application fee. (This fee can be waived if your inability to pay can be demonstrated.)

If you are eligible for pro bono (free) services, the VLA will attempt to refer you to a volunteer attorney. If it's determined that you're not eligible, the VLA will assist you in locating an attorney who may be willing to provide legal services on a reduced fee basis.

The Massachusetts VLA can be reached at 617-523-1764. Outside of Massachusetts, call the main office in New York at 212-977-9270 for the VLA office nearest you.

Some law schools with an "Entertainment Law" track sometimes set up low- or no-cost artist services at the school so law students can get experience reviewing real contracts and advising artists on various legal matters. If there is a law school near you, check with it to see if this service is available.

Some legal issues will fall outside what these services can offer you. At that point, you will need to see an attorney specializing in music law. For guidelines on choosing an entertainment attorney, see the box on the next page.

Making arrangements for performing deserves special consideration and planning. Keep in mind that your ability to get your music out there will be enhanced by getting your business act together.

WHEN YOU NEED A MUSIC LAWYER

Sooner or later, you'll have to bite the bullet and seek out legal counsel as a musician, so it's important to know how to select the best lawyer for your needs. Here are a few tips to help you with the screening process:

1. **Get a specialist.** The value of a music attorney is determined in large part by the quantity and quality of his or her contacts in the music/entertainment field. Artists should be cautioned against the natural inclination to use a friend, relative ("My Cousin Vinny"), or family lawyer to fill their entertainment law needs. This is fine if they're qualified. However, the trend today is toward greater legal specialization than ever before because of the increased complexity of our commercial society.

   Unless a lawyer deals regularly with management, recording, and music publishing contracts; copyright protection and administration; and licensing of intellectual and artistic property, chances are that he or she won't understand or appreciate the entertainment industry and its peculiar problems sufficiently.

2. **Get referrals from other musicians.** A referral from a satisfied client is a good start, but also...

3. **Get references.** Always ask the attorney for at least two client-references and their phone numbers. This is a perfectly reasonable request and any balking at this should be your cue to exit.

   Be sure that the work the lawyer did for this client is similar to what you need, and also that the work was performed in the last six months to a year (this business changes too fast for sporadic legal excursions).

4. **Get the dirt (if there is any).** You can make two important phone calls to find out if there have been any complaints lodged in your city or state against this attorney. They're calls worth making:

  A. Secretary of State's office (look for the phone number in the "Government" section of your phone book).

  B. The Better Business Bureau (4200 Wilson Blvd., Suite 800, Arlington, VA 22203-1804; Phone: 703-276-0100; Fax: 703-525-8277; www.bbb.org/). The Better Business Bureau Online Directory lists the addresses and phone numbers of Better Business Bureaus in cities throughout the United States and Canada.

5. **Have a meeting.** Most attorneys will waive their usual hourly fee for the first consultation. At this consultation meeting you'll want to:

  A. Ask the attorney about his basic philosophy of life. Why? Because this will help you understand his world-view, a significant relationship component. If your world-view turns out to be diametrically opposed to the attorney's, it probably means you are not a good match for each other.

  B. Inquire about the extent and quality of the attorney's pertinent industry contacts.

  C. Find out how the fee structure would work to avoid any misunderstandings.

  A note on legal fees: Sometimes you'll need legal counsel for short-term projects like putting together the appropriate performance and partnership agreements, trademarking your business/band name, incorporating your business, and copyright registration. These kinds of projects are usually paid for as a "flat fee" based on the attorney's hourly rate. Longer-term projects and legal representation to the music industry (to labels, publishers, merchandise companies, etc.) are often paid in "points" (percentage points) of contract advances and/or future royalties.

6. **Feel the vibe.** Trust your instincts.

7. **Do-(some of)-it-yourself.** A lot of groundwork can be done by yourself when it comes to short-term legal needs. For example, modern communication technologies like the Internet let you do a national trademark search from your desktop. For tips on this and other do-it-yourself legal resources contact Nolo Press (www.nolo.com/) or call 510-549-1976 for their free self-help law books and software catalog.

Fifteen Ways to Get the Most Out of Every Gig

One of the keys to music business success is the ability to maximize limited resources. This simply means making the most of the time, money, and effort available to promote your career. Though your resources may be meager, it's what you do with them that really counts.

This principle applies to every aspect of a musician's life, but I want to focus on just one of them: *How to get the most out of every gig you play.*

Gigs are one of the most potential-rich avenues for bands and musicians, in terms of networking and exposure. Yet few take full advantage of the full opportunities they present. *Each gig should be seen as an occasion for expansion of your music and performing skills, your fan base, your media contacts, and your industry relationships, etc.* What follows are fifteen ways to get the most out of every gig.

BEFORE THE SHOW

You've just booked a gig at a new club, and it's two months away. Let's look at some of the things you can do now to maximize this performance before, during, and after the show.

1. **Find out all you can about** the room you're going to play. Know the stage size, what times bands are expected to sound check and to begin and end playing, and whether or not there's a dressing room. Find out about the sound and lighting systems, if provided, and talk to the engineers. If possible, ask other bands who have played the room for tips and pointers. Remember, you're there to perform a show,

not worry about all these details. Get the right information before the gig, and you'll have that much less anxiety during the gig.

2. **Rehearse your show straight through as if it were the real thing.** Pay attention to your stage presence as well as your stage sound. Practice any movements or dance steps you're planning to use at the gig. You may also want to hold a full dress rehearsal and have someone snap some photos or shoot a low-budget video of the group to see what the audience will see. This is always educational (and often humbling!). Remember, you're trying to make the most of this gig.

3. **Publicize the show.** If you already have a fan base, mobilize those fans to help you promote the show. They are your advance guard, and you should always engage them in moving your act forward. In addition, print up a bunch of flyers with all pertinent information, including contact number. You're competing with a lot of other events, so you want your flyer to stand out. Use colorful paper and eye-catching graphics. Seek the advice of a friend who's an artist, or go the extra distance and have a professional create a killer gig poster for your act, leaving a blank space at the bottom for all relevant info. Once you have your flyer in hand, it's time to send it out. First, send it to all your fans as an attachment via email, your primary support base. Ask them to redistribute the flyers to their friends. Second, send it to all music writers in the local media. To obtain this information, visit the reference librarian at your public library. Tell them what you need and you'll be directed to a number of useful directories. Two particularly good ones are *Gale's Directory of Publications and Broadcast Media,* which lists over 36,000 print and broadcast media, and the *Broadcasting Yearbook,* covering radio, television, and cable outlets in the United States and Canada.

4. **Write down all dailies, weeklies, and monthlies** within a ten-mile radius of where your show will happen. Your list should include music publications as well as mainstream press. Chances are, you've already started such a list (see chapter 6), but you want it to be as comprehensive as

possible. Record phone numbers as well as addresses. Then call each publication to find out two things: first, the name of the arts and entertainment editor to whom you will send your notice, and second, how much "lead time" the publication needs for printing a concert listing (i.e., when you need to send in your listing for it to be printed before your show). For more insights into working the media, see chapter 11. You'll also want to send a good photo of your act, if available. Your gig listing will receive a hundred times more attention with a photo. It's worth the extra expense. Make it as easy as possible for the editor to use the photo by finding out the exact specifications required for photo submissions when you call about the other items. As mentioned in chapter 6, in general, you should have two photos, each of these at 72 dpi for the Web, and also at 300 dpi for print use.

5. **Assemble a list of local radio stations.** Most stations have local concert listings as part of their news segment, and you'll want to target a flyer to each. Be sure the station receives your notice at least a week before the show. If the gig is extraspecial (e.g., a high-profile showcase room), you may also want to send out personal invitations and free tickets to local music industry representatives (record execs, booking agents, personal managers, entertainment attorneys, radio personnel, etc.). Remember, think *maximization* of the event.

6. Besides your mailings, you'll also want to **post your flyers** in music stores, hangouts, inside the venue (don't forget the bathroom stalls!), and on all community bulletin boards in the area. Email flyers as attachments to friends and fans.

7. **Create your own cool handstamps.** Instead of drawing Xs on people's hands with a permanent marker, consider making a custom handstamp. Custom handstamps can be made from materials at office supply stores. Consider stamping the link to your Facebook or MySpace account so people remember to add you when they get home after the gig. You could also include a graphic such as your band logo as a handstamp.

DURING THE GIG

At last, the night has arrived. You walk into the club, greet the sound and lighting engineers (you already know each other), park your belongings in the appropriate space, and proceed to set up on the familiar stage. Smooth. Now here are a few more things you can do to make tonight's show a standout:

8. **Hang a banner with the band's logo** behind the act, high enough to be easily read by all. You'd be surprised how many people will see and hear your act and never know who you are. A visible banner solves that problem.

9. **Place "table tents"** with interesting band information (trivia, song lyrics, etc.) and gig schedules on each table around the club. Use sturdy, postcard stock for best results. Not everyone will take these home with them, so be sure to help with cleanup at the end of the evening. This includes taking down any flyers. After all, it's *your* mess. Wait staff appreciate this.

10. **Set up a visible area for merchandise** (T-shirts, buttons, CDs, etc.). The most successful artists at selling their products are the ones who really plan their pitch, make it interesting, and time it appropriately within the set at various intervals. The person (nonband member) running the merchandising can also oversee the new fan mailing list. Be sure there are plenty of writing instruments and paper on hand.

THE 20 TOP SELLING MERCH ITEMS

Here's a detailed breakdown of the twenty most profitable merchandising items—pound for pound—based on average costs and expected retail price tags. The data comes from top merchandising provider Jakprints, which compiled and averaged the data from multiple band and retail sites.

Here's a detailed breakdown of average cost and retail price.

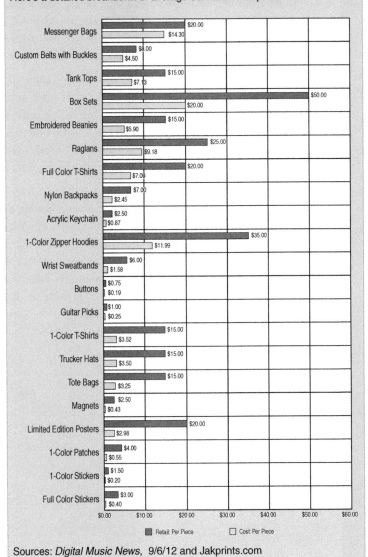

Sources: *Digital Music News*, 9/6/12 and Jakprints.com

If you're going to sell merchandise at shows, here are several tips to make it a smooth (and profitable) affair:

- **Have a sales rep.** This will usually be a band member or a fan or roadie, who greets the potential buyers and controls the sales transactions. Some bands give the rep a commission, say 5 percent on all sales.

- **Set up a sales table:** The longer the better, for accommodating more people and spreading out your wares. Also, use a *solid color tablecloth* that complements your CD colors and that "lifts" your merch off the table rather than makes it look flat.

- Offer a bowl of individually wrapped **candies** (required!).

- **Use flyer displays** that say what is available, along with pricing. You can get plastic-coated easel boards that hold your flyer and stand up on the table for easy viewing from stores like Staples or Office Depot. If you're selling t-shirts, try displaying them on hangers so people get a better look at them.

- Employ a method of getting names and email addresses for your **mailing list:** Depending on the crowd you're playing to, you can perhaps have a bowl with a sign that says, "Mailing List...Drop Your Card In," instead of having people write on a list.

- Have a stack of **postcards** people can take away with them that invite them to your website.

- Have plenty of **business cards** with a contact person's name and number in the pockets of all band members and support crew. Distribute them liberally.

- When you're on stage, remember to **make your show *visually* stimulating as well as *aurally* stimulating**. You and your band mates are on display and all your clothing, colors, movements, and lines should blend with the music you're playing. Give the people what they want—a feast of sight and sound. This is an essential part of "working the crowd."

- **Record all of your performances.** An audio or visual recording of your performances can be used for further promotional or educational needs. A previous band of mine used to videotape every performance and then analyze what was happening in terms of stage presence, crowd interaction, etc. This made us grow as a band. You also never know when a magical moment may happen onstage, which makes it the best performance of that song and can be used in the future. Having a visual recording will give you a glimpse through the audience's eyes and will make you more critical about yourself for future gigs. Not to mention it may become a valuable artifact years from now!

AFTER THE GIG

You just had a great gig! Congratulations. A lot more people know about you now than before this evening. There's a small buzz brewing, and now it's time to follow it up. But first, before you leave the club:

11. **Try to secure another gig** with the owner while you're fresh on the mind. At the very least, seek a verbal commitment and call within a few days to confirm and formalize it.

12. **Tip your waitresses and bartenders.** It doesn't matter what your policies are on tipping people when in the general public, but you should *always* tip when you are a guest performer in their establishment. Tipped employees remember those who do not tip and will hold it against you. Do not forget that they are working just as hard for you. I always tip 15 to 20 percent of my tab, but you can also consider giving your servers a flat fee for the entire band. Even if your entire tab is comped or you are just drinking water, you should leave a tip. This will establish good relations with your coworkers for the night (and future gigs), as well as keep things professional.

13. **Make sure the dressing room is in the same condition as that in which you found it.** While this may sound trite, it's a basic human consideration and will speak well of your act for future opportunities.

Then, after you leave the club:

14. **Strike while it's hot!** As soon as possible, follow up on any industry contacts made at the gig. Call to thank them for coming to the show. Build rapport. Network.

15. Finally, **send a personal email message to all new fans**, thanking them for coming to the show and informing them further about the band and other ways they can support you (for example, calling club owners, calling radio stations to request your song, telling their friends about you, etc.).

Of course, you can forget about all the above suggestions and just play the gig. After all, you're a musician, and that's what you do best. Granted.

But more and more, we are seeing the smarter bands being brought home because they know how to organize publicity, work the radio, boost promotion, and generally maximize and optimize their limited resources. After all, why should one gig equal *one* when it can equal *ten*? Maximization is the key. Go for it!

PART III

Rise Up

Mapping Your Media Plan

When "psychobilly" rockers the Cramps signed their first recording contract, they didn't do it in the standard office setting like everyone else. Instead, they marched over to the cemetery where Bela Lugosi is buried and ceremonially signed it on his grave. Needless to say, a photographer and journalist were in tow, and the event received major media attention. With such a creative idea, how could the media resist?

Publicity is the art of using the media (Facebook, Twitter, radio, press, YouTube, television, advertising, blimps, etc.) to expose your cause or event. Publicity includes all of the ways you can get noticed without buying expensive ad space or time. Publicity makes people talk, think, read, and hear about *you*. Since we all live in a dense media culture, the challenge today is finding a way to get your signal through all the noise.

"Media" is anything that can carry a message or content. It includes "traditional media" (radio, television, magazines, billboards, etc.) as well as "social media" (Facebook, YouTube, blogs, podcasts, etc.). The line between the two kinds of media has blurred, and any media plan you create today must include both traditional and social media in order to be effective.

Here's the good news. One thing all artists have in their favor as far as media goes is this: *The media has space to fill and depends on us to provide the filler.* Did you know that 75 percent of what you read in magazines, newspapers, and online news media is "planted?" This means it came to the media vehicle from *outside*, from people like you and me. Publicity, therefore, provides an open door for artist promotion.

Dollar for dollar, hour for hour, media publicity may very well be the best investment you can make for you marketing program. For example, if you were to purchase space for a 6 x 8 display ad in *The Boston Globe* newspaper, you would pay about $2,000 for a one-time run (*on top of* the costs to design the ad). But say you get a story written about you and your music in the same publication, and it takes up the same amount of space. You're now $2,000 ahead of the game!

Plus, publicity is more credible than paid advertisements. You can make any product claim you want when you place an ad, and consumers know this. A journalist or reporter, however, doesn't have to feature you in their publication, and by doing so, lends more credibility to what you're about. Of course, the downside is you don't control the message when you don't pay for it!

The key to successful media coverage is having a *strategic plan* that leaves no stone unturned in your efforts to get your signal through all the media noise out there. In this chapter, we'll lay out the ingredients for a successful media plan that includes both traditional and new media, and then continue the discussion in the next chapter as we explore the best ways of executing your media plan.

UNDERSTANDING YOUR MEDIA AUDIENCE

The first ingredient for a successful media plan is a clear understanding of your market audience: *who* they are, *what* they read and listen to, *where* they go, *how* they think. Each style of music is a subcultural world with its own outlook, values, organizations, and media. Your job is to understand this world as best you can, particularly its media.

For example, a jazz musician should be aware of the publications *Down Beat, Jazziz,* and *All About Jazz,* organizations like International Jazz Festivals, blogs like *JazzWax* and *a blog supreme,* various cable television and radio shows specializing in jazz performance, as well as the hundreds of generalist outlets for jazz music. Likewise, a reggae group will be acquainted with *The Beat, Rhythm Vibes Magazine,* and *Rootz Reggae & Kulcha,* record labels like VP, Heartbeat, and Shanachie, and organizations like Reggae Ambassadors Worldwide. The same thing applies to folk, metal, alternative, blues, classical, country, Latin, world, experimental, and all other music styles.

Through learning about the who, what, where, and how of your music's audience, you also learn about the best ways to reach that audience. This is the foundation for an effective media plan.

How do you find out about your audience's preferences? Observe. Ask questions. Another good way is to go through one of the better indie-oriented directories (*The Musician's Atlas* and *The Indie Bible* are excellent) and look for listings of organizations relevant to your style of music. These groups often serve as general information clearinghouses that can make your job easier. You can also request subscriber profile information from magazines to get a sense of reader demographics like age and location as well as preferences. Also, don't overlook *local* sources relevant to your style-audience.

Know Your Traditional Media

What kinds of media should you target when trying to get publicity? That will depend on the kind of audience you are trying to reach. Each media entity has an intended audience, whether it's a mass audience or a small group interested in a specific topic. But one thing is for sure: in order to cover your bases effectively today, you need to understand *both* traditional media *and* new media.

As you're doing your research, take notes. This leads to the second component of a successful publicity plan: *developing your media contact list.* "Media" is one of the three databases you began developing in chapter 6. Capture all this information into a contact management program like Act! (Sage) or, one designed more specifically for musicians, like *Indie Band Manager.* Staying organized is essential! A media list will forever grow and change based on your coverage needs.

The best approach is to start locally and then branch out from there. You'll be surprised at the wealth of publicity opportunities within your own backyard.

While checking out local *print media* watch for names of music editors, writers, and record reviewers relevant to your particular area too. Pay special attention to those writers who help break ground for new acts. You can get some reviewer names by visiting sites of independent artists similar to your style of music and observing which media contacts they cite.

The primary tool you use to connect with traditional media is the *news release* (also called a *press release*). It's a standard tool that works better than letters and phone calls and is universally used to publicize people and events. The release is essentially a pared-down news story that presents the outline of your event in a way that will grab an editor's attention. Anything newsworthy should be publicized. You should define "newsworthy" as creatively as possible. Special upcoming shows; formation of a new band; record release parties; production of a video; signing a management, agent, publishing, or recording deal; recitals; formation of your new indie label; involvement in a benefit; winning a band or songwriting contest—these are just a few types of events worthy of mention.

Always type and double-space the band's information, preferably on the band's own letterhead. Include all the pertinent details (who, what, when, where, and why). Use a bold and creative headline (see samples below). Be sure to include the date, your contact information, and the city where your act or news is based. You may also need to tweak or customize your release to a particular media outlet so it has the biggest impact. You may need to add a sentence or change the tone of the press release or highlight something that would specifically interest members of that particular outlet.

SAMPLE NEWS RELEASE HEADLINES

- GRAMMY-Nominee ARUN SHENOY Makes History as the First Singaporean Nominated for a GRAMMY® Award

- Artist/Producer/Composer's *RUMBADOODLE* Is up for Best Pop Instrumental Album; Proceeds Will Go to Aid India's Poor

- Matthew Schultz's Hot New Single "Money or Me" Was Selected to Be Featured on Kendrick Lamar's New Mixtape By Coast 2 Coast Volume 224

- New Artist Matthew Schultz selected to be featured on Kendrick Lamar's New Mixtape by Coast 2 Coast Volume 224 with His New Hit Song "Money or Me"

- Guitar Icon Orianthi to Play Alice Cooper's 12th Annual "Christmas Pudding" Benefit

- The Platinum Selling Artist and Guitarist Will Join Johnny Depp, Don Felder and More to Raise Funds for the Solid Rock Foundation

At the top, write "FOR IMMEDIATE RELEASE," and then send it off to everyone on your media list. Many editors and journalists prefer either faxed or electronic press releases. When you call for current contact information, be sure to also inquire about preferred submission formats, and obtain fax numbers and email addresses as needed. You can also use services like PRWeb or PR Newswire, which electronically distribute your news releases to targeted media. There are even music-specific services like *Billboard*'s Publicity Wire, you may wish to look into. More on these in the Resource Directory in the appendix.

Always visit the media outlet's website first before sending your material to verify contact information. Find out the names (with correct spellings!), direct phone numbers, and email addresses of all editors and writers in the areas of music, entertainment, and the performing arts. Also request a copy of their editorial calendar for upcoming months. This will alert you to what themes and topics it is planning so you can scope out possible story tie-ins with your band well in advance.

Radio also requires some research. Learn about the different formats of the various stations in your area and the types of programs they air. Consider who their target audiences are. Listen to the stations. Consult program guides (a station will send you one upon request). Check media reference books (see the Resource Directory) for station contact information. Talk with program and/ or music directors, producers, and DJs. Always ask if they feature local and new artists in any special programming section. Write it all down.

Information about commercial and college radio stations and the types of music they play can be found in *The Musician's Atlas*. There are also fairly complete lists of college stations online. See the Resource Directory for contact information on these. When you discover which radio stations play music from independents (usually called "open" or "varied" formats), phone to inquire about the configuration they use. Some will play only CDs. Others will also play vinyl, and some just want links to MP3s. Record all this information into your database. We'll look at your radio *strategy* in the next chapter.

When it comes to *television*, forget about MTV or VH1 (at least for now). They have the tightest playlists on the planet, catering exclusively to major label and high-charting artists. Focus instead on your own best bets: public television, local cable stations, and community programs. If your research shows that there are specialized programs devoted to issues that appeal to your target audience (environmental, women's issues, etc.), add the names of the producers to your lists. If your project is "newsworthy," the person to contact is the *assignment editor*. His or her job is to weed through the news and prioritize it for news programming. You can find out who these people are by phoning the station and requesting their names.

If you're involved with a nonprofit cause, organization, or event, you can get your event or program broadcasted as public service announcements ("PSAs") for free. Check radio and television (network affiliates and local cable) station deadlines and requirements. Submit all pertinent information to public affairs or the PSA director. Work with the benefit coordinator to make sure he or she has your band's information.

The geographical region covered by a media outlet, its frequency of publication, its ability to reach specialized markets, and its ability to provide color, sound, or video are all factors that need to be factored into your decision-making process.

HARNESSING YOUR NEW MEDIA CONNECTORS

Being a working musician without a label has not only become more possible, but cheaper than it has ever been before, thanks to social media. Sites like MOG and SoundCloud have replaced MySpace as a destination for listening to music, and Tumblr has offered a blogging space for bands. Twitter now provides artists with quick ways to give away tickets and merchandise to loyal fans, to promote themselves, or simply to communicate regularly with a potentially global audience. And services like Spotify, Pandora, and Rdio have provided a rich space for music discovery.

Social media has come alongside traditional media and revolutionized the media world forever. It has completely transformed the landscape of business and entertainment by allowing interesting content to spread quickly, and perhaps most importantly, for artists to have direct and immediate contact with their fans.

Caveat. Everything digital comes back to what's happening in the real world. I don't necessarily think social networking is absolutely essential to achieve music success today. In fact, many artists have sworn off or avoided social media entirely. I believe social media should be viewed as a *fan management extension*. Social networking's purpose is about building a bridge between you and your fans who will then (hopefully) share your name and music with others. This should be the focus, and used consistently, social media will amplify your name—positively or not.

With that said, what follows in this chapter assumes a basic understanding and familiarity of the key social media channels (Facebook, Twitter, and YouTube). If social media is an entirely new game for you, then you'll want to start slow. Your friends can show you around. Go to Facebook, and set up an account. It's easy and will give you a chance to get some experience with how it works. Do the same with Twitter. You've probably already viewed numerous videos on YouTube. Now you want to think about how you can use this video platform to further your music career.

Which Social Media Should You Focus On?

While MySpace has become less prominent as a destination for music in recent years, it was the first place that gave bands a forum for sharing music, writing blog posts, sharing live show details, and communicating personally with fans in a way that made them feel valuable and special. Major acts like Lily Allen, Colbie Caillat, Soulja Boy, and Sean Kingston managed to significantly expand their brand through the site. MySpace is trying to make a comeback and may end up as a significant player once again. Time will tell.

Since the debut of MySpace, many more options have become available, and the possibilities the Internet provides for musicians and music fans today are seemingly limitless. "On their own, social networking sites appear to be either blunt promotional tools or much too intense interpersonal tools," says John Flansburgh of the band They Might Be Giants. "But it doesn't have to be a one-on-one direct engagement with a stranger or 'here's our big rock video.' There's a middle ground. The trick is about finding a friendly and appropriate level of interaction."

Social media is a fluid and dynamic phenomenon. While new social media tools launch every month, most musicians will focus on the major players: Facebook, Twitter, and YouTube. Each should be integrated with your primary online asset: your website. We'll look at LinkedIn, Instagram, and other social media channels in more detail in chapter 13 ("Expanding Your Online and Mobile

Presence"), and explore your website development later in this chapter. But let's start with the Big Three social media outlets.

Facebook

Facebook launched in February 2004, went public in 2012, and, as of January 2013, had more than one billion active users. Users create personal profiles, add other users as friends, and exchange messages, including automatic notifications when they update their profile. Facebook users must register before using the site. Additionally, users may join common-interest user groups, organized by workplace, school or college, or other characteristics.

Again, the primary value of social media is the way it connects people, and a key success strategy for any business (especially bands and artists) is engaging its customers, fans, and followers. Here are several suggestions for using Facebook to promote your music and career:

- **First, switch your personal profile to a Facebook Page.**
  A Facebook Page is a better option for promoting your music. For one, using a Facebook Page allows you to keep your personal details private. Facebook Pages also have key features that will help you market your music. Note: You need to have a profile *before* you can create a Page.

- Apps such as ReverbNation and BandPage let you **stream music** *directly* from your fan page. Use them.

- Use **location targeting** to promote shows, tours, album release parties, and other events. Use it to determine where you'll have more success in terms of touring, physical CD distribution, street-team investment, and media coverage. Playing in Denver in two weeks? Develop a Facebook ad for the upcoming performance, and target it to Facebook users who fall into your demographics and who live in Denver.

- **Sell music and merch directly from Facebook.** Music store applications such as those from Nimbit, Topspin, and Reverb-Nation have store widgets that can be integrated into Facebook for sales directly from your fan page.

- By collecting additional contact information from your fans through **a sign-up form**, you can augment your Facebook campaigns with mass emails and mobile promotions. But, be sure to show your followers a side of yourself that enhances their connection to your music, and is not *solely* based on promoting it.

- Target **ads based on interests**. If you've been told you sound like Radiohead meets Bob Marley, target your ads to fans of Radiohead and Bob Marley, and be sure to communicate your similarities to those brands. Also, if a noteworthy music critic is the one who said this, be sure to include his or her quote.

- Many top musicians, including Coldplay and Shakira, create **separate Facebook events** for each of their concerts to drum up awareness and gain exposure for their Pages. This may seem like overkill for an indie artist, but there may be a high-profile show that merits it. With just a little foresight and coordination, you can easily invite everyone your band knows on Facebook. Just be careful to delegate one band member to post the event so fans don't receive multiple invites.

- **Live chats** allow you to webcast video of yourself responding to questions that fans pose through a text-based chat room interface. These provide vivid, intimate virtual face-to-face interaction with fans that is cheap in terms of dollars and an artist's time.

- By **hosting a forum** where users can interact with each other and voice their opinions, Pages like that of Jack Johnson and Amanda Palmer draw fans back by providing a sense of community in addition to more formal content.

- **"Serialize" your content** by spreading videos, MP3 giveaways, tour diaries, photos, essays, and status updates across your Twitter, Facebook, and other social profiles, as well as your blog. When you do, make sure folks know they can find other kinds of content in those other locations.

Facebook is a continuously improving social media platform, and keeping up with all the changes is an arduous task. Your best bet is a weekly visit to www.facebook.com/help, which informs users of these developments and suggests ways for how to best make use of them.

Twitter

Twitter is a Web service, owned and operated by Twitter Inc., offering a social networking and microblogging service, enabling its users to send and read messages called "tweets." Tweets are text-based posts of up to 140 characters displayed on the user's profile page.

Since its founding in 2006, Twitter has gained popularity world-wide and is estimated to have 600 million users, generating 400 billion tweets a day and handling over 2 billion search queries per day. It is sometimes described as the "SMS (short message service) of the Internet."

Twitter is not a social network *per se*, at least not in the classic sense that people perceive social networks. Twitter is a platform that is more closely aligned with IM and texting. Once this is grasped, it makes it easier to understand how to use it to reach your fans. Nothing beats an artist posting, retweeting, or replying. It is all about two-way communication; think about how you use IM or texting with your friends. It's a conversation starter or a quick update tool; either one works. An artist has to treat it every day like it's a "meet and greet."

"Word of mouth has always been incredibly important to us, and now, it's easier than ever to get the word out there," said David Emery of Beggars Group, a collection of independent record labels. "Different networks play different roles," he added. "Twitter is great for artists interacting directly with fans, like MIA, who has millions of followers and will do things like make a video on her phone and post it on Twitter. That is so much more powerful than traditional marketing. But Facebook is a powerful method of direct marketing. It's less personal, but fans don't seem to mind that."

Here are some ways musicians can use Twitter for self-promotion:

- **Take requests.** Some bands ask fans for cover song requests, or if they have a large catalog of original songs, they could just simply ask for requests of their own songs, a few hours or a day before an upcoming show.

- **Share.** Share photos and behind-the-scenes info about your band. Even better, give a glimpse of developing projects and events. Users come to Twitter to get and share the latest news, so give it to them!

- **Use hashtags.** Using hashtags is a way of putting your tweet into a stream of related tweets and conversations and helping them to spread further. That way all the tweets about a specific subject are united and therefore become a searchable category. This is done by putting the # symbol in front of the keyword to which your tweet relates.

- **Do market research.** Twitter allows you to do searches that can help you locate new potential followers who you can add, as well as conversations you may want to participate in, if you're to be seen to be relevant in your local scene. You may pick up fans, but you'll also establish that vital authority by passing on local information, supporting other local bands, venues, clubs, record stores, etc.

- **Ask fans to tweet about you.** Why not? But remember, people are far more likely to follow you because your conversation is interesting than because your music is great.

HEATHER MCDONALD, FROM ABOUT.COM, OFFERS THESE ADDITIONAL "GOOD THINGS TO POST ON TWITTER"

- Updates from the studio when recording
- Updates on the manufacturing process (announce when artwork is finished, when the master has been approved, when finished copies are delivered, etc.)
- Reminders about release dates, shows, and other news
- Updates from the road when you're on tour
- News about deals it's okay to talk about (for instance, "just arranged digital distribution with such and such company")
- Day-to-day work news (e.g., "just signed off on ad copy for magazine").

With Twitter, you have a chance to craft a voice—one that fits into 140 characters at a time. Work on developing that voice. Twitter isn't about following people you already know; it's about engaging interesting people from all over the music world and beyond.

The bottom line: Be authentic and true to your values, and you'll quickly become a valuable member of the Twitter community.

YouTube

Of all the online video options, YouTube.com is without a doubt the 800 lb. gorilla. It has been the launch pad for Karmin, Alex Day, Terra Naomi, Grayson Chance, and of course, Justin Bieber. I consider YouTube like a radio station because the first thing someone does today when they want to hear a new song is type that song into YouTube. That's why doing cover versions of songs can be so effective on this social media platform. Warning: Doing covers without a license is copyright infringement. Sure, everyone does it, but YouTube has begun shuttering accounts upon the request of the Warners and Universals of the world, so beware!

Founded in 2005 and acquired by Google for $1.65 billion in 2006, YouTube is an ever-growing online community that allows you to post video clips on the Web, and watch a huge array of clips in hundreds of categories. Over 2.5 billion video clips are viewed on YouTube every single day.

What makes YouTube a hit is its ability to transcode anything and produce an easy-to-watch and easy-to-embed streaming flash movie. You simply upload a video you made on a digital camera or camcorder, and YouTube's computers turn it into a flash video. Producers, the public, wannabe actors, corporations out for publicity, clip collectors, and bands all use YouTube.

Take the country act Lady Antebellum. Since the group's earliest days, they've been shooting video and posting it online under the moniker "Webisode Wednesdays." What started as a low-cost way to build the brand now involves a full-time videographer and professional editing because these webisodes have become important bridge builders between the band and its fans.

YouTube is your chance to create minimasterpieces, but the "music video" isn't the only way to get your music exposed on YouTube. Once you've created an account, here are some other ways you can use YouTube to further your career:

- **Create your own YouTube channel.** This allows you to customize the presentation of selected videos and engage your fans through social interaction features. Basically, your channel gives you the opportunity to brand your band the way you want, control the content, and share it with the world from one simple location. Once you have your own channel, set it to "Musician" in your Settings window. Now you can add performer information and publish a schedule of show dates (by enabling the "events dates" module). You can also *create a custom look* by clicking "Themes & Colors" and then "Advanced Options," where you can upload your own background for your channel page.

- **Tag it properly.** This is the process of listing words that relate to the video content you've posted. Put in your name, your band's name, your genre of music, venue names, song names, and other relevant keywords. Pick the words for which you want to turn up as the top search result and put them in the tags of your videos.

- **Use annotations.** Annotations allow you to overlay text onto your YouTube videos. Handy for adding your band URL and extra comments that you wish to convey to viewers.

- **Create a tour diary.** If you're an artist that tours, give updates from the road. All you need is a webcam, a laptop, and an Internet connection. Tell about last night's gig, where you're going next, your favorite (and least favorite) moments of being on the road. Show us the messy van with all the empties. Interview people who are at the show. Fans love this stuff.

- **Give a studio tour.** Next time you're in the recording studio, shoot as much video of the sessions as possible, and upload it to your channel. People love seeing what goes on in recording studios. Plus, it gives them a glimpse into your creative process.

- **Redistribute!** Whenever you put up a video on YouTube, be sure to put it everywhere else you can think of, too: Facebook, MySpace, Vimeo, Viddler, Blip.tv, and other relevant outlets. YouTube may be the 800 pound gorilla, but there are lots of other great niches where you can find audiences, too. See this book's Resource Directory for other suggestions.

These are just a few ideas on how you can use this amazing platform for your career. YouTube has also released its own *Creator Playbook* to help you learn the best tips for building your audience and taking your channel to the next level. Get it at: www.youtube .com/yt/playbook/index.html.

Your Own Artist Website

For some bands, their Facebook pages represent their primary online presence. But that's not really enough. At *Billboard* magazine's Future Sound conference in 2012, it was revealed that when you add one additional site, you get 50 percent more traffic. Adding two sites boosts your traffic by 75 percent. All the more reason to create your own artist website, in addition to using the various social media outlets.

Your website is home base. Everything starts from there because that's the only thing you have complete control over. No matter what new technology or cool app comes along, it's important to remember the only thing that's going to be constant is your website (and your email list).

There are six main reasons you work so hard on your social media and networking. Ultimately, you want people to:

1. Buy something

2. Join your mailing list and follow you

3. Donate to your band

4. Contact you

5. Come to your gig

6. Spread the word about you to others

Keeping these six reasons in mind, what follows are guidelines for creating your artist website.

Designing Your Website

Website design costs can range from free to tens of thousands of dollars, depending on the information included, the complexity of the design, and who does the actual coding of your site.

There are plenty of Web designers for hire, and costs are far-flung. But if you're a band on a shoestring budget, and nobody in the band feels ready to tackle HTML5 (the next generation of hypertext mark-up language), you're going to have to find an economical solution. One idea is to tap into the talent of your fans. See if there is someone on your mailing list who would like to help you create your band's site in exchange for a lifetime free pass to your shows and copies of your CDs. Or, look into art schools with New Media Design or Computer Graphics programs. Students in these programs are often looking for opportunities to grow their portfolios. For a quicker solution, tap craigslist.com, an international collection of local community classifieds and forums. Elance.com is another great source of design talent that operates through a bidding process.

Finally, you can opt for some of the free artist website templates at services like Nimbit.com or Bandzoogle.com. They provide good, low-cost solutions.

Whether you go for a Web designer or the freebie options, you'll want to follow some tried-and-true tips to help guide the process.

1. **Get organized.** Start visualizing your website before you ever turn on the computer. Think about what you want to put on your landing/home page, what you want the reader to immediately grasp, how the information will relate, and how you want everything to flow. Some Web experts recommend creating a storyboard or flowchart—sketches of each page in outline form—before you start writing. I like using the "journey" metaphor when designing. Take your visitor on a journey into your story.

2. **Take a look at other websites.** No sense reinventing the wheel. Check out which sites you like the best, put them in your favorites file, and then study them. What features make the site easy for you to use? What content appeals to you? What designs do you like best? Select the best elements of your favorite sites, and incorporate those features into your own.

3. **Add value.** Don't waste people's time with a page that provides only a list of links to other websites, unless, of course, that is your purpose. You should think about providing content that is of value to your site visitors. For example, if you're an avid blues lover and want to create a Web page on the subject, tell visitors where the best blues clubs are in your area and provide directions. *Pull* people in with useful information.

4. **Keep it simple.** The home page is to the rest of your website as a book's cover is to its contents, or as the front door is to

a place of business. The design should be bold and understandable at a glance. Don't clutter it up with unnecessary details or over-complicated layouts. Try to get everything for this page into one frame. A home page should not scroll forever. Also, having the word "Enter" on your home page is not usually helpful.

5. **Get visual.** Use imaginative layouts and good-looking typography to give your Web pages a unique and identifiable look. Graphical content should be of some practical value. Avoid empty window dressing. To save time, many users set their browsers to ignore graphics; all they see is text. It's essential that any important messages or links contained in graphics be duplicated in textual form. Test-drive your page in text-only mode to make sure it works. You may also consider creating a "text only" version for visitors who prefer this option. As for text style, don't use bold in large text blocks. This is difficult to read. Finally, be careful of the relationship between text color and page background. White on black, and black on white work well. Green on pink and yellow on blue, however, do not.

6. **Observe limitations.** Many people have "technologically challenged" hardware. The World Wide Web becomes the World Wide Wait when huge graphics or audio files are downloaded for viewing. Keep graphics to no more than 50 KB, and your site will be a delight to visit.

7. **Make it easy to navigate.** One of the home page's primary roles is as a navigational tool, pointing people to information stored on your website or elsewhere. Your site visitors will fall into three primary groups: fans you don't have yet, fans you do have, and members of the media and music industry. Keep these groups in mind as you map your site navigation. Make this function as effortless as possible. Also, don't bury information too deep in the page hierarchy. Stepping through five or more links can get pretty tedious. Finally, don't leave your visitors looking for bread crumbs to find their way to you. Provide clear email and social media gateways so people can contact you if they wish.

8. **Include the essentials.** Here are a few things most every home page should have: a header that identifies your website

clearly and unmistakably, an email address for communicating and reporting problems, and contact information, along with all your social media links. Another essential, in my opinion, is an embedded store widget from which you can sell tracks and other merchandise. The reason it's essential is because, unlike indirect sales via services like iTunes, you can capture customer information from direct sales. Some excellent online store widgets are available from Nimbit.com, Reverbnation.com, Bandzoogle.com, and Topspin.com. Finally, be sure to include a call to action. This can be a call to sign up to your mailing list, buy a CD, or just tell a friend about your band.

9. **Engage your visitors.** What causes people to come back for return visits? According to IntelliQuest, 56 percent return to entertaining sites, 54 percent like attention-grabbing sites, 53 percent extremely useful content, 45 percent information tailored to their needs, 39 percent imaginative sites, and 36 percent highly interactive sites. Engage!

10. **Be sure to title your home page** with a headline that will attract the most viewers to your website. Many search engines use the title as one of their main ways of selecting sites to show to requesters. The first paragraph of text after your title is also often used by search engines to rank listings, so be sure your first paragraph contains key words about the contents of your site. As a matter of practice, you should add proper titles to the rest of your pages as well. When embedding videos, be sure to contextualize them with titles and a brief description. These will also get picked up by search engines.

11. **Have a site-wide music player** so when people go from page to page at your site, the same music continues to play. You can do this by having the player in a separate frame that stays "glued" to a particular location on the page. (Most opt for the top of the page.) It's a little tricky, but it can be done. Should a site have "auto-start" music? Personally, I don't like this. Often, it clashes with what I'm already playing in the background. Also, many people Web surf at work, and if you're a metal band and they happen upon your page, they might bring unwelcome glances from coworkers. Finally,

since many browsers use tabs, the tab controlling the audio might get lost and it becomes a pain in the neck trying to figure out which one it is. So avoid auto-start music.

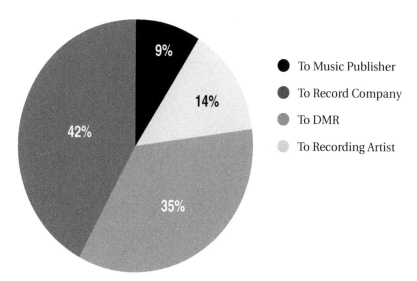

Fig. 10.1. How iTunes Divides Download Revenue Per Track. If the "Artist" is also the "Record Company" and "Music Publisher," then he or she also receives those shares, or about 65 percent of the total revenue.

12. **Keep it fresh.** Visitors could get jaded if your website never changes. Encourage return visits by giving them something new to look forward to. Include your website in your established publicity program, so that new information (such as press releases), appears concurrently on your Web pages.

Orchestrating Your Web Strategy

The chart on the next page provides a bird's-eye view of a basic social media strategy a band or artist can employ for raising their profile via social media, along with all the desired outcomes and best purposes for each tool. Note that your website (center) is the "grand central station" where you ultimately want to bring visitors.

BASIC SOCIAL MEDIA STRATEGY OUTLINE

This chart shows the primary movement of fans and the purpose of each tool.

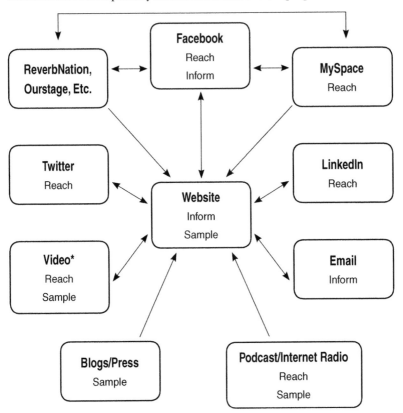

Fig. 10.2. Basic Social Media Strategy Outline. *Video sites include: YouTube, DailyMotion, MetaCafe, Blip.tv, Break, Google Video, Revver, Vimeo, AOL Video, Spike, Vevo, Collegehumor, FunnyOrDie, LiveVideo, Veoh, Ustream.

The six primary goals of a social media strategy for a band or artist are to reach more people, to keep their fans informed, to allow people to sample their music, to sell their music and merchandise, to have content that people pass along to friends, and to engage their fans to encourage continued interest. Each goal can be reached with the following popular tools. Of course, there are dozens of others that are not included here as well.

- **Reach:** Twitter, video, blogs/press, Facebook, MySpace, Reverbnation, Ourstage, LinkedIn, podcast/Internet radio

- **Inform:** Facebook, Twitter, MySpace, Reverbnation, Ourstage, LinkedIn, website, email

- **Sample:** Facebook, MySpace, Reverbnation, Ourstage, website, video, blogs/press, podcast/Internet radio

- **Sell:** Facebook, MySpace, website

- **Pass-along:** video, blogs/press, social bookmarking (tagging)

- **Engage:** video, Twitter, LinkedIn (groups), website/artist blog, email.

Social networking is not the only way to make it as an artist. In my opinion, social media is simply a fan management extension. Social networking's purpose is about building a bridge between you and your fans who, in turn, will use word of mouth to promote you. Therefore, it's better to look for your fans and build up your online social presence. The main objective is to get your fans to your website and take them on a journey into your story. That way they can discover you, share, interact, and eventually, buy.

Tracking Your Social Media Presence

One can easily begin to feel out of control when it comes to social media. In fact, due to the explosion of social media, *reputation management* has now become a crucial component in one's career management. We all know that one of the first things hiring managers check when someone applies for a job is their social media presence. If you ever posted a less-than-admirable photo of yourself, or if you released an unfiltered stream of consciousness rant on some topic, or even a "prank" video, it might later come back to bite you. We are all leaving digital footprints.

The best way to fight this is, of course, to never post anything unsavory. But if there is personal stuff online you don't like, you can suppress unwanted content by flooding the Web with good, positive content. This content might include a solid, professional LinkedIn profile, a blog, a personal website, and more. The important thing is to keep this content clean and professional, without anything that might raise a potential employer's eyebrow. That's a career tip you can take to the bank.

Tracking all the conversations, band mentions, fan questions, comments, and feedback can become almost impossible for one person (even one band!). Thankfully, some services have emerged to help with the online bustle. Here are a few that savvy artists are using to monitor their mentions in social media:

- **Google Alerts.** Set up multiple Google Alerts for your company, band, name, products, leaders, industry terms, etc. The alerts will get delivered directly to your email inbox at the frequency you indicate (e.g., daily or as they happen), and they are a great way to help you track mentions of your brand and relevant keywords on the Web on news sites, in blogs, etc.

- **Twitter.** Monitor mentions of your brand on Twitter with tools like Twitter Search or HootSuite. CoTweet is also a great tool to help manage multiple tweets.

- **Artist Data.** Artist Data (which was acquired by Sonic Bids) actually allows you to update everything from your profile info and status to things like music and events on all of your existing social networks like Facebook, Last.fm, Reverbnation, and a whole list of others.

- **Ping.fm.** Similar to Artist Data, Ping.fm allows you to update information on many different social networks (ping.fm/networks/). The difference here is that Ping.fm is for general use, and not specifically for artists, so while it has a much larger reach to more social networks and blogging platforms, it has less capability to meet the specific needs of an artist.

- **Facebook Insights:** Helps you stay on top of and participate in discussions occurring on your company's Facebook Fan Page. Use your Fan Page's "Facebook Insights Dashboard" (found in the left sidebar when you're on your page as an administrator) to show you stats, such as fan growth and page views, to gauge your page's interaction and engagement.

Notes to the Social Media Optimist

Social media isn't the only way to market your band or brand, though you have to wonder, in light of all the press it gets. This is the number-one mistake because it can absolutely cripple a band from ever finding success. Some artists are sitting out the Twitter revolution completely (i.e., Mumford & Sons), and others are finding it a distraction no longer worth the time ("[Twitter] started to make my mind smaller and smaller and smaller. And I couldn't write a song," said John Mayer).

Far too many artists forget that social media is a device to be used within a strong, well-rounded marketing campaign. If you, as an artist, expect to just sit in front of your computer, friend thousands of people, and wait by the phone for the call from a talent scout, you will be severely disappointed when that call never comes.

Too, social networking is causing artists to draw clear lines between what is public and what is private. They have to be careful not to overuse any one social media platform and censor the type of information they share. Promoting a contest or showcasing new merchandise for the tour? Awesome. The lead singer's girlfriend when they're on a date? Not so much.

In the music business, there are two things that matter more than anything. Those are your reputation and the relationships you create along the journey. Traditional and social media allow for the gradual nurturing of relationships through generosity and creative communication. How you communicate through these media networks, will follow you for the rest of your career. Be smart, plan well.

CHAPTER 11

Working Your Media Plan

Market visibility for an independent artist tends to be a cumulative rather than an "overnight" experience. It is generally not one big event somewhere that creates a strong, national following for an artist, but instead:

- a number of stories in smaller, regional publications
- a buzz online via ezines, blogs, YouTube, and forums
- pockets of heavy rotation airplay, usually on reporting college stations
- several high-profile performances and hundreds of local or regional gigs
- perhaps, a few television interviews.

This is the media "boot camp" phase of an artist's rise to prominence.

In previous chapters, we looked at the basic ingredients of mapping out your media plan: researching your niche audience and the media preferences of this audience, developing your media contact database based on this research, and assembling your publicity tools, including photos, EPKs, and press releases. This chapter lays out some guidelines for organizing your publicity efforts and some effective ways for executing your media plan.

ORGANIZING YOUR MEDIA WAVES

Before sending anything out to media, get yourself one of those "year-at-a-glance" wall calendars. They can be obtained at any well-stocked office supply house, like Staples or Office Depot. This will serve as your publicity map for the whole year. By the way, can you remember what the lead feature was on the evening news two nights ago? All self-promoting bands take heed! People have miniscule attention spans, and memories that are even shorter. This is why your publicity objectives can only be realized through successive "waves" of media exposure.

Each wave "coats" your market, raising the awareness of your audience. These waves must come at regular, considered intervals so that your offerings are perceived as inevitabilities. How many waves should you launch and how often? It used to be three or four times per year; now, it's a good idea to try to release something newsworthy at least once a month, if not more often.

Each wave needs a promotional spearhead. For musicians, this spearhead can take many forms: a high-profile performance, record release party, impending tour, hiring a new band member, important contract signing, endorsement deal, contest award, etc. The more of these you have, the more waves you can organize. All of this assumes a good amount of planning. This is where your wall calendar comes in. Set some goals for yourself for the coming year, and mark their realization dates on your calendar: I want to set up a small tour for my act, I will record a full-length CD, I will organize a show to benefit the environment. Whatever it is, you'll want to incorporate it into your publicity wave strategy. Ten to twelve well-organized waves per year will reap exposure aplenty for your act or business.

TYPES OF PUBLICITY TO SEEK FOR ARTISTS AND THEIR MUSIC

- Calendar listings (performance dates)
- Reviews of recordings
- Reviews of live shows
- Interviews with the artist: in print, radio, and television
- Stories about the artist: music or consumer press, or other related niche
- "Associational" publicity: partnering with another artist or with a cause you support.

Here's a tip for generating publicity: link your project (or event, or news) to something that already has media movement. For example, take a look at the calendar. Can you tie your story or event in with a holiday or other special day? What about Earth Day, St. Patrick's Day, Valentines Day? All of these already have momentum and media attention. How can you hitch your wagon to them?

And don't just limit yourself to the standard calendar everyone knows. Sometimes, the more far-fetched the better. Check out some of the more unusual calendar dates too. For example, did you know March is "Music in Our Schools Month," and March 9 is Barbie's birthday? August is "Foot Health Month," October "Hispanic Heritage Month," February 26 is "Tell a Fairy Tale Day." There are thousands more.

You and your team will have to do some brainstorming on this but it'll be worth it. Try finding a common ground, a resonance point, where you can tie in with what's already happening, and then pitch that to the media. It's fun, creative, and economical.

Plus, it can generate some valuable buzz for your project.

30 WAYS TO CREATE NEWS FOR YOUR COMPANY

1. Tie in with news events of the day.
2. Work with another publicity person on cross-promotional opportunities.
3. Tie in with a newspaper or other medium on a mutual project.
4. Take a poll or conduct a survey.
5. Issue a special report in your field, genre, etc.
6. Arrange an interview with a celebrity.
7. Take part in a controversy.
8. Report unusual or human-interest stories.
9. Announce novel observations and discoveries.
10. Make an analysis or prediction.
11. Start a networking group.

12. Hold a demo derby.
13. Announce an appointment for a new staff member.
14. Celebrate an anniversary.
15. Issue a summary of facts.
16. Tie in with a holiday.
17. Link up with a social organization or burning social issue.
18. Sponsor an award.
19. Hold a contest.
20. Give a valuable but unusual donation.
21. Secure a high-visibility performance opportunity.
22. Stage a special event.
23. Write a controversial letter to an editor.
24. Establish a Seal of Approval or Best/Worst list.
25. Adapt national reports and surveys for local use.
26. Stage a debate or discussion.
27. Tie into a well-known week or day.
28. Honor an institution.
29. Organize a tour.
30. Compile a list of hot tips or fascinating facts.

GETTING YOUR MUSIC REVIEWED

Getting people to listen to, review, and write about your recordings or performances should be a high priority in your overall music promotion efforts. You can pull juicy words and quotes from reviews and use them for further promotion of your music. Of course, we'd all like to have our tracks reviewed in *Rolling Stone* or *Entertainment Weekly*, but you'll probably want to aim for closer targets at first.

Remember, 75 percent of what you see in magazines, newspapers, and blogs is planted. This means the information came from outside of that particular media vehicle, from people like you and me. This also applies to music reviews.

1. Your first step is to **describe your music.** What makes your music so special? Why do people listen to it? I remember a few years back at a music conference, a guy came up to me, handed me his CD, and described it as "hillbilly flamenco." That description hooked my interest, and I couldn't wait to listen to it (and it didn't disappoint!). If you describe your music creatively, rather than as simply "rock" or "folk" or "jazz," it will have a much greater chance of being heard.

2. **Revisit your audience profile** from chapter 10. At this juncture, you want to ask: where does my audience, and people like my audience, go to feed their musical appetite? Where do they go to learn about new bands and artists? What media vehicles convey this information to this audience? For some, it will be music magazines like *Under the Radar* or *Fader*. For others, it will be "lifestyle" magazines like *Utne Reader* or *Guideposts*. Still others will strictly visit blogs and vlogs for all their music needs.

3. **Compile your list.** Make a list of these and also any local or regional media outlets that review recordings or performances. These will include everything from the musician-oriented *Performer Magazine* (with northeast, west, and southeast editions), to newsweeklies like New York City's *Village Voice*, to your own town's daily or weekly newspaper. Write down also the name of the person at the publication who handles music reviews along with any "submission guidelines" they have. You can usually find out this information at their website or in publications like *The Musician's Atlas* or *The Indie Bible*.

To locate blogs that might review your music, check out resources like Google Blog Search (blogsearch.google.com) and Elbo.ws. (elbo.ws). Google Blog Search functions similarly to a regular Google search, but with one enormous difference: it only searches content published within the blogosphere. Elbo.ws is a music blog aggregator, which basically means that it reposts the newest and most popular music from a handpicked selection of music blogs around the globe. The site is artistcentric, so do a couple searches for bands that sound like you and you should find some great hidden gems. Other helpful blog search tools are Captain Crawl (captaincrawl.com) and the Hype Machine (hypem

.com). Just as with magazines, don't forget about "lifestyle" blogs that may have an affinity with your music.

Enter all this information into a spreadsheet and stay organized!

4. The next thing to do is **send a strong pitch letter.** Use a strong subject line and first talk about *them*. This is a principle you should practice in all your marketing and promotional activities. Mention your admiration for their writing style and how they introduced you to some of your favorite bands. This is what they live for, so be sure to acknowledge their work before talking about yours. Simply request they give your music a listen and provide download links to your music and include full contact information so they can get back in touch with you. Wait two weeks. No response? Send the *same* email a second time, and then follow up again. Getting reviewed is a game of persistence. Hang tough and be consistent.

5. Finally, when reviews start appearing, start **tracking the results** and stay involved. Use the same tools for tracking media mentions as you would use for tracking your social media presence (see chapter 10). Since your website will often be included in any reviews or features, you will want to additionally tap into the power of *Google Analytics* (www.google.com/analytics/), so you can see where new people are coming from to your website and what actions they are taking on your website. Most bloggers will automatically share their freshest content to Facebook, Twitter, and other popular social networking sites, which is definitely a nice way to amplify the buzz. Be sure to always send a thank you note for any reviews you get.

One more thing: don't ever argue with the music reviewer. He may find your vocals "nasally" or your arrangements "derivative" but just remember, this is only one person's opinion and arguing with him will just get your future submissions pitched into oblivion. Be courteous and stay professional, always.

GETTING RADIO AIRPLAY

Radio has lost some of its music discovery power but is still the second most important vehicle for breaking new acts (next to word of mouth), so it continues to be a worthwhile promotional vehicle for independent artists.

There are five types of radio:

- Commercial Radio
- Colleges/Nonprofit Radio
- Community Radio
- Satellite Radio
- Internet Radio/Podcasts

In the U.S., independent record labels represent over 80 percent of the releases every year and 30 percent of digital (internet and satellite) radio plays, according to SoundScan. But in traditional radio broadcasting, indies come in at only 5 percent. Why? Because there's a logjam at radio and a serious weighting towards the major record companies: three labels control 95 percent of radio spins! This makes traditional terrestrial, commercial radio a virtual closed door to indies.

College radio, on the other hand, is music minded to the extreme. Freed from commercial constraints and funded by school budgets, college radio has unbridled license to indulge every musical taste, and it does. So, for indie recording musicians, college radio will be the best bet, followed by internet radio and, finally, satellite radio. Public radio (like NPR) is another possible outlet, but only once you've achieved a certain level of notoriety.

College Radio

Since college stations receive dozens of CD submissions weekly, you'll have to work smart to ensure that your music gets to the right person and that they will give it a chance for some airplay.

Where to Start

Getting the right information is your first task. There are hundreds of college radio stations in the United States. You'll want to target your efforts. To begin, pick a small number of stations (twelve or so) in a two-hundred-mile radius of your base, and concentrate on these. You probably already have a pretty good idea which local stations would be receptive to your music. Contact these first. Find out the names of the program director (PD), the music director (MD), and DJs who have shows that play your style(s) of music. You can get this kind of information from resources like *The Musician's Atlas* and *The Indie Bible.*

Commercial radio formats (Contemporary Hits Radio) are quite formal and inflexible. College radio, on the other hand, is much less formal, and its eclectic programming allows for a mix of formats or styles. Each college station has numerous "shows" within its flexible format. These can include segments devoted to everything from a capella to zydeco. So you should know generally where your music fits in with a particular station's programming. Visit the station's website, look at recent playlists for each show, and note who the DJs are for each. Being colleges, station personnel change fast so double check all contact information before sending anything out.

College radio also has "charts" that are kept and monitored by CMJ (*College Media Journal*). If your release gets wide airplay across several college stations, it may merit a chart position in CMJ, though this is usually the result of hiring an independent radio promoter and may not be the best way to spend your precious dollars. More on this later.

Just as with music reviewers, keep good records on all your radio outreach (see sample radio phone log figure 11.1).

Station call letters: _____ Station frequency: _____

Wattage: _____ Trade reporting: _____

Station owner: _____

Station address: _____

Fax: _____

Station email: _____

Station Web address: _____

Program director: _____

Music director: _____

Key DJs:

name: _____ show: _____ date/time: _____

name: _____ show: _____ date/time: _____

Communication log:

Date	Outcome

Fig. 11.1. Radio Phone Log

The Radio Mailing

Which format is most appropriate for radio airplay? By far, the best is CD. Second best is vinyl (currently experiencing a resurgence) and, only as a last resort, MP3s. The reasons for CDs are the ease with which a song can be cued and the general durability of the product. Some stations may prefer DAT (digital audiotape) or reel-to-reel, but these are the exceptions.

Even though you'll be submitting a sound recording containing numerous songs, you'll want to select the one song you deem best for radio and push that one. MDs and DJs are busy people. Make their jobs easier by telling them which cut to play. The person receiving the package is going to want current information about the artist or band. You should include a brief cover letter referring to your initial phone conversation, a biography, photo (best to incorporate onto bio), and any favorable press about the act. Make each piece graphically interesting. Talk to printers for ideas. Also include mention of any other stations that have agreed to play your music, as well as information on the record's availability online and in local stores. Make sure your name and address are on every item in your package. Remember, MDs receive tons of new music—fifty to a hundred CDs each week! One way to make your recording stand out is to enclose something unique in the package, like a hip calendar with your logo printed on top or some other promotional novelty that will make your name memorable. Be creative. You're aiming for attention. Another important item to include is a DJ Response Card. I use printed postcards, self-addressed and stamped.

Side 1

Thank you for taking the time to listen to **"Little Warrior"** from **Shea Rose**. Please answer the following questions so we may service you better. A stamp is already attached to make it as easy as possible for you. Thanks again!

Will this CD receive airplay at your station? _____

If so, which cuts? _____

Would you be interested in interviewing Shea Rose either in person or by phone?

   ❑ In person   ❑ By phone

Would you like to receive upcoming releases and news from Shea? _____

What trades does your station report to? _____

Comments: _____

_____

Your name: _____

Phone: _____

Side 2

WMUS
100 Radio Street
New York, NY 11223

stamp

You
123 First Avenue
Anywhere, CA 12345

Fig. 11.2. DJ Response Card

On the card, print three questions: Will the record receive airplay at your station? Which cuts? Would you be interested in an interview with the artist? At the bottom, leave room for comments (to be used in subsequent promotion), their name, station address, phone number, and best time to call. The rate of return for these cards is about 30 percent. They can provide crucial feedback for your ongoing radio promotion (see figure 11.2 "DJ Response Card"). Follow up all positive comments with a phone call. Use this to remind them of your recording. Tell them of other stations' response to it and any current information about your act. People talk. Work to create that buzz. Any invitations for interviews (in-studio or over the phone) should be followed up immediately and scheduled, preferably in tandem with an upcoming gig in the area.

Whenever you release a CD locally, your radio promotion should be tied into your other efforts encompassing retail presence, performances, and publicity. This four-prong approach ensures the greatest amount of exposure for your music. Here are some additional ways to maximize your college radio airplay:

1. **Push a single.** Because of the sheer quantity of music at college radio stations and the natural time constraints of student DJs, make their job easier by telling them the cut you want played. Some will ignore your choice and make their own selection, but most will take your lead and play that cut. Having a single repeatedly play over several weeks is often more effective than airing multiple cuts. Your single should be the strongest song on the CD and should not exceed four minutes.

2. **Know the rules.** Most program and music directors accept calls only during specified hours. Ask their assistants for their "call hours," and call then and only then to pitch your material. These call hours apply to everyone—major labels, indie labels, independent promoters—so be prepared to be put on hold for an extended period of time. Call once, just to make sure the PD or MD received your package. Don't bug them before they've had a chance to form an opinion!

3. **Line up song requests.** This should not be underestimated. Without getting obnoxious about it, you, your brother, your mother, your boyfriend/girlfriend, your Aunt Sally, and your bandmates should all be on a "request schedule," each person taking a different day to request your song. Even if the song isn't played when requested, you've filled an ear with your act's name and song one more time, each time. This too is promotion.

4. **Give thanks.** Send a letter to thank the radio station for playing your song. This proves you were actually listening, which will encourage them to play it again.

5. **Discuss related opportunities.** Ask the MD what other opportunities exist for bands and artists at the station—live music weeks, benefits, annual fundraisers, etc. Get involved!

6. **Provide PR for the station.** In exchange for airplay, mention the station with thanks in all your promotional literature. Tell the station manager and MD you will do this. It can't hurt.

7. **Network.** While working a college station, try to network yourself into the school's entertainment scene by contacting those who hire talent for various events, and mention you're getting airplay at the college's radio station. You can locate these entertainment buyers through the student activities office.

8. **Distribute giveaways.** Provide the station with giveaways: records, CDs, T-shirts, tickets to shows, whatever. Station personnel love this.

9. **Continue scouting out key stations.** Subscribe to a national publication specializing in your music style to see what radio stations in your region are industry leaders. Make sure you send your record to them as well. For example, if your music is primarily acoustic, then peruse *Sing Out!* out of Pennsylvania. If it's thrash rock, look into *Alternative Press* out of Cleveland, OH. If it's world music, check out *Songlines* out of London. If it defies categories, see *Under the Radar* out of Virginia.

10. **Hire an independent radio promoter.** If you really want to make a splash on college radio, you can hire an independent radio promoter. Independent promoters know the ins and outs of breaking a record on radio and can save you a lot of time. More importantly, independent promoters already have relationships with MDs and DJs. Getting a record played is a lot easier for them than it would be for you. Independent promoters aren't cheap (ranging from $300 to $500 per week for a 6- to 8-week period) and should only be considered once your distribution lines are established and you have money in the bank. You can find promoters in *The*

Musician's Atlas. Be sure to ask the promoter for references from recent clients so you can hear from artists themselves about their service and effectiveness.

11. **Leverage your assets.** Be sure to include a list of all radio stations that play your music in future promotion.

Internet Radio

The Internet is a wild frontier with plenty of ways to enjoy radio. Pandora is definitely the standout in this bunch, but there are numerous other worthy contenders who broadcast completely online. Some broadcast 24/7 like traditional radio, others can be found in the form of podcasts.

Accordingly, Web radio has grown from 178 stations in 32 countries in August 1996, to more than 115,000 stations worldwide by mid 2009. Arbitron, radio's audience measuring service, has expanded its service to now include Internet radio. That information is coveted by advertising firms, the financial engine behind conventional radio, and may lead to new interest in 'Net radio.

In appearance and feel, Internet radio is similar to regular radio. Instead of turning a dial, you enter a URL. Anyone with a broadband Internet connection can hear CD-quality audio (called, "streaming audio")—better sound quality, in fact, than with traditional FM radio. Even dial-up users can get sound quality roughly analogous to AM radio. Another key difference is that under federal law, Internet radio stations are responsible for paying per-performance royalties for each track they play (that they do not own the rights to). Regular radio stations are not responsible for per-performance royalties on sound recordings.

Part of the attraction of 'Net radio springs from real-world radio's current straits. Consolidation has largely left over-the-air radio in the hands of multistation networks, with computer-generated playlists, controlling consultants, and fierce competition for ratings. The results are cookie-cutter programming and stifled innovation, leaving a prime opportunity for competition on the 'Net. On the 'Net, you'll find such idiosyncratic radio shows as "Sweet and Soulful Motown," "'80s Funk," "Evening Melancholy" (vocal jazz), and "Smooth Jazz Piano & Keyboard." Narrowcasting, but global.

Internet radio operates on a different, radically decentralized model: individual DJs decide what music they like and what music to play. And music fans listen; they even pay a premium to listen to ad-free content.

US WEEKLY INTERNET RADIO LISTENERS, 2009-2015
Millions of Internet Users

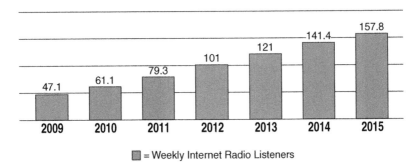

= Weekly Internet Radio Listeners

Fig. 11.3. US Weekly Internet Radio Listeners, 2009 to 2015. Source: Arbitron, Inc. and Edison Research.

Internet radio also makes it simple to track listening behavior, accurately gauge total listener hours, and gather demographic data on listeners. For example, you can easily use the Live365 website to see which stations are playing your music and how many listening hours they have had over the past month—valuable information you could never obtain from traditional radio. Plus, webcasters are obligated to identify song, artist, and album when playing a recording, and radio shows get archived for up to two weeks. Many also link the album to Amazon.com and other retailers so that people can purchase the music they're listening to.

Such 'Net radio companies as Grooveshark and major players such as TuneInRadio, Last.fm, and the aforementioned Live365 are building a strong presence. They offer artists and genres not heard on conventional radio, commercial-free programming, and the ability to break down the geographic boundaries of conventional radio. Particularly in music selection, such features are a big change and play very nicely into the segmentation tendencies of today's music market.

You can locate net radio shows relevant to your style of music most easily by visiting the shows listed in iTunes.

Podcasts

As its name suggests, a podcast is an iPod (or some other form of a portable music device) combined with a broadcast. It is essentially a radio show that is frozen and time-shifted. Podcasting makes audio files available online in a manner that allows these files to be automatically downloaded to a subscriber's computer (or portable music device) at the user's leisure.

EMarketer reports that in 2010, 45 percent of all Americans were aware of podcasting, while 23 percent listened to podcasts, an increase from 11 percent in 2006. In addition, video podcasting viewership was up to 20 percent for Americans in 2010. It is estimated that 70 million people have listened to or viewed a podcast.

No interest is too small for the podcast universe, and they provide an open door for new music, especially music whose rights are cleared. As with Internet radio, a good place to find appropriate podcasts for your music is the podcast section in iTunes, where you'll discover music podcasts of all shapes and sizes featuring just about every genre you can imagine. Also look into Podcast Alley (podcstalley.com) and Podcast Pickle (podcastpickle.com) for appropriate outlets. Stick with those that are active and podcasting regularly. Listen to several shows before sending anything out. Follow submission guidelines, and contact the podcaster. If you get played, promote it by linking to it on your Web, social, and mobile presences, and always send a thank you!

Satellite Radio

When it was announced in October 2004 that shock jock Howard Stern would be jumping from free AM/FM radio to pay satellite radio, it brought instant attention to the young medium. It took four years to sell a million VCRs, three years to sell that many CD players. DVD caught on faster—a million units sold in just over two years.

Satellite radio has beaten them all: one million subscribers within twenty-three months. It used to be that there were two competing satellite radio services: Sirius and XM radio. But in 2008, the two companies merged to form SiriusXM radio, with a huge selection of channels that were originally exclusive to one or the other. Boasting well over 200 stations that can be heard anywhere in the country and nearly 20 million subscribers, satellite radio could be a huge resource for unsigned independent artists to get a little music promotion and exposure.

You can think of satellite radio services like Sirius (which signed Stern) and XM Radio as something like a combination of satellite broadcaster DirecTV and premium pay channels such as HBO, says Michael Harrison, publisher of *Talkers,* a trade magazine covering the radio industry. Like DirecTV, these companies bounce their signals off satellites to beam high-quality digital service coast-to-coast. Like premium television channels such as HBO, they offer exclusive ad-free programming (well, for the most part).

A look at satellite radio:

1. **Something Different.** Similar to the way FM radio grew against dominant AM radio, satellite radio is becoming known for "edgier" alternative programming. In addition to Stern, SiriusXM has signed "Opie & Anthony," New York DJs who were kicked off the air due to their raunchy antics. Also, in sports, SiriusXM have exclusive National Football League NASCAR packages.

2. **Start-up Costs.** Potential subscribers have to start by purchasing special receivers and antennas. The sky's the limit for fancy gear, but a typical start-up package sells for about $150. Units are available for homes, cars, and boats, but each unit requires a separate subscription. Some portable units can move from car to home and back again.

3. **Subscription Costs.** Besides buying hardware, consumers also have to subscribe to Sirius XM. Subscriptions start at $18.99 per month or $199 for a year. There are also "Premier" and "Select" packages available.

4. **Niche Programming.** The companies are creating an array of channels to appeal to every taste. As of January 2013, Sirius XM offers over 200 channels, including commercial-free music channels, news, sports, talk entertainment, and weather/traffic channels.

5. **Getting into the Dashboard.** Sirius XM has exclusive deals to offer its gear and service as original equipment in General Motors, Acura, Audi, Ferrari, Honda, Nissan, Toyota, BMW, and Ford Motor models. It expects to be offered in over eighty vehicle models in 2013, as well as Avis and Hertz rentals.

Making Contact

First, determine which satellite radio stations are appropriate for your style of music. While you might be able to contact specific stations directly, the official way to be considered for SiriusXM radio airplay is by sending your materials to their Music Programming Department in New York City. Get your press kit together, make sure everything is in order, and write up a cover letter introducing yourself. You might even want to mention some of the stations you think your music would be a good fit for. Mail your package to:

Attn: Music Programming Department
SiriusXM
1221 Avenue of the Americas
New York, NY 10020

TIMING A MEDIA CAMPAIGN FOR A HIGH-PROFILE PERFORMANCE

Say you've booked a high-profile gig, and it's a month away. Here's a sample publicity schedule you may follow to maximize the media exposure of this performance.

3 to 4 Weeks Prior to Performance

- Mail out a press release and bio to everyone on your media and blue-ribbon list. Follow this mailing with a phone call, two to three days after you think your materials have been received.

- Put up posters and flyers, as allowed, in high-visibility areas.

- If you have a recording, send it along with a press release and bio to radio stations that your research has indicated might play it. Include a personal invitation to the gig. When you make your follow-up phone call, ask if the station might be interested in interviewing a key person in your band on the day of the show.

2 to 3 Weeks Prior to Performance

- Send out the same release (or a longer one with more information) and a photograph (captioned with time, place, date and price), and other graphic materials. Include a personal letter of invitation. The personal letter might also contain a sentence or two of blatant hype pleading for attention and saying why it is important for the person to show up. Keep it short. This is also the time to request an interview or longer feature story.

- Send email messages to your fans.

- To other than media people (i.e. booking agents, record label staffers, etc.), send a personal letter inviting them to the performance, together with the press release and other publicity materials.

- Follow up with phone calls.

- Check the places where you placed flyers and posters to make sure that they are still there. Repeat if necessary.

Day of Performance

- Make sure that people who are invited are on the "guest list" (at the entrance to the bar or club or at the gate or ticket booth). I've seen quite a few embarrassing situations where key people showed up only to find that the band had forgotten to place their names on the list. No good!

- When you get reviews, reprint them on your letterhead stationery. Include them in mailings. Hype breeds hype. When the media sees favorable reviews and articles on your band, it stimulates them to join the bandwagon.

- Two other nice ways to use reviews: make up a page of favorable quotes, and blow up a review so that words are more easily read. Use favorable quotes in posters, flyers, and on recording materials.

- Do these steps for every gig until you get results. Perseverance and repetition works.

- The eighth time a club owner or record company executive sees a press release about a band, they will realize that you are consistently performing. The fifth time a critic is invited to a gig, they may actually show up. The tenth time you send a press release and photograph announcing a gig, you may be surprised to open up the newspaper and see it printed word for word. You are trying to cut your own path through a dense media jungle. *Consistency* and *perseverance* are the key.

Track the success of your media campaign the same way you track your social media mentions, using Google Alerts, site analytics, and other available tools. You also want to follow up on *all* your media outreach. It's a dirty little secret in the music business that, unless you follow up two or three times, the other person will assume you are *not* really serious. Strange, but true.

THE MAGIC OF FOLLOW-UP

Following up on all your media publicity is critical. Follow-up allows you to monitor your coverage, maximize the benefits of good reviews, and maintain good relations with the press even after less-than-favorable reviews. Opportunities for follow-up include when you:

- **Acknowledge good reviews** with a thank-you note. Have a stack of these stamped and ready to go on your desk. Good manners go far in the world of business and a hard-copy note has stand-out power in today's digital economy.

- **Politely correct errors in reviews.** All publications work under tight deadlines, and many don't spend the time to check every fact in the article with the sources. That's a sad fact, but true.

- **Respond to bad reviews.** Look as objectively as possible at what's being said in the review. Learn from it, and thank the writer for the feedback.

- **Build on positive reviews.** The real value in a review, release announcement, or news story is not merely its immediate impact on the publication's readers. It's the impact you create by subsequently sending reprints of that article to anyone you choose: labels, agents, tastemakers, new leads, outside contacts, etc. To stay on the right side of the law, be sure to contact the publication to obtain the rights to reprint the article.

- **Keep in touch.** Help media people remember you by calling them periodically. You won't develop rapport overnight. It takes time. Until you feel you've established rapport, call only when you have news. Always have a goal in mind and a legitimate purpose for your call.

Another good planning tip, mentioned in the previous chapter, is to obtain the editorial calendar from the publication you're planning to contact. This document will tell you what articles the publication is planning to print, the deadlines, and in some cases, the editor in charge. By obtaining the editorial calendar, you'll learn what the publication is planning to write, when, and who their audience is. Use this knowledge to submit appropriate information about your product or event well in advance of the publication's deadlines.

MAKING THE MOST OF INTERVIEW OPPORTUNITIES

While some artists may be "naturals" at creating strong, positive images for themselves through the media, others must be coached by publicists and put through a "media school" where they are taught the basic skills of effective interviews, including how to answer awkward or touchy questions, how to always present their best side to the media, and making the necessary points regardless of what the interviewer asks.

Once you've got the media's attention, you'll want to make sure your message comes across effectively. You need to make sure you get your main points across loud and clear, whether you're being interviewed in the newspapers or on the Internet, television, or radio.

Here are some pointers to ensure that interview sparkles:

- **Prepare.** Write out the key points or message you want to convey to the audience.

- **Keep the audience in mind.** Find out as much as you can about who will be reading, watching, or listening to your interview.

- **Don't try to sell yourself or your business.** Guest appearances and other interviews are not commercials, and the media is very sensitive to this distinction. Your job in an interview is to *inform* and to do so in an entertaining way.

- **Arrange in advance for the audience to be able to contact you.** If appropriate, ask before the interview whether the interviewer would be willing to let people know how they can contact you for more information. Such a plug will be far more valuable to you than self-promotion.

- **Restate the question in beginning your answer.** For example:

  Q: "Which song is most requested when you play out?"

  A: "The most requested song when I play out is..."

  This helps the audience stay with you and gives you a chance to focus your thoughts.

- **Keep your answers brief and to the point.** Radio and television interviews are a conversation, not a monologue, so if your response to a question lasts longer than 30 to 60 seconds, you are probably overanswering. Print allows a bit more room for stretching out on answers.

- **Talk personally, concretely, and colorfully.** Avoid academic, theoretical, abstract, and clinical language.

- **Be positive and speak with enthusiasm and conviction.** Don't dwell on the negative aspects of your message. Provide info that inspires hope, encouragement, and confidence, and end each segment on an upbeat note.

THE PROFESSIONAL PROMOTER: WHEN TO SEEK OUTSIDE HELP

There is only one correct time to seek the help of a professional publicist or promoter: When you yourself have become thoroughly familiar with the self-promotional universe, but because of manifold commitments and the lack of time, you fail to access all the opportunities available to you. It's crucial for the do-it-yourselfer to have at least introductory experience working with the media. That way, you're in a better position to evaluate a professional's record and, once having done so, realistically evaluate just what is being done on your behalf.

Where do you find a promoter or publicist? Start by asking for local recommendations. Also notice which bands and musicians are getting a lot of quality press coverage or radio airplay. Contact the media outlet and inquire about who the artist's professional is. Those professionals specializing in music will often advertise in music magazines. Shop around. Never take the first person who's available. You have nothing with which to compare his or her skills. Prices vary as does creativity.

Once you've found several possibilities, use the following guidelines to be sure you get exactly what you need. Consider:

- Is the individual or firm inventive? Can they create distinction and dimension in an artist's story?

- Is the individual or firm interested in what you're doing?

- Is the individual or firm so overwhelmed by current clients that their ability to take on new work is limited?

- Does the individual or firm now serve clients with whom you compete?

- What will it cost?

It's completely reasonable to request samples of their work and client references. (BTW, the same applies to *all* service providers you are considering spending your hard-earned cash on.) After all, it's the musicians they've worked with who can give you the most relevant feedback about that professional's work.

Understanding how the media works is not merely a matter of idle curiosity. Whether you're a band, a soloist, a personal manager, booking agent, or other music professional, having access to the media on a continuing, positive basis is a decided advantage. A positive media relationship can be measured in enhanced prestige, greater recognition, and ultimately, larger profits.

Media exposure can get you noticed, convince customers to buy from you, encourage other media to cover you, and expand your business. All in all, it's one of the best uses of your marketing time and dollars.

The Self-Promoting Songwriter and Composer

My guess is most people reading this book aren't just music performers but writers as well. You may express your writing in lyrics or in music. Then again, you may be the complete songwriter and create both the lyrics and the music. You may see yourself primarily as a film music composer, or a commercial jingle writer, or a jazz arranger.

If you are both a performer and a writer, then you have parallel career paths to cultivate. And, while both paths will often work in tandem, the writing side will also have its own particular needs and require its own particular strategies to move it toward success. To ensure long-term career success as a songwriter, an understanding of subjects like music rights, music publishing, and music licensing will be crucial. Many songwriters and composers have suffered over the years because they neglected to learn about these subjects. Don't let that be you.

The first thing you want to understand is copyright.

COPYRIGHT 101

Before tackling some strategies for marketing your songs, let's review the meaning of "copyright."

First, a work is copyrighted (not, copy*written*) when it is fixed in some type of medium. In a sense, then, a work is "copyrighted" when it is created (drawn, filmed, played, written, or recorded). You do not obtain a copyright from the Library of Congress in Washington, D.C.; you merely *register* your copyright that already exists.

A song is a "bundle" of rights. Each right is exclusive (owned and controlled by the writer), and each right is also divisible (that is, assignable to different parties). Over a hundred years ago, some very discerning people figured out what each of these rights are. A copyright gives the owner five exclusive rights.

The owner can:

1. **Reproduce the work.** Make and sell the work in any form.

2. **Distribute copies of the work.** One illustration of this would be a record company that hires a plant to manufacture their CDs. The plant gets the right to reproduce the songs (item 1 above), but not the right to distribute copies of them.

3. **Perform the work publicly.** It doesn't matter whether the performance is by live musicians or a DJ playing records; you get to control this right.

4. **Make a derivative work.** A derivative work is a creation based on another work. An example is a parody lyric set to a well-known song (e.g., "Gangster's Paradise," which Weird Al parodied as "Amish Paradise"). The new work is called a derivative work because it's *derived* from the original. By the way, Weird Al did not have to obtain the permission of the original writer and publisher to create these derivations, because parodies fall under "fair use laws." Al, however, takes it upon himself to request permission. If he doesn't get it, as in the case with Eminem, he doesn't go forth with the parody.

5. **Display the work publicly.** This doesn't really apply to music; it's the right to put paintings, statues, etc. on public display.

Songwriters often worry that other people will steal their songs. They worry about sending their songs to publishers or entering songwriting contests.

While it's smart to be alert to copyright issues, it's also important to maintain perspective. Outright attempts to steal songs in today's music business are actually quite rare. And thanks to modern copyright law, songwriters have safeguards to help protect their rightful ownership of songs they create.

Duration of Copyrights

Copyright protection begins on the date of creation and, in most cases, lasts for the lifetime of the author *plus* seventy years. So, if you write a song in 2013, and die in the year 2050, the copyright will last until 2125.

What about songs written before January 1, 1978? These originally fell under the Copyright Act of 1909 which gave the song 28 years of protection with the right to renew it for another 28. The Copyright Act of 1976 extended the life of pre-1978 copyrights to 75 years from the date of creation.

Copyrights

For an easy-to-follow chart on the various lengths of copyrights go to: www.unc.edu/~unclng/public-d.htm

What Can and Cannot Be Copyrighted

The following works can be copyrighted:

❏ Musical compositions

❏ Recordings of musical compositions

❏ Arrangements of musical compositions

❏ Works of literature

❏ Recordings of works of literature

❏ Adaptations of works of literature (e.g., screenplays)

❏ Logos (trademarks)

❏ Original pictures

❏ Original photographs

❏ Original illustrations

❏ Film, video, and animation

❏ Software

❏ Clothing and product designs.

The following works cannot be copyrighted: Any idea, procedure, process, system, method of operation, concept, principle, or discovery—regardless of the form in which it is described, explained, illustrated, or embodied—in an original work, cannot fall under copyright protection.

For example:

- ❑ An improvised speech where a recording or prewritten script doesn't exist;

- ❑ Titles, names, and short phrases (unless these items form a part of a trademark);

- ❑ Ideas, methods, and procedures (unless protected by patent);

- ❑ Lists of common information (such as calendars, or items taken from public domain sources).

Of course, as with all matters of "intellectual property," there are many grey areas, many exceptions to the rule, and many complicated scenarios that can twist your mind like a pretzel. I would point you to the Resource Directory for plenty of further resources to satisfy your intellectual property curiosity.

ILLUMINATING TRIVIA
Did you know that...
...John Fogerty's "The Old Man Down the Road" sounded so much like his Creedence Clearwater Revival hit "Run Through the Jungle" that he was sued for copyright infringement of his own song by CCR's label, Fantasy Records?

How to Register Your Copyrights

It is *not essential* to register your copyrights with the government's copyright office, but it is *advisable*. Registration creates a clear paper trail in the event of an infringement on your copyright. Plus (and this is ultimately most important), formal registration allows you to collect statutory damages as well as attorney fees from the infringer when you win your case.

There are five music-relevant copyright registration forms obtainable from the Library Of Congress. They are:

- Form PA (Performing Arts)

- Form SR (Sound Recording)

- Form TX (Nondramatic Literary Works)

- Form VA (Visual Arts)

- Form CA (Corrections and Amplifications).

A CD project can easily involve every one of these forms. For example, when the tracks were just "unpublished" songs on a rough lead sheet, you could have registered each one with form PA. When the tracks were recorded, you could have filed an additional SR form to register the sound recording version of the songs registered under the previous PA form. (BTW, an SR form will cover *both* the recorded version of the song *plus* the underlying composition.) You may have some special liner notes written for the CD which can be registered using form TX, and the CD graphics registered using the VA form. All of the forms you need are obtainable from the U.S. Copyright Office (copyright.gov).

Fortunately, the process has gotten more streamlined via online registration through the electronic Copyright Office (eCO) at a reduced fee of $35.

What about the CA Form?

Well, listen up and save some dough.

A person may register as many songs as they wish on a PA or SR, call it "The Collected Works of Joey Singer, Vol. 1," and be granted full copyright protection for each song listed on the form. This is great because for one $45 fee, each song gets protected.

But what if someone hears one of these songs and wants to cover it? How will they be able to find it in the Copyright Office records?

"They won't," says Page Miller, a senior copyright information specialist in D.C. "This is why we created the CA form." The CA (Corrections & Amplifications) form allows you to "amplify" your PA or SR filing so that each of your songs can be individually indexed at the Copyright Office.

Now, if a band or artist wants to cover a song you've written or recorded, they would be able to look up your name as the song's copyright owner. If the song in question was merely one of, say, twenty songs registered on a PA or SR form, it would be protected but it would not allow a person to find it in a copyright search. A CA form registration has nothing to do with giving the song additional protection; it just provides a tracking path to the song's author.

You file the CA after you receive your registration number back from the first filing. The total process can take several months.

So, for a total amount of $160 ($45 for initial registration and $115 for the CA), you can register and protect all your songs, and provide a tracking route to them as well.

OFFICE OF COPYRIGHT CONTACT INFO

Download any form you'll need at: **copyright.gov/forms/**

If you want to speak with an information specialist at the office of Copyright call: **202-707-5959.**

Recording Copyrighted Songs (Covers)

Copyright law gives the owner of a copyrighted song the exclusive right to make the first sound recording of the song. However, once the song has been recorded and distributed to the public, others are entitled to make their own recordings of that work. How so?

In the early 1900s, the disruptive technology was player pianos. Manufacturers of player piano rolls purchased a single copy of the sheet music of a song, hired someone to record the music, and then sold these mechanical reproductions to consumers. The songwriters held that this was copyright infringement, while the piano roll manufacturers pointed out that they had paid the appropriate copyright fees when they purchased the sheet music. As often happens, lawsuits ensued.

Though the Supreme Court found in favor of the piano roll manufacturers, it invited Congress to consider new legislation on the issue. Congress responded with the Copyright Act of 1909, which created a new form of intellectual property known as "mechanical reproduction rights."

So now, if you want to record a previously published song, you *do not* need to obtain permission from the copyright owner directly. The law does, however, require you to make account to the copyright holder and to pay fixed rates per song for each record manufactured and sold. This is accomplished through the issuance of a compulsory "mechanical license," and the "rate" is set by Congress. In other words, anyone who wants to record a cover of a song may do so without permission, but needs to obtain a mechanical license.

There are three ways to obtain a mechanical license:

1. First, find out who owns the copyright on the composition by contacting BMI (212-586-2000 or www.bmi.com), ASCAP (212-621-6160 or www.ascap.com), or SESAC (800-826-9996 or www.sesac.com). Armed with this info, you can contact the publisher and negotiate your own rates. This, however, is very time-consuming.

2. If you don't want to negotiate your own rates, contact the Harry Fox Agency (nmpa.org/hfa.html), which is authorized to issue mechanical licenses at the current statutory rate set by Congress. Current rates can be found at the Harry Fox website.

STATUTORY ROYALTY RATES (OR "MECHANICALS")

As of January 1, 2006, the statutory mechanical rate is as follows:

9.10 cents for songs 5 minutes or less, or 1.75 cents per minute or fraction thereof over 5 minutes.

For example:

5:01 to 6:00 = $.105 (6 x $.0175 = $.105)

6:01 to 7:00 = $.1225 (7 x $.0175 = $.1225)

7:01 to 8:00 = $.14 (8 x $.0175 = $.14)

This rate will remain in effect until the next schedule of mechanical licensing rates is determined.

In some cases, Harry Fox does not administer publishing rights, and you must find the individual publisher who owns the publishing rights. This can oftentimes be much more difficult, especially with defunct and obscure record labels. Again, if you have the original release, you can look in album credits for publishing information.

If you do not have the original recording, a good place to start is the *All Music Guide* (www.allmusic.com). This website can help you find album and/or song credits for many artists, even those on small independent labels. Once you contact a publisher, you must prove that you have begun the process of obtaining the proper mechanical license, and you intend to complete the transaction. In some cases, the publisher may give you written permission without any fee. In either event, it is recommended that you obtain written permission on company letterhead.

3. If you can't afford the standard fee, contact a group like the Volunteer Lawyers for the Arts (call 215-545-3385 for the chapter nearest you). They can often help negotiate reduced royalties for schools and nonprofit groups. Go to: www. pdinfo.com.

Public Domain (PD) Music

Music and lyrics published in 1922 or earlier are in the public domain in the United States. No one can claim ownership of a song in the public domain, therefore public domain songs may be used by anyone. For more info on public domain music go to: www .pdinfo.com/.

"Flexible Copyrights" with Creative Commons

 "Creative Commons" (CC) is a concept and set of licenses developed by Harvard Law School professor Lawrence Lessig as a reaction to our increasingly litigious society. CC developed out of a desire to add some gray between the extremes of reserving no rights (public domain) and reserving all rights (in standard copyright agreements).

Lessig doesn't see Creative Commons as replacing copyright, but complementing it. It may make sense to license some of your works one way and some another. And Creative Commons licenses themselves are quite flexible, allowing you to choose what the consumers of your music can do with it.

You create your own license by combining these four conditions in a way that works for you:

• **Attribution:** You let others copy, distribute, display, and perform your copyrighted work — and derivative works based upon it — but only if they give credit the way you request.

• **Share Alike:** You allow others to distribute derivative works only under a license identical to the license that governs your work.

• **Noncommercial:** You let others copy, distribute, display, and perform your work—and derivative works based upon it—but for noncommercial purposes only.

- **No Derivative Works** You let others copy, distribute, display, and perform only verbatim copies of your work, not derivative works based upon it.

There are a lot of possibilities. Learn more at creativecommons.org

MUSIC PUBLISHING 101

The writer is the first link in the music industry food chain, the earth from which everything springs. The writer faces an empty page, and from the factory of his or her mind, creates words and music that weren't there before.

But once that song is written, and assuming the writer wants to move it beyond the four walls of his or her bedroom, the next step is *publishing* it.

Music publishing is the sleeping giant in the record world. It takes people a while in this business to realize that the real money isn't on the *record* side, it's on the *music* side. Records go up and down the charts, but the publishing goes on forever (well, almost forever).

To most people, the term "music publishing" connotes a business concerned with *print* music. And, in fact, this was what early music publishing was. However, over the years, the importance of popular sheet music sales has declined in inverse proportion to the success of recordings.

In fact, most music publishers today don't manufacture product in any physical form, nor do they sell product directly to consumers. Instead, music publishers *license* other companies *the rights* to use, perform, copy, and sell songs in various types of media. It's primarily a B2B (business to business) rather than a B2C (business to consumer) kind of business.

It might have been a logical step for music publishers to issue music on records, but as things unfolded, *record companies* emerged to "publish" recorded performances by musicians and singers. That meant that record companies had to obtain permission from the music publishers who owned the songs performed by the recording artists.

The upshot was that, instead of selling product per se, music publishers began dealing in *rights*, and so it remains primarily a *service*-based business.

ILLUMINATING TRIVIA

Did you know...

...that for five years Bob Dylan did not publish songs in order to avoid sharing an exorbitant percentage of the income with his manager Albert Grossman?

(*Rockonomics: The Money Behind the Music*, by Marc Eliot)

Here are some additional facts about the music publishing business.

- **Publishing is the "real estate" of the music business.** It can be subdivided into many smaller pieces and owned by many parties. In this scenario, the publisher is similar to a landlord or managing agent, who exploits the property and receives money from those using the property, and then distributes the income to the owners.

- **Since most music publishers, then, have no physical product, copyrights constitute their sole stock in trade.** Copyrights are intangible assets (i.e., they don't have physical properties you can see or touch). Music publishers "rent" the rights to intangible properties (songs) to *users,* such as record companies, artists, record producers, broadcasters, film producers, ad agencies, software developers, etc. The users can make physical copies of the songs and sell them to consumers (after paying the appropriate licensing fee, in this case, a mechanical license).

- **Until the 1960s, the work of music publishers involved signing songwriters and then placing their songs with singers** who would use them for commercial recordings or public performances. The publisher would then receive an income from sales of the recordings and sheet music, and revenue from performance rights.

The emergence of rock music radically changed the relationship of publishers to popular music production. In the Tin Pan Alley tradition, there was a clear-cut distinction between writers and publishers on one side, and performers and record companies on the other.

The success of artists such as the Beatles and Bob Dylan, and the emergence of the rock aesthetic that placed great emphasis on individual expression, resulted in performers increasingly writing their own songs. And so it remains today.

In all styles of music, the big-name publishing companies are no longer dominating the industry. Writer/producers who do most of their production work at home aided by MIDI and Pro Tools studios have pop hits on a regular basis with a variety of artists.

MUSIC PUBLISHING REVENUES

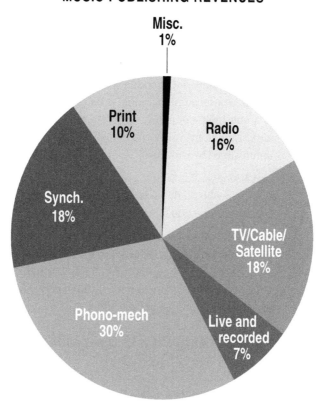

Fig. 12.1. Music Publishing Revenues

There are approximately 70,000 music publishing companies in the U.S. alone, though a great many of these are largely inactive. In fact, only a few hundred publishers have songs on the U.S. charts each year. Anyone can set up a music publishing house, but the value of a publisher lies in how effectively they are able to "exploit" (i.e., market) their copyrights. With the rise of the "digital common" along with the "every business is a music business" trend, many businesses are beginning to develop music publishing subsidiaries. From radio stations to ad agencies, airlines to online licensing services, they are all waking up to the riches that lie within the uses of music.

Types of Music Publishers

There are essentially four different kinds of music publishers:

1. **The Mega Pubs.** These are the major publishing companies affiliated with a multinational record or film company (such as Warner/Chappell, EMI, BMG, Sony/ATV, MGM, Rondor, Jobete, Famous Music, etc).

2. **Major Affiliates.** Independent publishing companies, fully staffed, whose "administration" is handled by a major record or publishing company (e.g., Quincy Jones Publishing administered by Warner/Chappell; or, Interscope Music, administered by Universal).

3. **Stand Alones.** Publishing companies not affiliated with a major but who do their own administration—that is, collect their own money, do their own accounting, etc.

4. **Writer/Publisher Owned Companies** (e.g., Bruce Springsteen, Bob Dylan, Sting, Diane Warren). They pocket the lion's share of the publishing and pay a 5 to 8% administration fee to a major company to handle the paperwork, typically known as an "administration deal."

THE ROLE OF PERFORMING RIGHTS ORGANIZATIONS (PROS)

One of the several rights in a song is the "performance right." This is the right to *perform* the work publicly; whether the performance is by live musicians or a DJ playing records, the writer gets to control this right. A performing rights organization's (PRO) function is collecting performing rights royalties on behalf of its members: composers and music publishers. The PRO then distributes these royalties to its members, minus the PRO's administration costs. Every serious songwriter or composer should join one of the PROs.

There are three in the U.S.: ASCAP (ascap.com), BMI (bmi.com), and SESAC (sesac.com).

PROs license public performances of their members' music, which includes network television, cable television, cable movie channels (HBO, Showtime, etc.), and use in nightclubs, stores, restaurants, and other public performances. PROs only license performing rights, and only nondramatic performing rights. Dramatic Rights—including performances you would see on Broadway—are negotiated directly with either the composer, the publisher, or their representative.

WHERE SONGS ARE PUBLICLY "PERFORMED"

Radio	Music in Businesses
Television	Racetracks
Amusement Park	Resorts
Arenas	Restaurants
Auditoriums	Retail Stores
Bowling Alleys	Shopping Malls
Colleges & Universities	Sports Bars
Concerts	Stadiums
Convention Centers	Taverns
Country Clubs	Theme Parks
Dance Studios	Water Parks
Festivals	Websites
Health & Fitness Centers	Hotels & Nightclubs

Public performances of songs and music are licensed and monitored by performing rights organizations like ASCAP, BMI or SESAC.

This is just a brief introduction to performing rights organizations. For further information, you should contact each PRO directly.

A newer trend in publishing is the signing of writer/performers to "development deals." More and more publishers are providing the service of artist development that record labels have relinquished. For example, the band Everclear signed a publishing contract with Rondor Publishing, and Rondor helped promote the band to *CMJ*, an influential industry trade magazine. They also helped the band buy new equipment and offered some tour support. This was Everclear's "back way" into visibility, and eventually, a recording contract. Similar deals were made for Alanis Morissette, Coldplay, and James Blunt, all of whom had publishing arrangements before signing recording contracts.

SONG MARKETING: FINDING OUTLETS FOR ORIGINAL MUSIC

Everything written in previous chapters of this book concerning marketing applies here. Perhaps the most important principle earlier discussed to guide your song marketing is the principle of *targeting*.

Because there are literally hundreds of potential markets for songs, it's virtually impossible to exploit them all. Each market has its own values, procedures, influencers (or tastemakers), dynamics, and culture. If the key to successful marketing is effective communication, then it's imperative for you to pick one or two markets and work *them*.

This means studying all the mainstream (and often marginal) information sources for each market. Anything you can discover about that particular market will, in turn, help you market to it more effectively. For example, if ad agencies are your target, then publications like *Ad Week* and *Advertsing Age* will be at the top of your reading list.

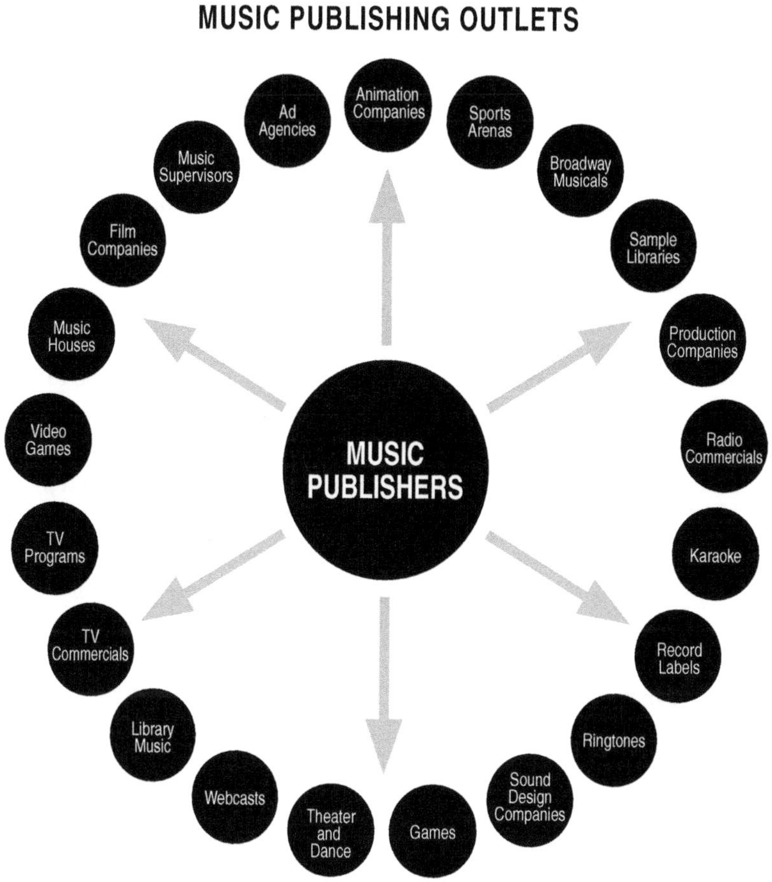

MUSIC PUBLISHING OUTLETS

Fig. 12.2. Music Publishing Outlets

As the whole business world goes *multi*media, the demand for audio in all its manifestations increases. In response to this need, numerous kinds of music suppliers have emerged: jingle houses, music libraries, specialty labels, even individual artists (think Moby). Sometimes these suppliers deal with companies one-on-one when brokering deals; more commonly companies hire agents of various kinds to facilitate the process. These "agents" can be music supervisors, music specialists at libraries, composer representatives, producers, or ad agency staffers with a focus on musical content.

Let's look at some of these agents and how to best approach them.

Music Supervisors

Music supervisors find music for television shows and film projects. They have built strong relationships with both film directors and television producers, and songwriters and composers, so they can be counted on to deliver what their clients need, often at a moment's notice. Ingrid Michaelson, whose story opened this book, got her start with a well-placed song on the popular show, *Grey's Anatomy.*

Since that time, many more singer-songwriters (not to mention thousands of bands and composers) have been trying their hand at getting song placements. I'm told some supervisors get 100 to 200 CDs *per week* from artists, leading to an oversupply of music in this space.

Indeed, the numbers game is stacked in the wrong direction, at least from the artist perspective, though a well-placed slot can open some doors. A successful show can generate lots of new fans, especially on bigger series and films. Additionally, those artists that own their publishing can quickly finalize deals and reap the rewards of downstream usage payouts (i.e., performance royalties). So how can you stand out?

Here are some tips.

- **Understand how music supervisors work.** The music supervisor has come to be the person responsible for all the musical elements—technical, creative, and administrative—that are exclusive of the score and its production. But there's no "one size fits all" approach.

  Stay on top of the different needs from company to company and person to person, while continuing to streamline your approach to the world of music supervision with every new conversation, letter, license request, or email. After all, if you demonstrate that you know how a particular person likes to communicate, you're also making his or her job easier, and it just may make the person feel inclined to tip a negotiation your way.

- **Connect.** As with everything in music, business is driven by relationships. So first, think of all the people you know or know of, even remotely connected to the film and television industries. Start networking with these people. This means reaching out with polite, purposeful letters, emails, faxes, and phone calls. Ask questions, read online and offline, and respond. To locate music supervisors, go to the Internet Movie Database (imdb.com). Check out a show you think your music would be appropriate for, and bring up the full "Cast & Crew" details. Do a quick find on the page for the word music or music supervisor, and voila! Another idea is to consult the amazing (though very expensive) *Film/TV Music Guide* (see Resource Directory for details).

- **Use the side hatch.** Find out who the leading film and video editors are and send them your music. Editors often put their own "temp" music track on films they're working on to liven up the cuts and sometimes they and the directors become so enamored of it, they end up using the music and the final score.

- **Deadlines, deadlines, deadlines.** A rock star can work on a record for as long as he wants. Soundtrack and music supervisors are working on strict timetables. Usually, they need it "yesterday."

- **Make it easy.** Music publishers are also making better use of the Internet to expedite the music supervisor's search process. The Royalty Network (roynet.com) is just such a publisher, with an online "Music Supervisor's Request Form" that allows you to submit a request, with criteria including:

- Genre sought
- Timing
- Term
- Scheduled release date
- Brief description of scene

- Type of use
- Territory
- Budget
- Media requested

Upon receipt of the form, publishers will search for applicable material in their catalog and quickly get the selections to the music supervisor for their review.

Other services like Soundcloud (soundcloud.com) and MOG (mog.com) make it easy to display your tracks and link directly to them in an email message. If you send a CD use a regular jewel case and not a slimline. People like stacking CDs as they listen, and they want spine labels that shows the artist name. Slimlines tend to get lost in those stacks.

MUSIC LICENSE FEE RANGES

Use in a National TV Commercial	
Sync Fee:	$15,000 to $100,000
Master Use Fee:	$15,000 to $100,000
Use in a One-Hour Episode of a Primetime Series on TV	
Sync Fee:	$500 to $2,500
Master Use Fee:	$500 to $2,500
Use in a Promotional Trailer (TV)	
Sync Fee:	$2,000 to $2,500
Master Use Fee:	$2,000 to $2,500
Use in a Daytime Drama on Network TV	
Sync Fee:	$100 to $500
Master Use Fee:	$100 to $500
Film Festival Use	
Sync Fee:	$0 to $250
Master Use Fee:	$0 to $250
Use in a Feature Film with Distribution by a Major Studio	
Sync Fee:	$7,500 to $17,500
Master Use Fee:	$7,500 to $17,500
Use in a Promotional Trailer (Theatrical)	
Sync Fee:	$4,000 to $7,500
Master Use Fee:	$4,000 to $7,500
Use in an Independent Film with Distribution	
Sync Fee:	$250 to $750
Master Use Fee:	$250 to $750
Use in a Basic Cable TV Program (MTV, Lifetime, etc.)	
Sync Fee:	$0 to $250
Master Use Fee:	$0 to $250

Fig. 12.3. Music License Fee Ranges

MUSIC TO VISUALS

Like screenwriting or professional athletics, this is a field where the available slots are few, and the hopefuls are many. Whether you're in Los Angeles, or other parts of the country or world, film scoring communities are being saturated with more and more composers. To that end, here's some helpful advice that will help you stand out.

- **Network around film schools**, find the most talented director, offer to put your music on his movie, and forge relationships with the people who will be the next generation of biggies. The UCLA Graduate Film Students Program approached Warner Bros. Records for someone to score first-time director Jeff Fines' *No Easy Way,* and ended up with American Music Club's Mark Eitzel.

- **Substitute.** Take a movie by a director you'd like to work with and create your own score for it. When Robert Rodriguez first asked Los Lobos to do the score for his movie *Desperado,* he suggested they get a tape of his first film, "El Mariachi," and put their own music to it as an exercise.

- **Be tech savvy.** Gain music technology and music production fluency; be able to produce top-caliber, "broadcast quality" music from your own studio with no live players beyond your-self, or almost no live players (less than four or so). Hone your craft so that you can produce quality in high quantity!

- **Connect the dots.** Let your publisher, ASCAP, or BMI know you are interested in film work. Performance Rights agencies are in touch with the film community and know if a movie is coming up that is looking for someone to do a soundtrack.

- **Establish a distinct musical identity**, but be prepared to abandon it in favor of diverse vocabulary. Sound like yourself. Artists such as Hispanic-American Los Lobos and Irish-Amer-ican Seamus Egan originally broke into films of very specific ethnic genres, but have managed to convince directors they can either work outside that style or make the style work apart from its normal connotations.

- **Be able to work as part of a team and accept direction.** Your typical modern pop artist is used to being his own boss, answering to no one and having absolute creative freedom. In

movie, television, or commercial soundtrack work, the musician must answer to a director, a producer, or a client.

There are so many factors that go into making it as a composer,
and only a few of them have to do with music. Are you smart, do you
have a good personality, can you meet deadlines, do you know how
to work with filmmakers? Someone who has all those ducks in a row
has incredibly better odds than a social misfit who writes crappy
music. If you have your act together, write really good music, and
have the financial ability and determination to stick it out, the odds
are you'll make it, because there are so few people who meet those
requirements.

Music Libraries

With the explosive rise of indie music and the Internet, there has
been an equal explosion of music licensing services to hit the
scene. Zynch Music, Sorted Noise, CopyCat Music, Killer Tracks,
Primary Elements, and Omni Music are just six of the numerous
services that have popped up. Each of these "indie consolidators"
are set up to take your tracks and license them to media producers
in all markets, including film, television, radio, telephony (music
on hold, ringtones), advertising, Web, and interactive and game
productions. They are essentially *music libraries.*

Music libraries act as "middlemen" between composer and
production companies who have built previous relationships
with music supervisors and find opportunities for composers and
publishers to have their music placed in film, television, and advertising. Some ask for an upfront fee; some take a percentage of the
licensing agreement from the composer or copyright owner.

Most of these are nonexclusive deals (meaning you can be
licensing the same tracks to more than one service at the same
time), allow you to retain full ownership, and pay you a 50 percent
commission on each licensing fee. This is certainly fair since they
act as your publisher, "booking" your track with a specific music
user. Fees are generally on the low end, anywhere from $50 to $300
per license.

As with any music service, the proof is in the pudding. Before
signing on with any of them, ask about "success stories" they've
been part of, and also request some references of composers who
they've worked with. A large part of working with these companies

is trust because you *never* fully know how much money your songs and tracks are earning under their negotiations. So, make sure you speak with enough people and get enough questions answered to your satisfaction before signing on.

Finally, stay organized. Create either an Excel file, Word document, or simply buy a notebook to keep specific information about the company and the company representatives you work with. Make a column for each of the following; name, contact information, film and television shows or commercials they've worked on, format they prefer, notes, and action taken.

Music Producers

Perhaps you have songs, beats, arrangements, demos, or master recordings you'd like to pitch to producers or labels. Maybe you would like to get a track on a top-shelf compilation CD. Or perhaps, you play an unusual instrument or possess a unique vocal style a producer may find useful for upcoming recording projects.

Producers come in all shapes and sizes with a vast range of production "styles," from microsound management to laissez-faire coaching.

Depending on where they fall on that continuum, producers can be perceived as the Svengalis of the business, responsible for transforming raw talent (or lack thereof) into artists and hit makers, or as Zen Masters, unobtrusive in the process of letting the particular genius of their musicians shine through.

Let's look at some ways you can interact with producers and labels to help forward your career and business.

- **Build your own production strength first.** Many great songs today don't make it simply because the production doesn't yield the emotional tone, upbeat or not, that the song implores. We all wish the day was back when a great song stood on its own, but many a song demo is actually the track used for the final artist record cut today. You can no longer get away with "fairly" good sounding tracks. They have to sound like a record cut.

- **Producers are not always easy to locate.** If you're looking for a producer for a recording project, you want someone whose work you already resonate with. Butch Vig or the Neptunes may be out of reach for now, so concentrate on those who have produced recordings you dig from the indie music world. Their names are easy to find on a recording's liner notes. Try to connect with producers via artists they work with. Use all the networking techniques discussed in previous chapters.

- **Work smart.** The role of the producer as creative and business person has expanded. Whether you produce dance tunes in your bedroom, work with a chart-topping act on a major label, or produce bands in a local studio, you'll need to be familiar with the legal and contractual side of your business, if you're to stay in the game and get paid for your efforts.

The sad reality is that music in most projects is an afterthought. While it is vitally important, it is also the last thing on the minds of the production team most of the time. Usually, the entire project has been shot and basic video edits have been done when the team members finally remember that they need good music and music supervisors. You could easily get hired in the last stage of production, having to quickly get a grip on the decision-makers' preferences, the feasibility of licensing music, and the limitations of the budget. It's intimidating, but it's a part of the profession. If you're passionate, focused, and up for the challenge, the pressure will never be a problem.

With twenty-five years in the business behind me, I've seen a lot of things come and go, and honestly, luck always plays a part in any songwriting success. But as the old saying goes, "Luck is where preparation meets opportunity." The *preparation* part is up to you. Create the best material you can, make it relevant, and make it competitive. Learn the ropes, build lots of relationships, and persevere. The *opportunity* part means that you will probably need to be in Los Angeles, Nashville, or any other large market that allows opportunities to occur, at least in the early stages of your career.

CHAPTER 13

Expanding and Deepening Your Music Career

Once your career is established and you have a steady stream of revenue flowing into your bank account, you want to sit back on your laurels and rest, right?

Well, maybe for a few hours.

Having a sustainable career in music means continual review of your career assets and exploration of ways you can improve and enhance your services and products for your fans and customers. Even if you plan to always work from home, you'll probably eventually need to expand. You might want or need more money. You might need to diversify your offerings, just to keep up with your competition. If nothing else, you know that some of your customers will eventually disappear, and the cost of doing business will continue to rise. So, expansion isn't just an ambitious dream; it's a real-world necessity.

Business expansion usually follows a "vertical" path, meaning the business will try to sell more of its current product or service. It makes sense because the effort usually requires few major adjustments or risks to what you are currently doing. For example, a retailer who sells drums will always try to sell more drums. If the market is hot, that's all he needs to do.

But the market is probably not hot enough for him to sell *only* drums. So, the shop owner expands "horizontally" by adding related merchandise: DVDs, accessories, cases, instructional materials, or any other complementary item that his customers might want. In this way, he not only gains more sales from customers who buy drums, but also from those who might only want a road case or a cowbell.

The principle is no different for a home-based business. A self-employed performing musician might decide to also market music lessons or other services, as well. A songwriter may decide to branch out into commercial jingle writing or even article writing for publications. A festival organizer might branch out into special events planning, awards ceremonies, and office parties.

SWOT YOUR CAREER

I recommend artists at this juncture should pause and take a good look at what they've built so far. An excellent tool to use for this is called the SWOT Analysis.

STRENGTHS	WEAKNESSES
What advantages does your career and/or company have? What unique or lowest-cost resources do you have access to? What do people in your market see as your strengths?	What could you improve? What are people in your market likely to see as weaknesses? What factors lose you sales?
OPPORTUNITIES	THREATS
Where are the good opportunities facing you? What are the interesting trends you are aware of? How can you turn your strengths into opportunities?	What obstacles do you face? What is your competition doing that you should be worried about? Is changing technology threatening your position?

Fig. 13.1. SWOT Analysis

SWOT is a powerful technique for understanding your Strengths and Weaknesses, and for looking at the Opportunities and Threats you face. The essence of the SWOT analysis is to discover what you do well, how you could improve it, whether you are making the most of the opportunities around you, and where there might be changes in your market—such as technological developments, mergers of businesses, or changes in suppliers—that may require corresponding changes in your career approach.

Used in a business context, it helps you carve a sustainable niche in your market. Used in a personal context, it helps you develop your career in a way that takes best advantage of your talents, abilities, and opportunities. What makes SWOT particularly powerful is that, with a little thought, it can help you uncover opportunities you are well placed to exploit. And by understanding the weaknesses of your business, you can manage and eliminate threats that would otherwise catch you unawares. So, look objectively at your company, and use the chart below to assess your business before making any decisions to expand it.

The SWOT exercise will help you get the necessary read on where you are at currently before considering any growth strategies for your business. With this in mind, you can assess which of the expansion strategies in the chart below may make sense for you. We won't look at all of these growth strategies, but will consider several in this chapter.

TEN WAYS TO EXPAND YOUR BUSINESS

Consider these suggestions:

1. Expanding your line of products
2. Importing products
3. Expanding the services you offer
4. Franchising your business
5. Offering consulting services
6. Partnering with another business
7. Exporting your product or service
8. Opening a second location
9. Buying an existing business to expand
10. Offering seminars, workshops, or training services.

DIVERSIFYING YOUR ACTIVITIES AND REVENUE STREAMS

As your career activities grow in one area, you may want to consider diversifying into other areas. Say you perform regularly with several bands. Besides the performing skills you use regularly you may also have a trove of music theory knowledge. This other set of skills can transfer into teaching music, either in a school setting or privately. Or, perhaps, you have a small recording studio. Some typical expansions for recording studios are: record label services, music distribution, music publishing, promotional services, even venue development.

This kind of business expansion is illustrated in the development of New Jersey's Silk City Recordings (http://www.silkcitycd.com/services.html).

Silk City Recordings prides itself in offering "End to End Capabilities" for music clients.

DIVERSIFYING YOUR REVENUE STREAMS

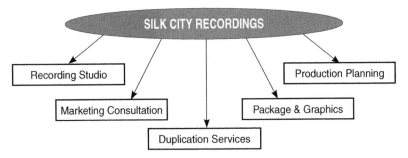

Fig. 13.2. Diversifying Your Revenue Streams

The idea at Silk City is to provide clients with a "soup-to-nuts" solution for their music recording needs. This is Silk City's niche. While many service providers in the industry are very good at producing *individual pieces* of this solution, Silk City differentiates itself in taking clients "end to end" with one team effort, as seen in figure 13.2.

Silk City's line of services include:

- **Consultation:** Helping clients with goals and direction.

- **Artist Development:** Creating a development plan defining all of the required activities and milestones.

- **Production:** Ensuring the best possible physical and emotional environment available to enhance client creativity in the recording process.

- **Recording:** Offering a wide range of studio and remote recording solutions that can be custom configured around client goals (and project budget).

- **Mixing:** Top-notch analog or digital mixing.

- **Mastering:** Offered through a strategic alliance with state-of-the-art digital mastering lab, Luna Sound.

- **Graphics and Graphic Design:** Offers complete layout and design for client projects in a Mac/Quark-ready format, templated for compact disc manufacturing, complete with bar code (UPC). They also offer photography sessions as part of their graphics design services.

- **Manufacturing:** Using state-of-the-art duplication/packaging facilities, Silk City can deliver a "retail ready" product in any format.

- **Distribution:** Provides online retail store distribution for select products and artists, and consultation on best online distribution options.

Of course, each stop on the pipeline is another revenue stream for Silk City Recordings. Many other music companies are offering similar "service packages" to music clients. With smart management, these extra services can grow and develop, and even be spun off or sold as separate businesses as the "mother" company desires.

Artists themselves can also create multiple streams of income. Take Annie Clements, bass player for the band Sugarland. Annie gets the lion's share of her revenue from touring and performing with Sugarland. But she also does vocal session work, teaches singing, and makes music-related jewelry. Each activity brings in additional income, and if the Sugarland gig ever ends, she will be able to continue generating revenue to sustain her career through these other "streams" or profit centers.

If you rely on only one main product or service, especially in this economy, you are like the investor who has just one stock. That stock may go up, but it also may go down. It's risky. You need to diversify your career portfolio. Here are some guidelines for developing your own additional profit centers.

- **Look for compatibility.** Whatever new profit center you choose, be sure that it complements what you are already doing. You need to choose a new endeavor that does not confuse your customers.

- **Look at line extensions.** Offering extra products or services— creating line extensions—often is the best way to create additional profit centers. The key to extending your line is to correctly assess what products or services you can add that complement and expand your current offerings.

- **Start with baby steps.** Whatever additional profit center you offer, be sure to start small. Do not just jump in without first really testing the waters. Start small, and test, test, test. See what works. Project how much money you can make. See what it will cost. Once you are certain that the plan will work, you can then devote more time, money and effort to the project.

42 Different Ways Musicians Can Make Money

This has become a running list from the Future of Music Coalition (FOMC), which now counts forty-two different, discrete revenue streams that artists can exploit. Take a look; add your own.

Songwriter & Composer Revenue

1. **Publisher Advance.** Bulk payment to songwriter/composer as part of a publishing deal.

    Paid to: songwriter/composer by publishing company

    Rate: varies according to deal

2. **Mechanical Royalties.** Royalties generated through the licensed reproduction of recordings of your songs—physical or digital.

    Paid to: songwriter/composer by publisher, label, Harry Fox, or digital aggregator like CD Baby

    Rate: 9.1 cents per manufactured copy of song/composition

3. **Commissions.** Typically a request from an ensemble, presenter, orchestra, or other entity for a composer to create an original work for them.

4. **Public Performance (PRO) Royalties.** Revenue generated when your songs are played on radio, television, and in clubs or restaurants.

   Paid to: songwriter/composer/publisher by ASCAP/BMI/SESAC

5. **Composing Original Works for Broadcast.** Typically a commercial request to compose an original jingle, soundtrack, score, or other musical work for a film, a television or cable show, or an ad agency.

6. **Synch Licenses.** Typically involves licensing an existing work for use in a movie, a documentary, television, video games, the Internet, or a commercial.

   Paid to: songwriters/composers either via publisher or record label, or via a direct licensing deal with the licensee (movie studio, ad agency, etc.) if you are self-published

7. **Sheet Music Sales.** Revenue generated by the sale of songs/compositions as sheet music.

   Paid to: songwriter/composer by publisher, or directly from purchasers if you are selling it on your website or at performances

8. **Ringtones Revenue.** Generated from licensing your songs/compositions for use as ringtones.

   Paid to: songwriter/composer via your publisher, your label, or Harry Fox

9. **ASCAPlus Awards Program.** Awarded by ASCAP to writer members of any genre whose performances are primarily in venues outside of broadcast media.

10. **Publisher Settlement.** Payment from publishers to writers for litigation settlements.

Performer & Recording Artist Revenue

11. **Salary as Member of Orchestra or Ensemble.** Income earned as a salaried member of an orchestra or ensemble.

12. **Shows/Performance Fees.** Revenue generated from playing in a live setting (for nonsalaried players).

13. **Record Label Advance.** Paid to artist as part of signing a deal.

14. **Record Label Support.** Money from label for recording or tour support.

15. **Retail Sales.** Revenue generated from selling physical music in retail stores or via mail-order.

    Paid to: artist/performer by your label, or digital aggregator like CD Baby or Tunecore

16. **Digital Sales.** Revenue generated from selling music digitally/online.

    Paid to: artist/performer by your label, or digital aggregator like CD Baby or Tunecore

17. **Sales at Shows.** Revenue generated from selling recordings of music at shows/live performances.

    Paid to: artist/performer directly by fans

18. **Interactive Service Payments.** Revenue generated when your music is streamed on on-demand services (Rhapsody, Spotify, Rdio).

    Paid to: artist/performer by your label, or digital aggregator like CD Baby or Tunecore

19. **Digital Performance Royalties.** Revenue generated when your sound recordings are played on Internet radio, Sirius XM, Pandora.

    Paid to: performers by SoundExchange

20. **AARC Royalties.** Collected for digital recording of your songs, foreign private copying levies, and foreign record rental royalties, distributed to U.S. artists by AARC.

21. **Neighboring Rights Royalties.** Collected for the foreign performance of your recordings.

22. **AFM/Secondary Markets Fund.** Paid to performers on recordings used in television and other secondary uses.

23. **AFM/Sound Recording Special Payments.** Paid to performers for the sales of recorded music.

24. **AFTRA Contingent Scale.** Payments paid to performers when a recording hits certain sales plateaus.

25. **Label Settlements.** Payments from labels to recording artists for litigation settlements (MP3.com, Limewire).

Session Musician Revenue

26. **Session Musician/Sideman Fees for Studio Work.** Revenue paid to you for playing in a studio. Paid by label, producer, or artist, depending on situation.

27. **Session Musician/Sideman Fees for Live Work.** Revenue paid to you for playing in a live setting. Paid by label, producer, or artist, depending on situation.

28. **AFM/AFTRA Payments.** Payments from the AFM/AFTRA Intellectual Property Rights Distribution Fund, which distributes recording and performance royalties to nonfeatured artists.

Knowledge of Craft: Teaching & Producing

29. **Music Teacher.** Revenue generated from teaching your musical craft.

30. **Producer.** Money from producing another artist's work in the studio or in a live setting.

31. **Honoraria or Speakers Fees.** Revenue generated from speaking opportunities at schools, colleges, and symposia.

Brand-Related Revenue

32. **Merchandise Sales.** Generated from selling branded merchandise (t-shirts, posters, etc.).

    Paid to: artist/performer by fans

33. **Fan Club.** Money directly from fans who are subscribing to your fan club.

34. **YouTube Partner Program.** Shared advertising revenue.

    Paid to: partners by YouTube

35. **Ad Revenue.** Or other miscellaneous income from your website properties (click-thrus, commissions on Amazon, etc.).

36. **Persona Licensing.** Payments from a brand that is licensing your name or likeness (video games, comic books, etc.).

37. **Product Endorsements.** Payments from a brand for you endorsing or using their product.

38. **Acting.** In television, movies, commercials.

Fan, Corporate, & Foundation Funding

39. **Fan Funding.** Money directly from fans to support an upcoming recording project or tour (Kickstarter, Pledge Music).

40. **Sponsorship.** Corporate support for a tour, or for your band/ensemble.

41. **Grants.** From foundations, or state or federal agencies.

Other Sources of Revenue

42. **Arts Administrator.** Money paid to you specifically for managing the administrative aspects of a group that you are a member.

SETTING UP A PRIVATE MUSIC INSTRUCTION SERVICE

I estimate that between 40 and 50 percent of professional musicians have "private teaching" as one of their revenue streams. Some may take on only one or two students per week. Others fill most of their nongig hours with private lessons. Either way, teaching music is an in-demand service and worth considering as another piece of your career as well as another revenue stream.

There are no set qualifications for private music teachers. In practice, however, most have a degree, and many have further teaching and/or performance and theory qualifications. The most important qualifications are musical competence and knowledge of your instrument plus a commitment to and understanding of the teaching and learning processes.

As a music teacher, you will also need:

- patience, perseverance, and excellent communication skills; much of your time will be spent with a range students all at different musical levels as well as with their parents

- high standards of professionalism and professional ethics

- excellent self-management and organizational skills

- the courage to be frank and businesslike when discussing money

- willingness to try new directions and be flexible

- readiness to do the routine jobs as well as the exciting ones.

If you feel like you have the above ingredients, then follow these steps for breaking into this activity.

Get Teaching Experience

Just because you know what a diminished 7th is or can arrange a four-part harmony, doesn't mean you can teach music. Some musicians are naturally gifted for this; others are pedagogically challenged. My suggestion for the latter is you get some experience first by working at an established studio or store-based service (e.g., Guitar Center). This way, you can focus on improving yourself as a teacher without having to worry about running and marketing your own service too.

Choose a Location

If you are willing to travel to student's homes you can either raise your price or stipulate an additional travel fee. You will also want to get a sense for the experience of the other teachers in your area and raise your price accordingly. If you have a music degree and many years of previous teaching experience, this can all improve the appeal of your services.

Teaching out of your home or apartment can save you a lot of time and money, though it presents its own set of challenges. The most difficult part is balancing your personal schedule with your students' schedules, and to really stick to the policies you create. You are using your home as a facility of learning, and so the quality of education you are providing these new students will lie solely in your hands.

Set Your Fees

One of the most important things to consider when setting up a freelance private music lessons business is that the income may be variable at times depending on students coming and going, but there are things you should do to limit this. You need to have control of your clients in any freelance business and not let them control you. Instead of having your students pay per lesson, try having them pay a month at a time so that you can count on a monthly income rather than not knowing if they will show up next week.

How much should you charge? A rule of thumb is to see what other music teachers in your area are charging, and then go with a general average of these. Google "Music studios in (your town name)," "guitar lessons," "private teachers," "guitar studios," and any other combination of these words. Browse through Craigslist in the "music" section too. Call a few to get their rates.

Underbidding the competition could backfire on you, since people generally know that "you get what you pay for," and too low a price might shout "Amateur"! Focus on the *value* you deliver, and keep your fees competitive.

Advertise Your Service

In order to develop a good clientele, you need to recruit students who are interested in taking music lessons privately. In order to target students, you need to first target their parents, since the majority of your students will more than likely be kids. Far and away, the most effective method for reaching your market today is via Internet marketing.

Boston-based musician Greg Arney (see box on next page) has these suggestions: "Upload your ads to Craigslist.com and Backpage.com, on a daily alternating schedule, every week (three times per week on Craigslist, three times per week on Backpage)." Also, "Sign up for Google Local, Yahoo Local, Bing Local, Yelp, InsiderPages, MerchantCircle, YellowPages. These are local business listings. Use the same information in each listing." Also, become a part of the takelessons.com, getlessonsnow.com, privatelessons.com, learningmusician.com, and worldlearningguide.com online indexes. The point is, people search for services at these places just as they once searched in the Yellow Pages.

Many successful private instructors encourage using SEO (search engine optimization) to help their service come up higher in online search results. This, of course, assumes you have a website that can be optimized. (Website design is covered in chapter 10.) For more on SEO, see "Expanding Your Online and Mobile Presence" later in this chapter.

Here are a few additional tried-and-true methods for advertising for your private lessons:

- Distribute flyers to people's newspaper boxes or hang them on their doorknobs. (Keep out of mailboxes, however.)

- Create brochures to put on people's cars or hand out at your local grocery stores.

- Contact your local school district and speak to the music department faculty to spread the word.

- Contact music stores in your area and ask to be put on a private teacher list for music lessons. (Some stores hire their own teachers for private lessons, but others will accept inquiries and direct parents to you if you are on a teacher list.)

- Make business cards and post them on local store advertising bulletin boards.

- Write a parent letter (if you are a music teacher in a school) that explains what private lessons entail, price information, scheduling information, and contact info.

What One Fabulously Successful Private Music Teacher Recommends

Boston-based guitarist and songwriter, Greg Arney, shares his insight on how to maintain a thriving private instruction practice. See more at Bostonguitarlessons.net and Musicianswages.com

1. **Outshine the competition, and you will outlive them.** Do you want to succeed, and be in control of your life? Commit that energy to becoming better than your competition. Most small businesses pop up to make a buck. If you bring something exciting to the market, you will win. How? You're a creator. Be creative!

2. **Don't ever forget about student acquisition.** This is the most important thing to remember, when you're starting out and *every day after that.* Stay focused on getting new students. If you end up with too many, you can raise your price, hire a sidekick, or become more choosy about who you accept.

3. **Mind your student retention.** This is a repeat-customer business. Satisfied students stick around, often for years. The correct outcome is this: most students who meet you will sign up for lessons, stay a long time, pay you even when they miss their lessons, and tell all of their friends about you, perhaps for life. Your studio is not a funnel that puts money into your pocket, but a foundry where musicians are forged. Until your studio has these qualities, it needs more work.

4. **Charge your students a monthly "tuition" charge.** Most teachers start out by charging only the students who show up, but this quickly sinks the ship. Do you only pay rent when you're at home, or do you pay it all of the time? Don't underestimate what people will pay a good teacher.

5. **Use technology for leverage and automate everything.** You don't have time to learn accounting or funds to hire a secretary. Use the power of technology to reduce the time drained by all nonteaching activities. Charge your students automatically every month for their tuition. Collect their contact info in an online Web form. If there is a need for constant rescheduling, deploy an online service to manage that as well. Be a teacher, not an administrator.

6. **Screen out unwanted students.** You can spend as much time as you want chasing down low-quality students. That path leads to vanishing returns. Let your competitors race each other to the bottom. You should reject unwanted students through a combination of: premium pricing, policies preventing the abuse of your time, and clearly explained "student requirements" that each new student agrees to. When you're doing it right, you won't be chasing them; they'll be finding you.

7. **Take risks and try new stuff, all of the time.** Read books on small business development for inspiration and new ideas to try. If something doesn't work, you can stop. The best indicator of your success will be how many new experiments you try, and how rapidly you can incorporate your findings.

ENDORSEMENT DEALS AND SPONSORSHIPS

Ravi is a guitarist and recording artist out of Connecticut who has gotten endorsements and sponsorships on almost every level, from free meals and hotel rooms, to premium guitars and sunglasses. Leveraging his mid '90s stint as lead guitarist on Hanson's world tour, Ravi went about strategically expanding his career by finding additional applications for what he can offer. These have included clinics, lectures, charity work, writing and, now, active participation in another of his passions, aviation.

"The key to securing sponsorships and endorsements," says Ravi, "is maintaining integrity in every aspect of the relationship. Offer potential sponsors maximum exposure through every channel you have, or can create." He recommends putting together "a concise and easy to skim proposal illustrating why this is a synergistic relationship, the details of what you need and the benefits *to them*, and why it is mathematically 'a no-brainer.'" His goal, he says, "is to make the recipient feel like he should be fired if he says 'no,' but promoted if he takes it to his boss!" See this contact as just one step in a long-term, mutually beneficial alliance. "Even if you only need to fund a specific project, the goal should always be to create long-term relationships—the key to any successful business."

Endorsements

It is fairly easy to get an endorsement from a company whose equipment you use. If you have a decent level of local visibility and a good track record of music accomplishments, then the company will often be fine letting you advertise that affiliation. No money or goods are exchanged. Remember, in these deals, *you* are endorsing the company's products, not the other way around. Most musicians, however, aren't thinking about their value to the company but rather, the company's value to them. They just want free stuff. That's not the right attitude.

In general, giving a local band equipment or money isn't necessarily a good deal for the company. Think about it. You are probably already using their equipment, and the people you are playing for aren't their customers. Your fans aren't going to go out and buy the equipment you are using.

Endorsements in 2013 are more about marketability than playing. It's more about relationships with the companies and what you can do for them. I have several friends that are not "big names" that do clinics for reputable companies. They have good endorsements, and their names get spread as a result. They are all competent players and have excellent business skills. Talk to reps at the NAMM (namm.com) show or visit some of your favorite companies online, and try to gather some of the endorsement application requirements. Don't ever be afraid to approach a company's artist relations representative to talk about your situation and your interests in promoting their product.

Finally, you can endorse many guitars, microphones, and keyboards, but can you really endorse two kinds of guitar picks or acoustic strings? Choose wisely so that the companies don't feel betrayed. I've seen musicians dropped from endorsing relationships because they seemed in the eyes of the companies to be backstabbing. Avoid these situations like the plague!

HOW TO BECOME A COMPANY ARTIST

Here is cymbal-maker Zildjian's criteria from its website:

The criteria for evaluating new artists [for an endorsement deal] includes a high profile playing situation, which provides maximum exposure for Zildjian. It also includes, but is not limited to, a record released on a major record label that is charting on Billboard's Top 200, a video in heavy rotation on MTV/VH-1, other television exposure, and headlining a major tour.

Sponsorships

If you are looking for more than just mutual recognition, then you are stepping into the realm of sponsorship. Sponsorships can be *financial-based* (companies pay you money to help support your band's project or tour) or the more common, *product placement sponsorship* (where you get merchandise in exchange for your band advertising a product or service).

Industries that are most likely to steer sponsorship dollars toward musicians include automotive, apparel, beverage, camera, insurance, and technology. If you have a growing audience, then you have sponsorship potential.

Here are some guidelines for securing these kinds of deals.

1. **Know your audience.** What can you deliver to a potential sponsor? Who are your fans? How many are there? What are their demographics? Does this match the company's target market? For company-brand marketers, it's all about reaching the right audience, so you must identify who your fans are. That way, the company can decide if your audience is the right fit.

What can you do for the company? In other words, what are the benefits for the company? These may include:

- Personal endorsement from a loyal customer (meaning, you would spread the good word with conviction!)
- Large and loyal following
- Banner at all gigs
- Advertisement in CD liner notes
- Making brochures available on merchandise table at shows
- Raffles and giveaways
- Stage mentions and testimonials
- Logo on printed materials (flyers, posters)
- Website promotion
- Promotion in band email.

2. **Gather your assets.** When your proposal does the talking for you, it minimizes the time that you have to spend selling the idea. Make sure you have a nice logo, perfect spelling, and clear evidence of your band's successful track record. Your aim is to demonstrate this is a sensible business prospect and is in the company's best interest.

Your proposal should follow this basic outline:

- Summary of the proposal
- What you bring to the table in terms of audience numbers, etc.
- The pitch: what you are seeking in terms of support (monetary and nonmonetary)

- All the benefits for the company

- Summary: This can include media clippings from the band and other success indicators.

Put it all on a single sheet of paper. You're dealing with very busy people and the more succinct you are, the better your chances will be of getting the company's attention.

3. **Think local.** Midwest band, Jakob Freely, locked in close to $1,000 from a local car dealership with a package and a personal testimony that told the story of how the band toured for a year in the type of car the dealership sold. In another example, they locked in sponsorship from a Monster Truck team who saw an affinity between what they sold and an outdoor festival the band was playing.

4. **Target with integrity.** Unfortunately one size does not fit all. It is virtually impossible to send one sponsorship proposal that can address the needs of *every* target company. Your big idea for an automotive brand does not resemble what you would pitch to a cosmetics company. Customize all your communications. Yes, this takes time and research, but the end result will be much more effective communications. Also, go for the companies you believe in, the ones you want your name associated with.

5. **Make contact.** Do you go directly to the brand? If so, do you hit up the brand manager, marketing director, CEO, PR director? Do you go to the brand's agency, and if so, which one? Their ad agency, PR agency, media agency? It's not always easy answering these questions. I recommend you start with the company's website and see if there are any links to sponsorship information. If nothing turns up there, call the company's marketing department, and ask about the procedure for submitting sponsorship proposals.

If you're new to sponsorships, start local. Music shops, cafes, bars, restaurants, and clubs are all prospects. Is the drummer's dad a dentist? Does the guitar player's mom run her own business? Go to these companies, and offer to put up a banner and add their name to your merch in exchange for them financing the goods.

Keep a detailed spreadsheet that records the name of every company you contact, the contact person at each company, and the current status of your communication. This can help you avoid double submitting and can prove useful if you plan on resubmitting at a later date.

Sponsorship through Grants

Another form of sponsorship is receiving grant support. While it is beyond the scope of this book to delve into the arcane world of grantsmanship (yes, it is a specialized skill set), there are some brief guidelines that can help move you in the right directions if you're interested in pursuing them.

First, *clarify exactly what your project is* and what kinds of benefits it holds for social and cultural enrichment (often a key qualifier for grant support). Are you looking to tour? Start a music educational series? Develop a recording lab for inner city kids? Each one of these requires a clear statement about purpose and outcomes.

Second, *investigate all available grants.* Tens of millions of dollars in grant money is left unclaimed each year either because no one applied for the grant, or because no one *qualified* applied. There are the highly visible grants (for example, the National Endowment for the Arts), and then there are the less visible, more idiosyncratic grants. To find out what kinds of grants are available, go to a well-stocked public or university library and find these two books:

- *The Grants Register*

- *The Annual Register of Grant Support*

Begin with grants for *anyone,* and then, using the terrific indexes of these books, zero in on grants specifically for what you're doing. You may find some grants available to only people who live in the town or city you reside in, or with your ethnic background, or who went to a particular high school. You'll be surprised how specific they can get!

Don't overlook nontraditional funding options too, like housing funds, community redevelopment projects, and human service outreach projects. Again, your local library can prove very helpful with these.

Third, *get some training* in how to write a grant proposal. Either speak to someone you know who has written one, or read a book on how it's done. Some cities, like Boston, have branches of the public library that specialize in providing grant resources and expertise to citizens (btw, it's called, The Associated Grantmakers of Massachusetts; 617-426-2606). Check with your own local library for similar organizations in your area.

There's plenty of great information online as well. Check the Resource Directory for more on finding and applying for grants, and developing sponsorship proposals.

EXPANDING YOUR ONLINE AND MOBILE PRESENCE

With the Internet, the information explosion of the past few decades has finally found a technological partner. Entertainment conglomerates and arts-grant bureaucrats still hold the strings to attractively fat purses. But their power is being tempered by the reach of the Web and the resourcefulness of creative minds paired with cheap, versatile tools.

The Internet adds networks of links over society, connecting people with information, action, and each other. It is in those connections that value is created, efficiency is found, knowledge is grown, and relationships are formed. Every link and every click is a connection, and with every connection, a network is born or grows stronger. That's how the Internet spun its web, as the network of networks.

Publishing in all its forms has been revolutionized by the 'Net. It's often been said that "freedom of the press belongs to those who own one." The 'Net enables everyone to own the press. Rather than competing with other media outlets for the public's attention, the media is suddenly competing with the public itself. Individuals can decide on their own what's important and what's not, set up their own information "filters" (rather than rely on the editorial judgment of faceless media conglomerates), and get closer to sources of information than ever before.

But that was only Web 1.0. Version 2.0 has arrived, *and in force.*

We are all an integral part of the Web 2.0 business economy because every time you click on Google, Wikipedia, eBay, or Amazon, you are sparking "network effects." Web 2.0 turbocharges networks because online users are no longer limited by how many things they can find, see, or download off the Web, but rather by how many things they can do, interact with, combine, remix, upload, change, and customize for themselves.

This seismic shift isn't just limited to how works are created. Already, digital technology has caused sweeping changes in how people gain access to creative works. Some venerable institutions, such as encyclopedias and newspapers, are disappearing because of the digital revolution. Newspaper publishers paid little attention to "a guy named Craig" until his list cannibalized a huge portion of the industry's most profitable revenues (classified ads). And the publishers of the *Encyclopedia Britannica* never anticipated that a loosely organized group of volunteers could create an online encyclopedia (Wikipedia) that would supplant their long-established reference work.

Independent musicians have long turned to the Internet in their struggle for recognition outside traditional industry channels such as radio and MTV. Many are discovering that savvy online marketing may never catapult them to stardom, but it can give their careers an important lift. Note the story of how Death Cab for Cutie's Ben Gibbard discovered an artist named Devin Davis on a site called Music for Robots (www.music-for-robots.com). He enjoyed Davis's music and began an email correspondence, which eventually led to Gibbard inviting Davis to open a show for his band.

You never know who is watching or who is listening on the 'Net.

Understanding Your Internet Power Tools

Internet marketing has quickly developed a sophistication that allows the online businesses to get a helpful peek into how people shop, what they're most interested in, and what works to make sales. We've already explored your social media toolkit. Now, let's briefly look at some other tools you can use to boost your online and mobile presence.

SEO (Search Engine Optimization)

Though this may sound as exciting as watching paint dry, search engine optimization is really a smart and relatively painless way to make your name or your company name come up higher in search engine results. Appearing on Google's first page ensures you a good measure of traffic volume. As a matter of fact, two-thirds of users click on the first page results and most of them don't go beyond the third page. Plus, two searches out of ten on Google are music-related, so this is definitely an area you want to spend some time on.

Musician Greg Arney (mentioned earlier in this chapter) applied some SEO principles to his guitar lesson service, and before he knew it, his site was coming up number 1 in Google in guitarist-saturated Boston. He now has more students than he can handle, and he is subcontracting work out to other instructors.

SEO can be divided into two separate categories: *on-page SEO* and *off-page SEO*.

- **On-page SEO** refers to how well your website's content is presented to search engines. This can often be improved immediately.

- **Off-page SEO** refers to your site's overall "authority" on the Web, which is determined by what other websites say about your site. This can take time to improve.

It is of prime importance to build your website according to SEO guidelines with a focus on on-page SEO in order to come up higher in the results. These guidelines include:

- Having some text (blog, content association, reviews) in order to incorporate "meta tags" that will get you listed on search engines.

- Using relevant key words within your content.

- No use of Flash (slows loading time).

SEO evolves rapidly, and its techniques are always innovating. The site, Searchenginewatch.com, will keep you updated on all SEO developments. You don't have to be a pro, but don't hesitate to seek professional advice via the many free resources available. See the Resources Directory in the appendix for some of the best.

Podcasting

For those unable to afford the multimillion-dollar price tag of a broadcast tower and FCC license, podcasting offers a fun, low-cost (sometimes no cost), and easy way to create and publish audio material for a potentially huge audience using downloadable audio files like MP3s.

A podcast is essentially a radio show that is frozen and time-shifted. Podcasting makes audio files available online in a manner that allows these files to be automatically downloaded to a subscriber's computer (or portable music device) at the user's leisure.

eMarketer (emarketer.com) reports that in 2012, 65 percent of all Americans were aware of podcasting, while 25 percent listened to podcasts regularly, an increase from 10 percent in 2008. In addition, video podcasting viewership was up to 20 percent for Americans in 2012.

Software called "podcatchers" can be easily programmed to continually search the Internet and find listener's favorite shows and then download updates automatically. It's sort of like a Tivo, but without the costly subscription service. Again, testifying to podcasting's popularity, Apple began including a podcatching function in its iTunes software (beginning with version 4.9).

How can *you* use podcasts? Performing songwriter/author Gilli Moon offers these suggestions from her trove of podcast wisdom:

- You can have it embedded in your own artist website, your Facebook page, anywhere you can manipulate the HTML code of a webpage you host on the Internet.

- Fans can listen to your podcast either through the Internet, there and then from your webpage, download the MP3s to their computers through a podcatcher, or download the podcast to their iPods through a podcatcher subscribed to a RSS feed so that every time you as the podcast host change your show, it automatically updates on their computer or iPod. (This is the coolest part!)

- Fans can also take the HTML code of your podcast and put it on their sites, thereby adding to the ultimate goal of spreading your music far and wide."

(Source: www.gilli.net/article-podcasting.htm)

Videocasting/Vlogs

The average Internet user watches an astounding 186 videos a month, according to comScore Inc., a global digital market measurement service. This includes news and entertainment clips, personal videos, advertising videos gone viral—you name it—and three quarters tell a friend or business colleague about it.

YouTube has become the go-to source for all things video, and you can review chapter 10 for some introductory info on this phenomenon. What makes YouTube a hit is its ability to trans-code anything and produce an easy-to-watch and easy-to-embed streaming Flash movie. You simply upload a video you made on a digital camera or camcorder, and YouTube's computers turn it into a Flash video. Producers, the public, wannabe actors, corporations out for publicity, and clip collectors all use YouTube.

Musicians and music-related companies—from "Obama Girl," who crooned about her crush on Barack Obama, to the tread-milling band OK Go, to lesser-known songwriters like Julia Nunes—are finding opportunities to connect on a visual (and emotional) level with potential fans and customers through online video.

Here are some tips for making the most of your online video presence.

Production

It all comes down to good planning, so hunker down and absorb the following advice:

- **Make it short.** Thirty to ninety seconds is ideal. Break down long stories into bite-sized clips.

- **Design for remixing.** Create a video that is simple enough to be remixed over and over again by others. Example: "Dramatic Hamster."

- **Don't make an outright ad.** If a video feels like an ad, viewers won't share it unless it's really amazing. Example: Sony Bravia.

- **Make it shocking.** Give a viewer no choice but to investigate further. Example: "UFO Haiti."

- **Use "fake" headlines.** Make the viewer say, "Holy Toledo, did that actually happen?!" Example: "Stolen Nascar."

Promotion

How do you get the first 50,000 views you need to get your videos onto the "Most Viewed" list? It'll take some work, but here are some tips:

- **Post to relevant blogs** (see section later in this chapter).

- **Post to relevant forums.** Even start new threads and embed your videos.

- **MySpace.** Plenty of users allow you to embed YouTube videos right in the comments section of their MySpace pages. Take advantage of this.

- **Facebook.** Share, share, share.

- **Email lists.** Send the video to a qualified email list. Depending on the size of the list (and the recipients' willingness to receive links to YouTube videos), this can be a very effective strategy.

- **Friends.** Make sure everyone you know watches the video, and try to get them to email it out to their friends, or at least share it on Facebook.

YouTube is a style now, an aesthetic of its own. It didn't take very long, but it has lodged itself into our consumer psyche as a recognizable visual, aural, and narrative convention. In that sense, it's a huge and notable success deserving of a special footnote in media history.

Performing Live Online

In early 2006, Scottish artist Sandi Thom traded in the traditional approach of squeezing in a van with her bandmates for a webcam. She then announced a run of twenty-one shows to be performed on consecutive nights in the basement of her flat in South London. Though her flat could hold only six people, 70 tuned in to the first performance over the Web. The next night it went up to 670, and by the middle of the second week she was performing to a peak audience of 70,000.

The best part about these shows is that they can be easily shared on social media, and give your fans a reason to talk about you. Also, each online show can be recorded and archived, giving you new material to use to promote in the future.

To put on a show online, try broadcasting your live show through a streaming service like UStream (ustream.com) or LiveStream (livestream.com). As long as you have a webcam or camera-enabled smartphone or tablet, all you need to do is log on, point, and shoot. Treat these like any other gig. Put them on your show calendar, and promote them to your fans so they know to tune in.

For more intimate shows, you can also use group video calling services like Skype or Google Hangouts, since these services usually limit the amount of viewers that can join in. Small online concerts like these are not only an online way to mimic the intimacy of a house concert, they're also a great way to reward your die-hard fans, and supporters.

WHAT MADE "GANGNAM STYLE" A HIT?

1. It captured the essence of pop in the YouTube era: It blended the perfect combination of weirdness, virality, dance moves, and catchy melody, and that made it one of the most popular pieces of entertainment in recent times.

2. Remixes: From a one-thousand person flash mob in Jakarta to cover videos from Ai Weiwei and Mitt Romney, hundreds of thousands of parodies have been uploaded to YouTube, some of which have tens of millions of views. In fact, fan tributes to "Gangnam Style" are now being viewed 20 million times every single day.

3. It delivered a bit of exotica from the Far East.

4. When news agencies started to pick it up in October 2012, the video just exploded. Everyone had to talk about it because it was a trending controversial video.

5. It cross-pollinated by getting picked up by Ellen, nighttime talk shows, etc.

6. It was fun to comment on. Everyone had an opinion, and soon fans and haters made spoofs and remixes.

7. One billion views and counting!

MP3 Blogs

Music blogs—weblogs that present audio files from their host's collections—are another opportunity for music promotion. Nobody's sure who came up with the first MP3 blog, and the evolution of the form was gradual enough that it's hard to pinpoint the date of its origin, although it was probably around 2002.

As recently as July 2004, there were only two dozen music blogs. Now (mid-2013), there are well over 10,000, with more appearing every day from all over the world, specializing in everything from hard-core punk to pre-World War II gospel. The music blogosphere has developed into a subculture with its own unofficial leaders and unwritten rules, and it is becoming a significant force in the recording industry, which mostly seems to be smiling on the phenomenon. In some genres, like hip-hop, blogs play the additional roles of scouting tool and virtual farm team.

The growing influence of blogs on the music industry is undeniable, and there are few better examples of a band thriving due to blog exposure than Passion Pit. The small Cambridge, Massachusetts band started innocuously enough, but once their first single "Sleepyhead" hit the blogosphere, it quickly spread all over the Web, garnering the band worldwide exposure in only a few weeks. Not so long ago, bands like Passion Pit had to fight to get their music on the radio, but today, getting music out to a large audience is done with simply the click of a button.

TEN POPULAR MUSIC BLOGS (MP3 AGGREGATORS)

1. Earvolution	6. MP3 Jackpot
2. Fluxblog	7. Mixtaper
3. HypeMachine	8. Lonesome Music
4. My Shared Folder	9. Some Velvet Blog
5. Stereogum	10. Totally Fuzzy

There's a relatively standard format for MP3 blogs that has unofficially evolved: one or two songs a day, each one accompanied by a paragraph or two about the song or the artist. Some bloggers also include photographs or links to places where their readers can buy the CD on which each song appears.

Most focus on little-known musicians or rare and out-of-print recordings. Few will post something that's already a huge radio hit or by a very famous artist, and it's frowned upon to post more than a single song from a given album.

Of course, one of the first questions a lot of people ask about MP3 blogs is if they are legal. The answer is that it's a gray area, and MP3 bloggers tend to work from the principle that it's easier to receive forgiveness than permission. No one has been sued, and nobody's yet talking about suing them. In fact, Universal Music Group's European division is paying Matthew Perpetua, the twenty-five-year-old curator of Fluxblog (fluxblog.com), to be a talent scout. (He sends them an annotated CD-R of his favorite new music once a month!)

All a prospective blogger needs is a site, a way to host the files, and a way to get the word out. The site is easy enough: free services such as Blogger.com or Wordpress.com provide the basic setup for a lot of music bloggers. The word can spread through friends' links, or through clearinghouse "metablogs" like MP3blogs.org. And YouSendIt.com, originally intended as a free tool for emailing large files, has also become a favorite resource for nascent MP3 bloggers.

Popular MP3 blog, *Earvolution*, is out to prove that music blogs can spawn the next record labels. Indeed, music blogs are organizing concerts, being quoted in television, and releasing independent albums—just like a record label. Music observer Eliot Van Buskirk agrees, and points out that these blogs, (1) have the audience, (2) fans already think of them as tastemakers, (3) they have lots of experience in judging new music (hmm...that one's questionable), and (4) they can submit songs to digital distribution networks such as IODA, the Orchard, IRIS, Tunecore, and so on, just like anyone else can.

To the extent that all next generation entrepreneurs need a point of entry, blogs do provide that for free. Time will tell if they can indeed provide the A&R filtering and marketing dynamics traditional labels provided.

To find and research music blogs, use the search engine at hypem.com/blog or musicblog.wikia.com/wiki/Music_Blog_Directory.

Mobile Apps

There are around 110 million Americans who own a smartphone, and more are signing on every day. This is a huge audience and millions of potential new fans. Using mobile apps for music isn't that new anymore, so what can musicians do to offer up more than the regular music stream and tour schedule to help engage their fans?

Always pushing boundaries with music, touring, and technology, England's Dan Deacon was bound to bring something fresh to the table. Renowned for live gigs that invite participation, interaction, and huge amounts of fun, Deacon decided to take things one step further and create a mobile app that lets fans in the crowd become part of the audiovisual show. Inspired by audience-based cell phone interactive pieces he has performed in the past, Deacon approached programming and instrument friends to develop an application that turns your phone into a synchronized light display and accompanying instrument at upcoming Dan Deacon gigs. The colors and sounds change depending on the location within each venue.

Berklee College of Music professor and top-selling smooth jazz artist Walter Beasley took a different approach with his two apps, *Sound Production for Saxophone* and *Circular Breathing.* They are essentially instructional videos in an app format. But the real beauty of this format is how it allows you to do a deep dive into some very specific or niche knowledge. It gives you "inside information" that would have otherwise taken years to glean via in-person lessons, music classes, and simple osmosis. Beasley continues to roll out a new app about every two months and his audience continues to grow.

For some clear, nontechnical instruction on how to build an app from scratch, check out www.theappbuilder.com.

CODA

To make it in music, you must have that fire in the belly, that burning desire to succeed. You must believe that no matter what the odds, no matter what others say, you will persevere. You will do what it takes. You will learn to do the business stuff, the networking, the bookkeeping, the planning, and the scutwork. You will bounce back from rejection, depression, and obsession. Because disappointments, highs and lows, and critics are everywhere. Not everything will feel like a masterpiece (or even be well received). In a way, that's good. You'll keep trying to improve.

Self-promotion means "DIY," and this typically means "do it yourself." This sounds nice, but hides a dark reality too. Doing *everything* yourself is a recipe for burnout. At the GRAMMY Awards, the winners thank their mentors, family, and friends. They are the first to say they didn't do it alone. "Self-promotion" doesn't necessarily mean doing everything yourself. That approach often leads to an overly heavy burden few musicians are capable of handling— one which a lot of musicians soon discover requires more than they are willing (or able) to give. It may be better to understand DIY as "decide it yourself." Musicians today have the opportunity to decide what path they wish to pursue, using the amazing array of tools and resources available to them.

And despite the many resources available for the DIY approach, artists are still drawn to record companies for affirmation and support. They may have the tools to record, publish, and distribute their own work, but they still want record labels as partners to support their professional careers. Of course, the nature of the "record deal" is evolving. Big money advances to new signings are harder to find, but at the same time labels have adapted their services to new areas such as brand partnerships, merchandising, and live music where they share revenues with artists.

So, though the "industry" may change, the music "trade" remains the same: artist sharing music with audience who then supports artist. The key, as always, is to be authentic in your music and consistent in your career and business development. That's a formula that ensures long-term music careers. You bring the former and, hopefully, this book will help with the latter.

Forward!

Resource Directory

CHAPTER 1. BEYOND THE NEW MUSIC BUSINESS

BOOKS

Anderson, Chris. *The Long Tail: Why the Future of Business Is Selling Less of More.* New York: Hyperion, 2006.

Barabasi, Lazlo. *Linked: How Everything Is Connected to Everything Else and What It Means.* New York: Plume Books, 2003.

Carr, Nick. *The Big Switch: Rewiring the World from Edison to Google.* New York: Norton & Co, 2009.

Goodman, Fred. *Fortune's Fool: Edgar Bronfman, Jr., Warner Music, and an Industry in Crisis.* New York: Simon & Schuster, 2010.

Knopper, Steve. *Appetite for Self-Destruction: The Spectacular Crash of the Record Industry in the Digital Age.* New York: Free Press, 2009.

Pink, Daniel. *A Whole New Mind: Why Right-Brainers Will Rule the Future.* New York: Riverhead Trade, 2006.

Tapscott, Don, and Williams, Anthony. *Macrowikinomics: Rebooting Business and the World.* New York: Portfolio, 2010.

ONLINE

AllMusic: allmusic: www.allmusic.com. The online "Grand Central" of all things musical.

Billboard: www.billboard.com. Core industry news.

The Daily Chord: www.sxsw.com/music/daily_chord

The Hollywood Reporter: www.hollywoodreporter.com

Leonhard, Gerd. *Music 2.0: Essays*. Media Futurist, 2008. www.mediafuturist.com

Variety: www.variety.com

Wired and Wired News: www.wired.com

MUSIC INDUSTRY BLOGS

Hypebot: www.hypebot.com

Music Ally: www.musically.com

Music Biz Blogs: www.musicbizblogs.com

Music Career Juice (author's blog): www.mcareerjuice.com

New Music Strategies: www.newmusicstrategies.com

CHAPTER 2. GETTING READY TO DO BUSINESS

BOOKS

Brodsky, Norm, et. al. *The Knack: How Street-Smart Entrepreneurs Learn to Handle Whatever Comes Up*. New York: Portfolio, 2008.

Durst, Christine, et. al. *The 2-Second Commute: Join the Exploding Ranks of Freelance Virtual Assistants*. Pompton Plains, NJ: Career Press, 2005.

Kao, John. *Jamming: The Art & Discipline of Business Creativity*. New York: Harper/Business, 1996.

Spellman, Peter. *Indie Business Power: A Step-by-Step Guide for 21st-Century Music Entrepreneurs*. Boston: MBS Media, 2008.

ONLINE

Business Owners' Idea Café: www.businessownersideacafe.com

Entrepreneur: www.entrepreneur.com

Fast Company: www.fastcompany.com

Forbes: www.forbes.com

Fortune: www.fortune.com

Springwise: www.springwise.com

Zero Million: www.zeromillion.com

ORGANIZATIONS

Freelancers Union: www.freelancersunion.org

National Association for the Self-Employed: www.nase.org

SCORE (Service Corps of Retired Executives): www.score.org

U.S. Small Business Administration: archive.sba.gov

CHAPTER 3. PLAN YOUR WORK, WORK YOUR PLAN

BOOKS

Adams, Rhonda. *The Successful Business Plan: Secrets & Strategies, 5th ed.* Palo Alto, CA: The Planning Shop, 2010.

Beam, Lisa Sonora. *The Creative Entrepreneur: A DIY Visual Guidebook for Making Business Ideas Real.* Minneapolis, MN: Quarry Books, 2008.

Boldt, Laurence. *Zen and the Art of Making a Living.* Revised edition. New York: Penguin Books, 2009.

Field, Shelly. *Career Opportunities in the Music Industry, 6th ed.* New York: Checkmark Books, 2009.

—*Managing Your Career in the Music Industry.* New York: Checkmark Books, 2008.

Guillebeau, Chris. *The $100 Startup: Reinvent the Way You Make a Living, Do What You Love, and Create a New Future.* New York: Crown Business, 2012.

Lee, Jennifer. *The Right-Brain Business Plan: A Creative, Visual Map for Success.* Novato, CA: New World Library, 2011.

Spellman, Peter. *Plan Your Band! Sample Business Plan and Investor Agreement All-in-One.* Boston: MBS Business Media, 2009.

ONLINE

Biz Sugar: www.bizsugar.com

Bplan: www.bplans.com. Business plan examples.

Business Owner's Toolkit: www.toolkit.cch.com

CEO Express: www.ceoexpress.com

CHAPTER 4. SMART MANAGEMENT FOR THE PROFESSIONAL MUSICIAN

BOOKS

Beach, Jim, et. al. *School for Startups: The Breakthrough Course for Guaranteeing Small Business Success in 90 Days or Less.* Columbus, OH: McGraw-Hill, 2011.

Chandler, Lynette, et al. *Solopreneurs are Smarter: Why Solopreneurs Rock the Online Business World.* Amazon Digital Services, 2012.

Horowitz, Sara, and Sciarra Poynter, Toni. *The Freelancer's Bible: Everything You Need to Know to Have the Career of Your Dreams—On Your Terms.* New York: Workman Publishing Co., 2012.

Marcone, Stephen. *Managing Your Band, 4th ed.* Milwaukee, WI: HiMarks Publishing Co./Hal Leonard Corp., 2006.

McBean, Bill. *The Facts of Business Life: What Every Successful Business Owner Knows that You Don't.* Hoboken, NJ: Wiley, 2012.

Urquhart-Brown, Susan. *The Accidental Entrepreneur: The 50 Things I Wish Someone Had Told Me About Starting a Business.* Saranac Lake, NY: AMACOM, 2008.

ONLINE: APPS, TOOLS, & PLATFORMS

Bandcamp: www.bandcamp.com

Free Management Library: www.managementhelp.org

Hourly Rate Calculator: www.freelanceswitch.com/rates

Indie Band Manager: www.indiebandmanager.com

Livewire Musician: www.livewiremusician.com

Nimbit: www.nimbit.com

CHAPTER 5. NETWORKING IN THE NEW MUSIC ECONOMY

BOOKS

Baber, Anne, and Waymon, Lynne. *Make Your Contacts Count: Networking Know-How for Business and Career Success*. Saranac Lake, NY: AMACOM, 2007.

Burg, Bob. *Endless Referrals: Network Your Everyday Contacts into Sales Money, 3rd ed*. New York: McGraw-Hill, 2005.

Edwards, Paul, and Edwards, Sarah. *Teaming Up: The Small Business Guide to Collaborating with Others to Boost Your Earnings and Expand Your Horizons, 5th ed*. New York: J. P. Tarcher/Putnam,1999.

Kimpel, Dan. *Networking Strategies for the New Music Business, 2nd ed*. Boston: ArtistPro/Publishing, 2011.

Zack, Devora. *Networking for People Who Hate Networking: A Field Guide for Introverts, the Overwhelmed, and the Underconnected*. Berrett-Koehler Publishers, 2010.

ONLINE

AAMPP: www.aampp.net

Brazen Careerist: www.brazencareerist.com

Facebook: www.facebook.com

Just Plain Folks: www.justplainfolks.org

Linked In: www.linkedin.com

TalentCom Media: www.talentspace.org

CHAPTER 6. ESSENTIALS OF MUSIC PROMOTION AND MARKETING

BOOKS

Ancowitz, Nancy. *Self-Promotion for Introverts: The Quiet Guide to Getting Ahead*. New York: McGraw-Hill, 2009.

Baron, Cynthia. *Creating a Digital Portfolio: A Guide to Marketing and Self-Promotion, 2nd ed*. New York: New Riders, 2009.

Budelmann, Kevin, et. al. *Essential Elements for Brand Identity: 100 Principles for Designing Logos and Building Brands.* Minneapolis, MN: Rockport Publishers, 2013.

Gordon, Kim. *Maximum Marketing, Minimum Dollars.* Chicago: Kaplan Publishing, 2006.

Levinson, Jay Conrad. *The Best of Guerilla Marketing.* Boston: Houghton Mifflin, 2011.

Mattimore, Bryan W. *Idea Stormers: How to Lead and Inspire Creative Breakthroughs.* Hoboken, NJ: Jossey-Bass, 2012.

Spellman, Peter. *Indie Marketing Power: The Resource Guide for Maximizing Your Music Marketing, 3rd ed.* Boston: MBS Media, 2012.

Weinschenk, Susan. *100 Things Every Designer Needs to Know about People.* New York: New Riders, 2011.

STREET TEAMS

Fancorps: www.fancorps.com. An online app that gives the artist (or manager or label) the ability to easily develop, organize, and maintain a street team.

Music Street Teams: www.musicstreetteams.com. Helps put together street teams in cities all over the United States.

CROWDFUNDING PLATFORMS

Artist Share: www.artistshare.com

CASH Music: www.cashmusic.org

Crowdfunding: www.crowdfunding.com

Fundable: www.fundable.com

Kickstarter: www.kickstarter.com

Pledge Music: www.pledgemusic.com

SERVICES TO HELP YOU SET UP YOUR EPK (ELECTRONIC PRESS KIT)

Bandcamp: www.bandcamp.com

Bandzoogle: www.bandzoogle.com

ePressKitz: www.epresskitz.com

Nimbit: www.nimbit.com

ReverbNation: www.reverbnation.com

Sonicbids: www.sonicbids.com

CHAPTER 7. FINDING GIGS IN ALL THE RIGHT PLACES: TAPPING THE SOURCES OF LESSER-KNOWN MUSIC WORK

BOOKS

Goldstein, Jeri, et al. *How to Be Your Own Booking Agent.* Revised edition. New Music Times, 2008.

Miller, Mary Fallon. *How to Get a Job with a Cruise Line, 5th ed.* St. Petersburg, FL: Ticket to Adventure, Inc., 2001.

Smith, Darren L. *Parks Directory of the United States and Canada, 3rd ed.* Detroit: Omnigraphics, 2001.

Weissman, Dick. *Making a Living in Your Local Music Market: Realizing Your Marketing Potential, 4th ed.* Milwaukee, WI: Hal Leonard Corp., 2010.

ONLINE

Armed Forces Entertainment: www.armedforcesentertainment. com

Bandago: www.bandago.com. Good deals on van rentals.

Concerts in Your Home: www.concertsinyourhome.com

Frybrid: www.frybrid.com. Diesel/vegetable oil fuel.

House Concerts: www.houseconcerts.com

Indie on the Move: www.indieonthemove.com. Venues database and tour booking contacts.

MusicNomad: www.musicnomad.com. Check out the "My Tour Manager" for mapping out and running music tours.

National Association for Campus Activities (NACA): www.naca.org

Pollstar: www.pollstar.com. Concert tour information database including all genres of music and other events.

Sonicbids/Baskstage: www.sonicbids.com. A rich database of performing and other music branding opportunities using an electronic alternative to the traditional press kit and lots more.

Festivals and Venues Online

FestivalFinder: www.festivalfinder.com

Festival Network Online: www.festivalnet.com

CHAPTER 8. PLAYING THE CLUBS: GETTING YOUR FOOT IN THE DOOR WITHOUT GETTING IT SLAMMED

BOOKS

Atkins, Martin. *Tour:Smart: And Break the Band.* Chicago: Soluble, 2007.

Galper, Hal. *The Touring Musician: A Small Business Approach to Booking Your Band on the Road.* New York: Watson-Guptil Publications, 2000.

Reynolds, Andy. *The Tour Book: How to Get Your Music on the Road.* Independence, KY: Course Technology, 2012.

Shih, Patricia. *Gigging: A Practical Guide for Musicians.* New York: Allworth Press, 2003.

ONLINE

The Musician's Atlas: www.musiciansatlas.com

The Indie Bible: www.indiebible.com

Meeting Professionals International Directory: www.mpiweb.org

CHAPTER 9. FIFTEEN WAYS TO GET THE MOST OUT OF EVERY GIG

BOOKS

Filichia, Peter. *Let's Put on a Musical: How to Choose the Right Show for Your Theater.* Revised & Expanded Edition. New York: Backstage Books, 2007.

Lane, Stewart F. *Let's Put on a Show! Theatre Production for Novices.* Subtext, 2009.

Shagan, Rena. *Booking & Tour Management for the Performing Arts, 3rd ed.* New York: Allworth Press, 2001.

ONLINE

Pollstar: www.pollstar.com. Concert tour information database including all genres of music and other events.

Volunteer Lawyers for the Arts: www.vlany.org. Organization providing low-cost legal services to artists and arts organizations.

CHAPTER 10. MAPPING YOUR MEDIA PLAN

BOOKS

Brogan, Chris, and Smith, Julien. *The Impact Equation: Are You Making Things Happen or Just Making Noise?* New York: Portfolio Hardcover, 2012.

Comm, Joel. *Twitter Power: How to Dominate Your Market One Tweet at a Time, 2nd ed.* Hoboken, NJ: Wiley, 2010.

Fidelman, Mark. *Socialized!: How the Most Successful Businesses Harness the Power of Social.* Bibliomotion, 2012.

Kabani, Shama. *The Zen of Social Media Marketing: An Easier Way to Build Credibility, Generate Buzz, and Increase Revenue, 2013 Edition.* BenBella Books, 2013.

Scott, David Meerman. *The New Rules of Marketing & PR: How to Use Social Media, Online Video, Mobile Applications, Blogs, News Releases, and Viral Marketing to Reach Buyers Directly, 4th ed.* Hoboken, NJ: Wiley, 2013.

ONLINE

Gigging & Touring Promo

Indie Band Manager: www.indiebandmanager.com

The Indie Bible: www.indiebible.com

The Musician's Atlas: www.musiciansatlas.com

College Radio Databases

A2zColleges.com:
   www.a2zcolleges.com/college_radio/radio_us_east.htm

The Record Industry.com:
   www.therecordindustry.com/collegeradio-AK.htm

Internet-Related Resources

• *Internet Stats and Surveys*

Internet World Stats: www.internetworldstats.com

Living Internet: www.livinginternet.com

• *Website Development Tools*

Bandzoogle: www.bandzoogle.com. Free website templates and more.

Nimbit: www.nimbit.com. Website management tools and hosting services designed for the entertainment industry. Free website templates.

The Starter League: www.starterleague.com. Intermediate-level resource for Web development

• *Website Resources*

ArtistServer: www.artistserver.com

Go Daddy: www.godaddy.com. Domain name registration and hosting.

Hostbaby: www.hostbaby.com. Hosting service of CD Baby (www.cdbaby.com).

Register.com: www.register.com. Domain name registration and hosting.

• *Sound Utilities for the Web*

GoldWave Inc.: www.goldwave.com

Harmony Central: www.harmonycentral.com

MAGIX Music Maker: www.magix.com/us/music-maker

TheFreeSite.com: www.thefreesite.com

• *Video Editing Tools*

Final Cut Pro (Apple): www.apple.com/finalcutpro

iMovie (Apple): www.apple.com/ilife/imovie

Movie Maker (Microsoft): www.windows.microsoft.com

Vegas Pro (Sony): www.sonycreativesoftware.com

• *Online Store Options*

Amazon Advantage Program: www.amazon.com/advantage

Get Shopped (Word Press): www.getshopped.org

Paypal Shopping Cart: www.paypal.com

Volusion: www.volusion.com

Yahoo! Stores: www.smallbusiness.yahoo.com/ecommerce

• *Online Advertising Options*

Burst Media: www.burstmedia.com

Google AdSense: www.google.com/intl/en/ads/

• *Advanced Internet Promotion and Marketing*

ClickZ: www.clickz.com

The eMarketing Digest: www.webbers.com/emark

The Internet Marketing Center: www.marketingtips.com

Web Marketing Today: www.webmarketingtoday.com

CHAPTER 11. WORKING YOUR MEDIA PLAN

BOOKS

Safko, Lon. *The Social Media Bible: Tactics, Tools, and Strategies for Business Success, 2nd ed.* Hoboken, NJ: Wiley, 2010.

Scott, David Meerman. *The New Rules of Marketing & PR: How to Use Social Media, Online Video, Mobile Applications, Blogs, News Releases, and Viral Marketing to Reach Buyers Directly, 4th ed.* Hoboken, NJ: Wiley, 2013.

Wilson, Don. *Facebook Demystified: The 10 Critical Components of a Viral Fan Page.* Donald G. Wilson, 2013.

Yudkin, Marcia. *Six Steps to Free Publicity.* Revised Edition. Pompton Plains, NJ: Career Press, 2003.

DIRECTORIES

Bacon's Publicity Checker. Chicago: Bacon Publishing Co., annual.

Gale's Directory of Publications and Broadcast Media. Farmington Hills, MI: Gale Research, Inc., annual.

Gebbie Press All-in-One Directory. New Paltz, NY: Gebbie Press, annual.

ONLINE PUBLICITY

Bill Stoller's Publicity Insider Links: www.publicityinsider.com/prlinks.asp

Creative Marketing Solutions: www.yudkin.com/publicityideas.htm

RADIO

Davis, Rick. *Get Media Airplay: A Guide to Song Exposure, Music/ Product Tie-Ins and Radio-Play Spins.* Milwaukee, WI: Hal Leonard Corp., 2006.

Geller, Valerie. *Creating Powerful Radio.* London: Focal Press, 2007.

Keith, Michael. *Radio Cultures: The Sound Medium in American Life.* New York: Peter Lang Publishing, 2008.

Radio Airplay 101. Series by Bryan Farrish: www.musicdish.com/mag/list.php3?author=78

Ramsey, Mark. *Fresh Air: Marketing Gurus on Radio.* Bloomington, IN: iUniverse, 2005.

RADIO ONLINE

FOLKDJ-L: www.folkradio.org. Lists folk stations, shows, DJs, playlists, and charts.

International Radio Station List: www.radio-locator.com. Lists
U.S., Canadian, European, and other international stations.

National Public Radio: www.npr.org

StreamFinder.com: www.streamfinder.com. Links to over 9,000
Internet radio stations.

INTERNET RADIO

Lastfm: www.last.fm. A portal to thousands of traditional and
Web-only stations.

List of Radio Stations on the Internet: www.radio-locator.com

Live365: www.live365.com

Pandora: www.pandora.com

PureVolume: www.purevolume.com

SHOUTCast Radio: www.shoutcast.com

Spinner: www.spinner.com

RADIO MONITORING

BDS (Broadcast Data Systems): nielsen.com/us/en/industries/
media-entertainment.html

RADIO SYNDICATES

Syndicates are networks that redistribute broadcasts to a variety of
radio stations around the country. One spin on a syndicate means
your music is heard on every station in that syndicate, making them
a cost-effective marketing tactic.

Echoes. Chester Springs. Syndicated to 135 public radio stations.
John Diliberto, Music Director. P: 610-458-0780.
echoes@well.com. www.echoes.org

E-Town. Broomfield, CO. Carried by over 100 stations nationwide!
Anne McConnell, Marketing Director. F: 303-443-4489.
www.etown.org

The Midnight Special. WFMT-FM, Chicago, IL. Rich Warren,
Producer. Second-longest running folk show in U.S.: 44 years.
Carried by 60 stations & 150 cable channels. P: 773-279-2000.
www.midnightspecial.org

Mountain Stage. Charleston, WV. Andy Ridenour, Producer. Carried by over 90 stations nationwide. www.mountainstage.org

A Prairie Home Companion. Carried on 356 stations! Two million listeners! 45 E. 7th St., St. Paul, MN 55101. Artists/Labels Contact: Stevie Beck. Radio Stations Contact: Katy Reckdahl. www.prairiehome.org

River City Folk. KVNO-FM 90.7. Omaha, NE. Tom May and Steve O'Gorman. P: 402-559-5866. F: 402-554-2440. www.tommayfolk.com/rivercityfolk/index.htm

Sheridan Gospel Network: The Light. 4025 Pleasantdale Radio. Suite 240. 770-416-2220. 888-467-7754. www.sgnthelight.com

World Café. Philadelphia, PA. Daily two-hour show on 111 affiliate stations. Bruce Warren, MD. P: 215-989-6677. F: 215-898-0707. www.npr.org/programs/world-cafe

CHAPTER 12. THE SELF-PROMOTING SONGWRITER AND COMPOSER

BOOKS

Adams R., Knatiuk, David, and Weiss, David. *Music Supervision: The Complete Guide to Selecting Music for Movies, TV, Games and New Media.* New York: G. Schirmer Inc., 2007.

Beall, Eric. *Making Music Make Money: An Insider's Guide to Becoming Your Own Music Publisher.* Boston: Berklee Press, 2004.

Bellis, Richard. *The Emerging Film Composer: An Introduction to the People, Problems, and Psychology of the Film Music Business.* Santa Barbara, CA: Richard Bellis, 2007.

Brabec, Jeffrey, and Brabec, Todd. *Music, Money & Success, 6th ed.* New York: G. Schirmer, Inc., 2008.

Davis. Richard. *Complete Guide to Film Scoring, 2nd ed.* Boston: Berklee Press, 2010.

Frederick, Robin. *Shortcuts to Songwriting for Film & TV: 114 Tips for Writing, Recording, & Pitching in Today's Hottest Market.* Los Angeles: TAXI Music Books, 2010.

Stim, Richard. *Music Law: How to Run Your Band's Business, 7th ed.* Berkeley, CA: Nolo Press, 2012.

Wentz, Brooke. *Hey, That's My Music!: Music Supervision, Licensing, and Content Acquisition.* Milwaukee, WI: MusicPro Guides, 2007.

Wilsey, Darren. *The Musician's Guide to Licensing Music: How to Get Your Music into Film, TV, Advertising, Digital Media & Beyond.* New York: Billboard Books, 2010.

Wixen, Randall. *The Plain and Simple Guide to Music Publishing, 2nd ed.* Milwaukee, WI: Hal Leonard Corp., 2010.

ONLINE

The Muse's Muse: www.musesmuse.com

SongU.com: www.songu.com. A unique opportunity to study songwriting with award-winning songwriters, make industry connections, and pitch your songs all from the comfort of your own home computer.

Songwriter Universe: www.songwriteruniverse.com

Songwriters Resource Network: www.songwritersresourcenetwork.com

Tip Sheets & A&R Services

Bandit A&R Newsletter: www.banditnewsletter.com

NOTC (New On the Charts): www.notc.com

Row Fax: www.rowfax.com. Country music mainly.

Songlink International: www.songlink.com

Taxi: www.taxi.com

Directories

Adweek Agency Directory, published by *Adweek* magazine: www.orderadweek.com

The Hollywood Music Industry Directory (Hollywood Creative Directories): www.hollywooddirectories.com

Music Publishers Directory, by The Music Business Registry: www.musicregistry.com

The Shoot Directory (annual Directory): www.shootonline.com

The Songwriter's Market. Writer's Digest Books, annual.

Commercial Music Markets

Adtunes: www.adtunes.com. Site that reveals the music behind commercials.

Devries, Henry. *Sold in Sixty Seconds: the Local Advertiser's Guide to Winning with Jingles.* AuthorHouse, 2005.

Fisher, Jeffrey P. *Cash Tracks.* ArtistPro, 2006.

Zager, Michael. *Writing Music for Television and Radio Commercials (and more): A Manual for Composers and Students.* Scarecrow Press, 2008.

TV/Film Music Markets

Film Music Network: www.filmmusic.net

The Film Music Society: www.filmmusicsociety.org

Film Music World: www.filmmusicworld.com. Home page for *Film Music Magazine,* Film Music Network, Film Music Store, Film Music Institute, and Film Music Online.

Film/TV Music Guide (annual), published by SRS Publishing (800-377-7411). Full contact information on music supervisors, music publishers specializing in film and TV placement, and music departments at all the major network studios.

The Hollywood Reporter: www.hollywoodreporter.com

Internet Movie Database: www.imdb.com. List of movies and TV shows with the complete cast and crew.

Mandy: www.mandy.com. Directory of creative talent and companies.

ProductionHUB.com: www.productionhub.com. An online resource and industry directory for film, television, video, and digital media production.

Video Game Music

Books

Collins, Karen. *Game Sound: An Introduction to the History, Theory, and Practice of Video Game Music and Sound Design.* MIT Press, 2008.

Gershenfelf, Alan, et. al. *Game Plan: The Insiders Guide to Breaking In and Succeeding in the Computer and Video Game Business.* St. Martins, 2004.

Marks, Aaron. *The Complete Guide to Game Audio: For Composers, Musicians, Sound Designers, Game Developers, 2nd ed.* Focal Press, 2008.

Michael, David. *Indie Game Development Survival Guide.* Charles River Media, 2004.

Salisbury, Ashley. *Game Development Business and Legal Guide* (Game Development). Muska & Lipman, 2003.

ONLINE RESOURCES

Gamasutra: www.gamasutra.com. The leading employment site serving the interactive entertainment industry.

Game Audio Network Guild: www.audiogang.org. A nonprofit organization established to educate the masses in regards to interactive audio by providing information, instruction, resources, guidance, and enlightenment not only to its members, but to content providers and listeners throughout the world.

Game Developers Network: www.gamedev.net

GameJobs: www.gamejobs.com. Another employment site serving the interactive entertainment industry.

Gamespot: www.gamespot.com

VIDEO GAME CONFERENCES

ACM SIGGRAPH: www.siggraph.org

Electronic Entertainment Expo (E3): www.e3expo.com

Game Developers Conference (GDC): www.gdconf.com

RINGTONES

IRIS: www.irisdistribution.com

Myxer Tones: www.myxertones.com. Make ringtones and wallpapers from files on your computer. Share and sell your own original content as ringtones or wallpapers. Deliver mobile content directly from your website or MySpace page.

The Orchard: Mobile Partnerships:
www.theorchard.com/marketing/orchard_mobile_partners.htm

Xingtone: www.xingtone.com

MUSIC LICENSING

Limelight: www.songclearance.com. A one-stop online tool that allows anyone to clear cover songs quickly and easily, for one low price.

Overview of Various Music Law Topics:
www.law.freeadvice.com/intellectual_property/music_law

CHAPTER 13. EXPANDING AND DEEPENING YOUR MUSIC CAREER

BOOKS

General

Arruda, William, and Dixon, Kristen. *Career Distinction: Stand Out By Building Your Brand.* Hoboken, NJ: Wiley, 2011.

Beeching, Angela Myles. *Beyond Talent: Creating a Successful Career in Music, 2nd ed.* Oxford, UK: Oxford University Press, 2010.

Clark, Timothy. *Business Model You: A One-Page Method for Reinventing Your Career.* Hoboken, NJ: Wiley, 2012.

Cutler, David. *The Savvy Musician: Building a Career, Earning a Living & Making a Difference.* Pittsburgh, PA: Helius Press, 2009.

Garfinkle, Joel A., and Goldsmith, Marshall. *Getting Ahead: Three Steps to Take Your Career to the Next Level.* Hoboken, NJ: Wiley, 2011.

Teaching

Boytim, Joan Frey. *The Private Voice Studio Handbook: A Practical Guide to All Aspects of Teaching.* Milwaukee, WI: Hal Leonard Corp., 2003.

Johnston, Philip. *The PracticeSpot Guide to Promoting Your Teaching Studio: How to Make Your Phone Ring, Fill Your Schedule, and Build a Waiting List You Can't Jump Over.* PracticeSpot Press, 2004.

Klingenstein, Beth Gigante. *The Independent Piano Teacher's Studio Handbook.* Milwaukee, WI: Hal Leonard Corp., 2008.

Osborn, Rebecca. *The Private Music Instruction Manual: A Guide for the Independent Music Educator.* Trafford, 2004.

Endorsements and Sponsorships

Grey, Anne-Marie. *The Sponsorship Seeker's Toolkit.* McGraw-Hill Book Company, 2008.

Karsh, Ellen, and Fox, Arlen Sue. *The Only Grant-Writing Book You'll Ever Need: Top Grant Writers and Grant Givers Share Their Secrets.* Basic Books, 2009.

Martin, Patricia. *Made Possible By: Succeeding with Sponsorship, 2nd ed.* Jossey-Bass, 2008.

Skildum-Reid, Kim. *The Corporate Sponsorship Toolkit.* Freya Press, 2012.

Tam, Simon S. *How to Get Sponsorships and Endorsements: Get Funding for Bands, Non-Profits, and More!* Simon Tam, 2012.

Arts Grants

Browning, Bev. *Grant Writing for Dummies.* Hungry Minds, Inc., 2008.

The Annual Register of Grant Support (annual, Information Today). Check your local library.

The Grants Register (annual, Palgrave Macmillan). Check your local library.

Online:

Arts Grants Opportunities: www.booksatoz.com

Arts International: www.artsinternational.org

National Endowment for the Arts: www.arts.endow.gov

National Endowment for the Humanities: www.neh.gov

Web and Mobile

Baker, Bob. *Guerrilla Music Marketing Online: 129 Free & Low-Cost Strategies to Promote & Sell Your Music on the Internet.* Spotlight Publications, 2012.

Cockrum, Jim. *Free Marketing: 101 Low and No-Cost Ways to Grow Your Business, Online and Off.* Hoboken, NJ: Wiley, 2011.

Moore, James. *Your Band Is a Virus - Behind-the-Scenes & Viral Marketing for the Independent Musician.* Create Space, 2011.

Mureta, Chad. *App Empire: Make Money, Have a Life, and Let Technology Work for You.* Hoboken, NJ: Wiley, 2012.

Olsher, Steve. *Internet Prophets: The World's Leading Experts Reveal How to Profit Online.* Morgan James Publishing, 2012.

Rosenblum, Michael. *iPhone Millionaire: How to Create and Sell Cutting-Edge Video.* McGraw Hill, 2012.

Turner, Kirby, and Harrington, Tom. *Learning iPad Programming: A Hands-on Guide to Building iPad Apps with iOS 5, 2nd ed.* Addison-Wesley Professional, 2013.

HELPFUL WEBSITES FOR MUSIC CAREER EXPANSION

Music Career Juice: www.mcareerjuice.com (author's blog)

Musician Think Tank: www.musicthinktank.com

MusicianWages.com: www.musicianswages.com

Sandbox: www.sandbox.fm

Index

AARC royalties, 232
accounting, 83–86
Accurate Records, 50
Act! software, 118, 160
Ad Week, 216
administration deals, 214
advertising, co-op, 144
Advertising Age, 216
advertising agencies, gigs at, 133
AFM payments, 232
AFTRA contingent scale, 232
agent license, 72
agents, booking, 138–42
Aguilera, Christina, 112
air and water pollution control permit, 72
alcohol, legislation on, 126–27
All About Jazz, 159
All Music Guide, 209
Allen, Lily, 164
All-Music Guide, 76
Alternative Press, 192
Amazon.com, 243
ambient light, 69
American Music Club, 221
American Society of Composers, Authors, and Publishers. *See* ASCAP
Andreozzi, Jay, 53
Andrews, Kyle, 7
Annual Register of Grant Support, The, 242
anti-hobby tax rule, 87–89
Apple Computer, 7
Arney, Greg, 235, 236–37, 245
Artist Data, 178
artist/band names, protecting, 76
Artistshare, 11
Artois Brewery, 7
ASCAP, 80, 209, 215

ASCAPlus Awards program, 231
assignment editor, 163
associations
    gigs for, 130
    joining, 109
audience
    empowerment of, 6–7
    engagement with, 11
    fan/customer database, 118–19, 165–66
    mobilizing, 149
    social media and, 163–69
    target profile, 159–63, 184, 240

Bacardi, 8
Backpage.com, 235
band members' agreement, 44
BandPage, 165
Bandzoogle.com, 172, 174
banners, 151
barcodes, 82–83
Barlow, John Perry, 14
Beach Street, 14
Beasley, Walter, 252
Beat, The, 159
Beatles, the, 213
Becket, Steve, 10
Beggars Group, 167
Better Business Bureau, 147
Bieber, Justin, 169
Billboard Publicity Wire, 162
bios (biographies), 121
blog supreme, a, 159
Blogger.com, 251
blogs, 118, 141, 159, 176–77, 184–85, 249–51
Blunt, James, 216
BMI, 80, 209, 215
bookers, 138–42

booking research worksheet, 129
bootlegging, 81
borrowing, creativity and, 39
Broadcast Music Incorporated. *See* BMI
Broadcasting Yearbook, 149
Buffett, Jimmy, 55, 112
business cards, 108, 153, 236
business licenses, 70–72
business name, 41–42
business planning and organization,
    17–61
    alternative approaches, 27
    business structures, 42–44
    career path description, 42
    components of, 39–60
    entrepreneurship and, 10–11, 18–23,
        27–34, 55–56
    expansion plans, 55–56
    facilities and equipment, 52–53
    financial plan, 56–60
    flexibility in, 60
    goal mapping, 35–39, 60
    goals and, 18–20, 29–31, 36–39
    information needed, 24–27
    marketing plan, 45–52
    operations plan, 52–56
    opportunities, 37–38
    organization dynamics, 54–55
    practical planning, 31–34
    project timeline, 56
    readiness check, 20–23
    risk assessments, 56
    self-assessment, 19–20
    summary statement, 40–42
    vision/mission statement, 36, 47
business structures, 42–44
businesses, gigs for, 130
Buyabarcode.com, 83

C corporation, 44, 93
cable television, 13
Caillat, Colbie, 164
calendars, "year-at-a-glance," 180–81
candies at gigs, 153
Captain Crawl, 184–85
CareerBuilder.com, 110
Caress, 8
CD recordings, mailing, 189
CDBaby.com, 83
Chamber of Commerce, 102
Chance, Grayson, 169
Circular Breathing app, 252
Clear Channel, 12
Clements, Annie, 229–30

clubs
    anti-drinking legislation and, 126
    booking dates in, 138–46
    changing scene, 126–27
    contests at, 142
    gig swapping in, 139–40
    liability insurance for, 126
    payment problems, 144–47
    promotion for, 141–42
CMJ, 216
Coldplay, 166, 216
college gigs, 133
College Media Journal, 187
college radio stations, 162, 186–93
commissions, 231
communication skills. *See also*
    marketing; social media
    booking acts and, 127, 138–39,
        140–42
    feedback and, 65
    forms of, 65
    importance of, 65
    marketing as, 65, 116–17
    press release and, 160–62
    spelling and grammar in, 65, 120
compact discs (CDs), selling at gigs, 151
competition profiles, 46–47
composers
    copyright basics, 203–11
    music publishing and, 211–14
    music to visuals, 221–22
    performing rights organizations,
        214–16
    revenue streams, 230–31
    self-promotion for, 203–24
    song marketing, 216–20
concert industry, revenues from, 6, 15
contacts. *See also* networking
    following up, 154–55, 192, 199–200
    marketing database, 117–19, 160,
        165–66
    networking and, 103–4
    targeted promotion to, 124–25
contracts
    performance, 134–37
    work for hire, 79
conventions
    attending, 108, 239
    playing, 131
co-op ads, 144
CopyCat Music, 222
Copyright Act of 1909, 205, 208
Copyright Act of 1976, 205

copyrights, 73–74, 78–83, 203–11
   correction and amplification form,
      207–8
   "covers" and, 208–10
   Creative Commons and, 210–11
   duration of, 204–5
   fees, 207, 208
   infringement, 81–82
   items protected by, 78, 205–6
   mechanical licenses, 80, 208–10
   ownership, 79–80
   registration procedure, 206–8
   rights covered, 203–4
   when to register, 78–79, 203
Corecommerce.com, 119
corporations
   C-type, 44, 93
   S-type, 44, 93
counterfeiting, 81
country clubs, gigs for, 131
"covers," 208–10
Craigslist.com, 235, 244
Cramps, the, 158
Creative Commons, 210–11
credits, performance/recording, 121
crowd-funding, 11, 233
cruise lines, gigs on, 132
Cruise Lines International Association
   (CLIA), 132
customer service policy, 51–52

Dangerbird, 14
Dariko, William D., *The Millionaire Next
   Door* (with Stanley), 18
Davis, Devin, 244
Day, Alex, 169
DBA (fictitious name) license, 70, 71
Deacon, Dan, 251–52
dead inventory, writing off, 93–94
Death Cab for Cutie, 244
Definitive Jux, 14
Delicious, 178
derivative works, 204
Digg, 178
digital performance royalties, 232
DirecTV, 196
disc jockeys (DJs), 118, 189–91
Domino, 14
Dorian Recordings, 9
Dory, Craig, 9
Down Beat, 159
dressing room, 148, 154
Dyer, Wayne, 102
Dylan, Bob, 212, 213

Earvolution, 251
eBay, 243
editorial calendar, 200
Educational Assistance Limited, 93
Egan, Seamus, 221
Eitzel, Mark, 221
Elbo.ws, 184
electronic Copyright Office (eCO) form,
   79, 207
Electronic Federal Tax Payment System
   (EFTPS), 91
electronic press kits (EPKs), 122–24
elevator speech, 111–12
Eli Lilly Co., 7
email, networking through, 111, 176–77
eMarketer, 246
EMarketer, 195
Emery, David, 167
"emotional bushwhacking," 19–20, 28,
   102
Encyclopedia of Associations, 130
endorsement deals, 233, 238–39
entertainment buyers, targeted
   marketing to, 124
entertainment lawyers, 146–47
Entertainment Weekly, 183
entrepreneurship, 10–11, 18–23
   information needed for, 24–27
   mindset, 27–34, 252–53
   musician skills favoring, 31
   personal and business goals, 55–56
   self quiz, 21–23
   setting goals, 29–37
   time division, 29
   time management, 95–97
equipment, 52–53
equipment insurance, 53
ergonomics, 69–70
events planners, 131
Everclear, 216
expansion plans, 55–56

Facebook, 102, 150, 164, 165–66, 176–77
Facebook Insights, 178
facilities, 52–53
Fader magazine, 184
fair use, 79–80, 204
fans. *See* audience
Faucher, Patrick, 60
Federal Express, 112
feedback, importance of, 65
fees, setting, 84–86
FileMaker Pro software, 118
film schools, 221

Film/TV Music Guide, 219
financial plan, 56–60
   forms needed, 57
   startup costs, 58
   three-year income projection, 58–59
Fines, Jeff, 221
fire department permit, 72
Flansburgh, John, 164
Flash, 247
Flickr, 178
Fluxblog, 251
flyer displays, 153
flyers, 149, 150, 197, 198, 236
Foreigner, 13
Form 1099-MISC, 90
Form CA, 207–8
Form PA, 206
Form SR, 206
Form TX, 206
Form VA, 207
Fueled By Ramen, 14
Future of Music Coalition, 230–33

*Gale's Directory of Publications and
   Broadcast Media,* 149
"Gangnam Style," 249
Geisel, Theodore, 112
general business license, 70
general partnership, 43, 93
Gershon, Russ, 50
Gibbard, Ben, 244
Gift-in-Kind Clearing House, 93
gigs
   association, 130
   booking research worksheet, 129
   business, 130
   finding, 126–37
   follow-up, 154–55
   high-profile, 197–99
   maximizing, 148–55
   non-profit organizations, 130–31
   payment problems, 144–47
   performance contract for, 134–37
   places for, 130–33
   promoting your act, 140–44
   publicizing, 149–50
   rehearsing, 149
   swapping, 139–40
   testimonials and, 132
goals
   long-range, medium-range, short-
      range, 38
   markers, 55–56
   setting, 29–31, 36–39

writing down, 30, 37
Golf Courses: The Complete Guide..., 131
Google, 243, 244–45
Google Alerts, 178, 199
Google Analytics, 185
Google Blog Search, 184
Google Hangouts, 249
grants, sponsorship through, 242–43
Grants Register, The, 242
graphic designers, 122
Grey's Anatomy (TV show), 3–4, 218
Groove Armada, 8
Grooveshark, 194
Grossman, Albert, 212
GS1, 82
guest list, confirming, 198
Guideposts magazine, 184
Guitar Center, 234

Hagar, Sammy, 13
Hall & Oates, 13
handstamps, 150
Handy, Charles, *The Age of Reason,* 28
Hanson, 13
Harrison, Michael, 196
Harry Fox Agency, 80, 209
hashtags, 168
Hawkins, Sophie B., 13
HBO, 196
headshots, 121
health department permit, 72
Heartbeat label, 159
Hibino, Norihiko, 83
Holiday Inn, 7
Home Office Deduction, 91
home-based businesses, 53
honoraria, 232
Horowitz, Sara, *The Freelancer's Bible,* 84
hotels, gigs at, 132
Hype Machine, 184–85

income, hiding, 86
independent contractor status, 90–91
Indie Band Manager software, 118, 160
Indie Bible, The, 160, 184, 187
indie record labels, 13–14, 186
Indiehitmaker.com, 82
industry database, 119
Instagram, 164
Instinct Records, 13
insurance
   equipment, 53
   liability, 126
intellectual property protection, 73–83

interest-based advertising, 166
International Jazz Festivals, 159
International Standard Recording Code
   (ISRC), 83
Internet
   artist websites, 171–75
   domain name search, 76–77
   expanding presence on, 243–52
   multiple presence online, 171
   music blogs, 118, 141, 159, 176–77,
      184–85, 249–51
   music promotion on, 3
   podcasting, 245–46
   power tools, 244–52
   radio, 176–77, 186, 193–94
   search engine optimization, 236,
      244–45
   social media, 150, 158, 163–69,
      175–77, 243–44
   video footage of band, 140–41
   videocasting, 246–48
interviews, 200–201
intrapreneurship, 23
introverts, networking and, 65–66, 101
IODA, 251
IRIS, 251
iTunes, 4, 194, 195, 246
iTunes revenue distribution, 175

Jakob Freely, 241
jazz, media for, 159
Jazziz, 159
JazzWax, 159
jingle houses, 217
Johnson, Jack, 166
Jones, Marc, 10

Kao, John, Jamming: The Art and
   Discipline of Business Creativity, 8
Karmin, 169
Kickstarter, 11
Killer Tracks, 222
King, Carole, 13
Kingston, Sean, 164

Lady Antebellum, 169
Last.fm, 194
law schools, 145
Lessig, Lawrence, 210
Levine, Brian, 9
Levi's Jeans, 7
libraries, public, 118, 149
lighting, office, 69
limited liability company, 43

limited partnership, 43, 93
LinkedIn, 102, 164, 176–77
liquor, wine, and beer license, 72
live chats, 166
Live365 website, 194
LiveStream, 248
location targeting, 165
logos, 122, 150, 151
Los Lobos, 221
Lucas, George, 112

mailing lists, 153
Mal's e-Commerce, 119
management, 61–97
   accounting, 83–86
   basics of, 63–66
   business licenses, 70–72
   communication, 65
   dealing with paperwork, 70
   incompetence in, 32, 61
   intellectual property protection,
      73–83
   networking and, 65–66
   organization and, 63–64
   oversight, 64
   self-, 62–63, 252–53
   setting fees, 84–86
   time, 95–97
   tips, 31–34
   workspace and, 66–73
   zoning laws and, 72–73
management description, 42
Mann, Aimee, 13
MapleCore, 14
Marcelo Productions, 132
markers, 55–56
market segmentation, 12–13
marketing
   communication skills in, 65, 127
   competition profiles, 46–47
   contact database, 117–19, 160
   customer service policy, 51–52
   electronic press kits (EPKs), 122–24
   essentials of, 114–25
   market description, 45
   mind-set development, 115–17
   mix, 49
   mobile apps, 251–52
   niche, 12–13, 49
   plan, 45–52
   positioning statement, 48–49
   presentations, 119–24
   pricing philosophy, 50
   primary market, 45–46

for private teachers, 235–37
referral markets, 46
sales/distribution methods, 50–51
secondary market, 46
semantics of, 117
song, 216–20
strategy, 48–52
targeted, 117, 124–25, 165, 166, 216
mass customization trend, 7
master use fee ranges, 220
Mayer, John, 179
McDonald, Heather, 168
mechanical licenses, 80, 208–10
mechanical royalties, 230
media. *See also* promotion and publicity;
    radio; social media; television
    database, 118, 124, 149–50
    following up, 199–200
    for high-profile gigs, 197–99
    market audience, 159–63
    online, 158
    publicity plan for, 158–79
    publicity waves, 180–83
    traditional, 158, 160–63
    types of, 158
*Meeting Professionals International
    Directory,* 131
merchandising, 151–54
    on Facebook, 165
    at radio stations, 192
    revenue streams, 233
meta tags, 245
Michaelson, Ingrid, 3–4, 218
Miller, Mary Fallon, *How to Get a Job
    with a Cruise Line,* 132
mobile apps, 251–52
Moby, 217
MOG, 163, 219
Moon, Gilli, 60
Morissette, Alanis, 112, 216
Moskowitz, Robert, 64
Mountain Dew, 7
MP3 blogs, 249–51. *See also* blogs
MP3 recordings, 121–22, 189, 245
MP3blogs.org, 251
MTV, 162
multimedia businesses, 217
Mumford & Sons, 179
Municipal Executive Directory, The, 131
music business promotion. *See also*
    networking; promotion and publicity;
    specific types
    crowd-funding, 11, 233

endorsement deals and
    sponsorships, 233, 238–43
expanding and deepening, 225–53
getting gigs, 138–46
new business models, 10–11
new trends in, 3–7
niche cultures and, 12–13
nonmusic business partners, 7–9, 38
QR codes for, 143
Radio's old role in, 3
revenue streams for, 228–33
small players' power, 13–16
for songwriters and composers,
    203–24
music consumers, empowerment of, 6–7
music description, 184
Music for Robots, 244
music industry
    careers, 37–38
    contact database, 119, 124
    legacy problems in, 10
    new business models, 10–11
    outside companies' involvement in,
        7–9, 38
    revenues, 6, 15–16
    sectors, 5–7, 15
    small players' power, 13–16
music libraries, 217, 222–23
music license fee ranges, 220
music producers, 223–24, 232
music products (physical), revenues
    from, 6, 15
music publishing
    basics of, 211–14
    copyrights as assets, 211–12
    development deals, 216
    home studios, 213
    Internet and, 243–44
    number of companies, 213–14
    outlets, 217
    revenues from, 6, 15, 213
    singer/songwriters and, 212–13
    types of, 214
music recordings, revenues from, 6
music supervisors, 218–20
music teachers, private, 233–37
    advertising, 235–37
    choosing location, 234
    getting experience, 234
    insights for, 236–37
    revenues for, 232
    setting fees, 235
Musician's Atlas, The, 160, 162, 184, 187,
    192–93

music-related business opportunities, 37–38

MySpace, 3, 150, 164, 176–77

NAMM show, 239

Naomi, Terra, 169

National Association for the Exchange of Industrial Resources, 93

National Association of Campus activities (NACA), 133

National Cristina Foundation, 93

neighboring rights royalties, 232

Neptunes, the, 223

networking, 100–113
    action steps, 113
    challenges of, 101–3
    contacts and, 103–4, 160
    defined, 100
    elevator speech and, 111–12
    importance of, 65–66, 100
    places for, 107–9
    at radio station, 192
    referrals and freelancing, 110–12
    rejection and, 112
    relationship growth, 105–7, 138–39
    small talk and, 107
    social media and, 101–2
    student advantage in, 103
    trade associations and, 109

New West Records, 13

niche music cultures, 12–13

nightclubs. See clubs

Nike, 7

Nimbit.com, 60, 119, 172, 174

noise levels clause, 136

noise permit, 72

non-profit organizations, gigs for, 130–31

NPR, 186

Nuclear Blast, 14

Nunes, Julia, 247

Obama Girl, 247

O'Connor, Sinead, 13

OK Co, 247

Old Navy, 4

Omni Music, 222

operations plan, 52–56

Orchard, the, 251

organization dynamics, 54–55

Ourstage.com, 176–77

Outlook software, 118

Palmer, Amanda, 166

Panay, Panos, 60

Pandora, 163

paperwork, dealing with, 70

Pardekooper, Kelly, 36

park programs, gigs for, 131–32

partnerships
    general, 43, 93
    limited, 43, 93

Parton, Dolly, 13

Passion Pit, 250

patents, 74, 206

PDF files, 122

performance contract, 134–37
    checklist, 135–36
    legal disputes, 144–47
    riders, 136–37

performance right, 214

Performer magazine, 184

performers. *See also* songwriters
    endorsement deals and sponsorships, 233, 238–43
    revenue streams for, 231–32

performing. *See also* gigs
    finding gigs, 126–37
    live online, 248–49
    mobile apps and, 251–52
    recording performances, 153–54
    venues for, 215
    visually stimulating, 153

performing rights organizations, 80, 209, 214–16

Perpetua, Matthew, 251

personal invitations, 150, 197, 198

personal licensing, 233

photos, 121

Ping.fm, 178

piracy, 81

pitch letters, 185

Plaia, Lou, 82

player pianos, 208

Pledgemusic, 11

Podcast Alley, 195

Podcast Pickle, 195

podcasts, 176–77, 195, 245–46

podcatchers, 246

postcards, 153, 189–91

posters, 149, 197, 198

PR Newswire, 162

presentations, marketing, 119–24
    components of, 120–22
    music description, 184

professionalism of, 127–28
    spelling and grammar in, 65, 120
press release, 160–62, 197–98
Pretenders, the, 13
pricing philosophy, 50, 84–86
Primary Elements, 222
primary market, 45–46
private parties, gigs at, 132–33
pro bono services, 145
product placement sponsorships,
    239–43
professionalism, importance of, 127–28
profit centers for musicians, 19, 229–33
project description, 42
project timeline, 56
promotion and publicity
    co-op ads, 144
    following up, 199–200
    generating, 182–83
    for getting gigs, 140–42
    for gigs, 149–50
    high-profile performance, 197–99
    interviews, 200–201
    location targeting, 165
    media plan, 158–79
    media waves, 180–83
    music reviews, 183–85
    presentations, 119–24, 127–28
    professional promoter, 201–2
    on radio, 3, 4, 150, 162, 186–97
    social media and, 163–69
    types of, 181
Proship Entertainment, 132
PRWeb, 162
public domain (PD) music, 210
public performance royalties, 231
public radio, 186
public relations firms, gigs at, 133
public service announcements (PSAs),
    163
publicity. See promotion and publicity
publisher advances, 230
publisher settlements, 231
Pussycat Dolls, the, 8

QR codes, 143

radio
    airplay, 186–97
    audience, 159
    college, 162, 186–93
    commercial, 186, 187
    DJ response cards, 189–91
    following up airplay, 192

Internet, 176–77, 186, 193–94
    mailings, 189–93
    phone log, 188
    previous role as primary
        promotional outlet, 3
    promoters for, 192–93
    promotion on, 4, 150, 162
    public, 186
    satellite, 186, 195–97
    stations, 141–42
"radius clause," 136
Rdio, 163
"record deal," 253
record labels
    decreasing importance of, 3–4
    indie, 13–14, 186
    legacy problems, 10
    lure of, 253
    major, 14
    organization chart for, 55
    publishing and, 211
Red Bull, 7
Red House Records, 13
referral markets, 46
referrals, 110–12
reggae, media for, 159
Reggae Ambassadors Worldwide, 159
rehearsals, 149
relationships, types of, 105–6
reputation management, 177
requests, online, 167
residencies, 144
results, tracking, 185
résumés, providing, 111
revenue streams
    developing, 8, 19, 37
    diversifying, 228–33
ReverbNation.com, 82, 165, 174, 176–77
reviews, music, 183–85, 198, 199
Rhino Records, 60
Rhythm Vibes Magazine, 159
ringtones revenue, 231
risk assessments, 56
Rodriguez, Robert, 221
Rolling Stone, 183
Rondor Publishing, 216
Rootz Reggae & Kulcha, 159
Royalty Network, 219
RSS feeds, 178

S corporation, 44, 93
sales rep at gigs, 153
sales table at gigs, 153
sales tax, 94

sales/distribution methods, 50–51
sampling, 81
satellite radio, 186, 195–97
Sound Production for Saxophone app,
 252
SBA. *See* Small Business Administration
 (SBA)
SBDCs. *See* Small Business Development
 Centers (SBDCs)
Schedule C, 90
Scherzinger, Nicole, 8
schools, gigs at, 133
SCORE. *See* Service Corps of Retired
 Executives (SCORE)
search engine optimization, 236, 244–45
secondary market, 46
self-assessment, 19–20
self-destructive impulses, 27–28
self-employment tax, 90
seller's (or resale) permit, 71
Service Corps of Retired Executives
 (SCORE), 26, 40, 57, 71
service mark, 74
SESAC, 80, 209, 215
session musicians, 232
Shakira, 166
Shanachie label, 159
Shapiro, Jake, 27
sheet music sales, 231
sign permit, 72
Silk City Recordings, 228–29
Simon, Paul, 15
Sing Out!, 192
SiriusXM, 195–96, 197
Skype, 249
Small Business Administration (SBA),
 25–26, 61
Small Business Development Centers
 (SBDCs), 25–26, 40, 57
small business tax write-offs, 92–94
small claims court, 144–45
small talk, making, 107
Smith, Fred, 112
social media, 163–69
 expanding presence on, 243–44
 Facebook, 165–66
 as fan management extension, 164
 focus for, 164–65
 networking on, 101–2
 overdependence on, 179
 promoting gigs on, 150
 publicity plan for, 158
 serializing content on, 166
 strategy, 175–77

tracking presence, 177–78, 199
Twitter, 167–69
YouTube, 169–71
software
 contact management, 118–19, 160
 for home-based business, 53
 podcatchers, 246
 spreadsheets, 57
sole proprietorship, 43, 93
 tax guidelines for, 87–94
song requests, radio, 191
SongFile.com, 80
Songlines, 192
songwriters, self-promotion for, 203–24
 copyright basics, 203–11, 211–14
 music to visuals, 221–22
 performing rights organizations,
  214–16
 revenue streams, 230–31
 song marketing, 216–20
Sonicbids, 60
Sorted Noise, 222
Soulja Boy, 164
SoundCloud.com, 121, 163, 219
SoundScan, 82, 186
Speakers' fees, 232
specialty labels, 217
sponsorships, 238, 239–43
 guidelines for securing, 240–41
 through grants, 242–43
 types of, 239–40
Spotify, 163
spreadsheets, 57
Stanley, Thomas J., *The Millionaire Next
 Door* (with Danko), 18
Star Search (TV show), 112
startup costs, 58
statutory royalty rates, 80, 209
Stern, Howard, 195
Stewart, Rod, 13
Stones Throw, 14
strategic plan, 159
streaming music, 165
streaming video, 246–47
success, defining, 36
Sugarland, 229–30
summary statement, 40–42
"sweat equity," 53
SWOT Analysis, 226–27
synch licenses, 231
synchronization fee ranges, 220

table tents, 151
Talkers magazine, 196

task lighting, 69
tax audits, 86
tax guidelines, 87–94
  anti-hobby rule, 87–89
  deductions, 91–93
  income tax and business tax
    deduction, 94
  independent contractor status,
    90–91
  record retention, 89
  sales tax issues, 94
  self-employment tax, 90
  writing off dead inventory, 93–94
television
  audience, 159
  cable channels, 13
  music placement on, 3–4, 218
  promotion on, 162–63
  "temp" music tracks, 219
testimonials, 132
thank you messages, 155, 192, 199
They Might Be Giants, 164
Thirty Tigers, 14
Thom, Sandi, 248
three-year income projection, 58–60
time constraints on networking, 101
time management tips, 31–34, 95–97
time/income factor analysis for
  determining fees, 85–86
Tin Pan Alley, 212
tipping waitresses and bartenders, 154
Tivo, 246
Topspin.com, 174
Toyota, 7
trade associations as networking
  centers, 109
Trademark Gazette, The, 78
trademarks, 73–78, 206
  company name as, 74–75
  formal registration, 77–78
  search, 76–77, 147
Trojan Records, 13
T-shirts, 151
Tumblr, 163
Tunecore, 251
TuneInRadio, 194
Twitter, 164, 167–69, 176–77, 178, 179
Two Ton Shoe, 27

UCLA Graduate Film Students Program,
  221
Ultimate Band List, 76
Under the Radar magazine, 184, 192
United States Patent and Trademark
  Office (USPTO), 74–75

Universal Product Code (UPC), 82–83
UStream, 248
Utne Reader magazine, 184

Vai, Steve, 13
Van Buskirk, Eliot, 251
variable labor, 54
verbal agreements, 145
VH1, 4, 162
Viacom, 12
video, Internet, 176–77. See also YouTube
  performing live, 248–49
  production tips, 247
  promotion tips, 247–48
  videocasting/vlogs, 246–49
Vig, Butch, 223
Village Voice, 184
vinyl recordings, 189
vision/mission statement, 36, 47
vlogs. See video, Internet
Volunteer Lawyers for the Arts, 80, 145,
  210
VP label, 159

W-9 tax form, 121, 136
Wall of Sound, 10
Warp Records, 10
webisodes, 169
websites, personal
  designing, 171–75
  use for, 176–77
Wikipedia, 243, 244
"winging" it, 60
Wordpress.com, 251
work for hire contract, 79
workspace, 66–73
  ergonomics of, 69–70
  lighting, 69
  L-shaped, 68–69
  optimizing, 69–70
  telephone in, 69
  work centers, 67–68

Yellow Pages, 118
YouSendIt.com, 251
YouTube, 121–22, 164, 169–71, 176–77,
  247

Zildjian, 239
zoning laws, 72–73
Zynch Music, 222

About the Author

Peter Spellman is director of the Career Development Center at Berklee, where he provides career-building resources, programs, and advising to students and alumni.

He is the author of several handbooks on music career development, including *Indie Business Power: A Step-by-Step Guide for 21st Century Music Entrepreneurs* (2009, MBS Business Media), *Plan Your Band!* (2009, MBS Business Media), *Your Successful CD Release* (with Dave Cool, 2010, MBS Business Media), and his latest, *Indie Marketing Power: The Resource Guide for Maximizing Your Music Marketing* (2012, MBS Business Media).

Peter has worked as a performer, arranger, producer, record label director, booking agent, artist manager, and music journalist. With over thirty years of experience as a performing and recording musician, he uses his vast experience to help musicians bridge their college experience to real-world opportunities in their chosen field.

Peter also performs with the ambient-folk-jazz ensemble, Underwater Airport (underwaterairport.com), a group that has been awarded two Berklee faculty recording grants.